Additional Praise

"Vicky Oliver has done it again! I love her savvy advice and the easy-to-read-and-refer-to format. As an industry consultant and a parent of a newly-minted college grad, I find *301 Smart Answers to Tough Business Etiquette Questions* incredibly relevant and a perfect guide to the wilds of the business world. This book belongs on every executive's bookshelf and on the bookshelf of anyone who wants to become an executive. Vicky Oliver's no-nonsense advice is timeless, easy to apply, and indispensable."

—*Victoria M. Amon, CEO, Building People Assets*

"In these tough times, getting the deal done is critical. This book provides the edge in those moments where impressions are formed and decisions are made."

—*Claude A. Chene, CEO, AllianceBernstein Limited*

"Vicky Oliver's advice will equip any young professional to make a great impression and stand out among the masses. Her guidance is critical to succeeding professionally in today's challenging economy."

—*Nicholas R. Wall, associate,*
Metropolitan Real Estate Equity Management, LLC

"Vicky Oliver's smart, career-saving advice guides you through all those workplace challenges that Emily Post somehow missed: virtual meetings and e-firings, business avatars and invisible doors, LinkedIn and Twitter, texting and blogging, email follow-ups after the interview, decoding the hidden hierarchy, staying on the radar, unspoken gender rules no employer will ever tell you, and much more. Ignore this timely book at your peril!"

—*Barbara Harrison, co-author of*
What to Do When No One Has a Clue: Advice for the Brave New World

301
SMART
ANSWERS
TO TOUGH
BUSINESS
ETIQUETTE
QUESTIONS

VICKY OLIVER

SKYHORSE PUBLISHING

Skyhorse Publishing books may be purchased in bulk at special discounts for sales promotion, corporate gifts, fund-raising, or educational purposes. Special editions can also be created to specifications. For details, contact the Special Sales Department, Skyhorse Publishing, 555 Eighth Avenue, Suite 903, New York, NY 10018 or info@skyhorsepublishing.com.

www.skyhorsepublishing.com

10 9 8 7 6 5 4 3 2

Library of Congress Cataloging-in-Publication Data

Oliver, Vicky.
301 smart answers to tough business etiquette questions / Vicky Oliver.
p. cm.
Includes bibliographical references.
ISBN 978-1-61608-141-6 (pbk. : alk. paper)
1. Business etiquette. I. Title. II. Title: Three hundred one smart answers to tough business etiquette questions. III. Title: Three hundred and one smart answers to tough business etiquette questions.
HF5389.O45 2010
395.5'2–dc22
2010021474

Printed in China

Table of Contents

IV. ETIQUETTE-CHALLENGED SCENARIOS

Foreword

The Ghost of Emily Post

The fun has gone out of etiquette. This is not what the late, great Emily Post intended. She was writing about Society, with a special emphasis on New York Society, and her observations were witty and sometimes barbed. She considered New York the epicenter of rudeness and wrote about it back in 1922:

New York's bad manners are often condemned and often very deservedly. Even though the cause is carelessness rather than intentional differences, the indifference is no less actual and the rudeness inexcusable.

Her pointed insights, sprinkled liberally throughout her book, *Etiquette in Society, in Business, in Politics, and at Home,* can't help but bring a smile to all but the most jaded. Emily portrays all types of boorish characters at her parties and luncheons, noting their manners violations with her literary "eye," but handling them with her trademark humor and forbearance. Almost a century later, these villains of rudeness are recognizable to modern readers from encounters in their daily lives.

Underlying Emily's devastating wit was always superb advice for getting along with others and bringing civilization to Society. The intention of this book is to fast forward the clock and shift the focus to the "society" (or lack thereof) that you will find at today's American workplace.

Here are 301 smart answers to any tough questions you might have about comporting yourself with dignity and poise with your workmates, bosses, clients, and customers. Inside, learn the up-to-the-nanosecond rules for engagement in the 21st century—whether you find yourself brainstorming around a conference room table, breaking bread at a business banquet, or glued to your computer screen communicating with a team three thousand miles away. You'll learn how wielding superb manners can help you impress your boss, make peace with your underlings, silence your dissenters, and annihilate your competition with kindness—so that you can *stay* at your job.

In deference to Emily Post's blithe spirit, the second aim of this book is to bring the joy back to etiquette. Becoming an office diplomat should—and can—be fun!

In the current climate of job scarcity, likeable, considerate, classy people are the only ones who get ahead, and this book, with the ghost of Emily Post as its guiding spirit, is poised to show you how to become one of them.

Introduction

Why Etiquette Is Not Like a Gold Watch

Etiquette—to the extent that you think about it at all, it's probably in the same way that you think about your gold watch.

You know the watch: 18-karat gold, stunning strap, but too intimidating to wear on a daily basis. The one you've owned for the better part of your life but haven't grown into quite yet. The watch that you either inherited from a dead relative right after the funeral or were given on a big birthday. To this day, the watch only comes out for important occasions, such as client dinners, visits from office dignitaries, and job interviews.

The watch you wear so infrequently that when you pull it out of the drawer, you always wonder if it will still work.

That watch.

And then, once the important occasion is over, what happens? Off come the Italian leather shoes and the fancy designer suit. You carefully lock the gold watch inside your jewelry box again, thoroughly relieved that you can now go back to being "your real self," unadorned. It's tempting to believe that etiquette can be taken off and put back on at will. Etiquette: the ultimate accessory!

And the truth is there is absolutely nothing wrong with thinking about etiquette as something that you trundle out for special occasions—if you truly need it only once in a blue moon, the way a hermit might.

But for most of us, life's little etiquette tests pop up every single time we interact with people, which is 99 percent of our waking lives. That's sixteen hours a day, 365 days a year. And with the average life expectancy at 77.7 years, that's a lot of people-interactions.

From the time we walk into the elevator in the morning, through meetings, appointments, and late nights burning out the fluorescent bulbs, in our office life and beyond, we must deal with people. For better or worse, they're *everywhere*. And each chance meeting is a time to impress them, or fail to.

If you are making a good impression, chances are you're also moving up, getting promoted, and regularly earning the kudos you deserve. If not, be forewarned: shoddy business behavior has a way of catching up with you. Workers are usually hired, fired, displaced, or promoted based on their personalities, rather than their particular talents for the jobs. Popular, well-liked people move up regardless of their competence. Unpopular, ill-mannered people lose their jobs even if they happen to be supremely competent.

In today's workplace, people skills trump other business skills, and mastering your business manners is a crucial career survival strategy. Ignore it, and you may soon find yourself pounding the pavement with millions of other people. But take these simple etiquette lessons to heart, and chances are you'll not only get to keep your job but also vastly improve your odds of moving up in the organization.

Still think you only need to mind your p's and q's on big, important occasions? Okay, Ms. Manners (or Mr. Manners), please take this short quiz. There are ten questions in all, and if you want to wear your gold watch as a good luck charm while reviewing the multiple-choice answers, that's entirely up to you. (Hint: There is only *one* correct answer to each question.) Good luck!

1. **One late night at the office, you accidentally discover who's been filching everyone's food from the fridge. What do you say to the thief?**

    A. "Aha! Caught in the act!"
    B. "Hey Stanley, I'm pretty sure that's Sheila's Fuji water, judging from the fact that she's written her name on the bottle in indelible ink. Why not put the bottle back and we'll just keep this between us?"
    C. Nothing.
    D. Nothing—but report the situation to HR.

2. **You're taking a taxi with three superiors from the office. You:**

    A. Get in first, and slide all the way over. (You've heard of apple-polishing. This is seat-polishing.)
    B. Get in second, so that you can take the uncomfortable middle seat.
    C. Get in third.
    D. Get in fourth, so that you sit up front with the driver.

3. **When you bump into your supervisor in the elevator, he asks how your latest project is faring. It's faltering. Do you tell him?**

    A. Yes. Honesty is the best policy.
    B. No. There could be spies from a competitive company lurking in the elevator.
    C. No. You promise him a conference report is in the works.
    D. No. Worried that the truth will lower your marks on your upcoming performance evaluation, you spin the facts to make it sound like there is still hope.

4. **You're chatting with your boss at a networking event when you spot your ex-boss. They have never met before. Who do you introduce first?**

   A. Your boss.

   B. Your ex-boss.

   C. Neither. Instead, you say something genial to your former boss, such as, "So nice to see you, Carl," and then let your current boss and ex-boss introduce themselves to each other.

   D. Neither. You dive into the hors d'oeuvres, hoping that your former boss won't notice you behind the crudités.

5. **When two people are discussing business, how far apart should they stand?**

   A. 10 feet. (Or even further—if one of them hasn't showered.)

   B. 7 feet.

   C. 6 feet.

   D. 3 feet.

6. **You're running five minutes late to a job interview. You:**

   A. Wait until the exact second when you were supposed to arrive, and then call your interviewer from your cell phone to apologize for your tardiness.

   B. Don't call. Instead, fib about the "security situation" downstairs.

   C. Don't call. Instead, set your *gold watch* back five minutes and carry on as if you were on time.

   D. Wait until five minutes before you were supposed to arrive, and then call your interviewer to say you're running a bit late. (This way, she can use the extra time to finish her tasks.)

7. **You eat spaghetti with a:**

   A. Fork.

   B. Fork and spoon.

   C. Fork, knife, and spoon.

   D. You avoid eating it at client dinners since you're not exactly sure of the protocol and you're worried about splattering it everywhere.

8. **You're at a client dinner at a posh restaurant when one of the clients walks in two hours late. The rest of you are finishing your main meal. You:**

    A. Say, "Hello, Jack, it's great to see you," and stay seated. Doing anything else would agitate your fellow diners.

    B. Rise. Just because he's rude doesn't mean that you need to be.

    C. Stay seated and signal the waiter so that your late client can be served promptly and, hopefully, catch up with the rest of you.

    D. Stay seated and keep talking to your dinner companion, so as not to disrupt the flow.

9. **On a plane, you overhear two passengers talking loudly and it's difficult to concentrate. What, if anything, do you do?**

    A. Politely ask them to keep their voices down to a dull roar.

    B. Ask the flight attendant to ask them to keep their voices down.

    C. Say nothing. Hushing them would violate the Great Etiquette Paradox™.

    D. Turn around and throw them glare darts with your eyes, hoping the two loud-mouths will get the message.

10. **Which American gesture is considered rude abroad?**

    A. Thumbs-up sign.

    B. Okay sign.

    C. Chin flick.

    D. All of the above.

Well, how did you do? If you didn't know the answers to at least *five* of these questions, your career could be stalled. But the good news is, you can get it unstuck by taking this opportunity to polish your business manners. Plus, you'll have an absolute blast doing it. (Keep reading to find out the correct answers. The answers to the Quiz can be found on page 364.)

I

Meetings

Life at the workplace may not feel like an exam until the week when performance reviews are handed out or the specter of an ax suddenly appears. Yet the fact remains, we are being tested on a daily basis on something that we never studied and never realized was important: business etiquette. These tests happen in all sorts of strange rooms too, such as elevators, office kitchens, and cubicles, not to mention boardrooms and client conference rooms. Part I examines how to ace those tests so that when the final exam rolls around we will be spectacularly well prepared.

CHAPTER 1

Random Meetings:
Proper Etiquette in Confined Spaces

City living can be crowded, congested, and contentious. Shoehorned into high-rise buildings that house our apartments, offices, and gyms, we are all on top of each other 24/7. Sometimes, just walking from place to place can feel like a negotiation for precious air space.

When a neighbor renovates an apartment, we count the days until the construction crew leaves our building. When a cube mate breaks up with a loved one, we cry right along with her. When a boss loses his temper, we can't help overhearing his tirade through tissue-thin walls. In these close quarters, boundaries stretch to the breaking point.

We may wish to remain cheerful, but sometimes we may also need to carve out some emotional distance to substitute for the lack of physical space. This chapter examines how to achieve the correct balance.

You'll learn the rules that apply—from dealing with doorways in matchbook buildings to proper protocol in constricted elevators to negotiating the bump and grind of a 737 airplane.

Just because quarters are cramped doesn't mean that your etiquette style need be. And if you can be civilized in these space-challenged circumstances, you will have achieved true serenity and poise.

1. *Elevators*

You step into the elevator this morning and, if you're incredibly lucky, you will have it all to yourself. Today, just maybe, the elevator will feel more like your private transporter. It's not that you're hermetic. You're as much of a "people person" as the next human being—once that first cup of java kicks in. But until it does, you'd prefer to crawl back into the womb and just stay there for a spell. In your view, space really *is* the final frontier. How are you supposed to cope when you have to share it with so many others?

1 **When the elevator door opens, it reveals your direct supervisor inside—just back from vacation. Eager to find out what he missed, he asks how your latest project is faring. It's withering on the vine. Do you tell him?**

A. No. There could be spies from a competitive company lurking in the elevator.

Think of yourself as an ambassador of your company, entrusted with its deepest, darkest corporate secrets, and you will always know exactly what not to reveal. Beware of sharing top-secret information about a client project with anyone. The world's most confidential information travels like a virus—often through random strangers in elevators. Let your supervisor know in a nice way that you'll circle back to him once he's had a chance to settle in. "Oh, I want to talk to you about that," you can say in a chipper voice that won't broadcast your news to any strangers in your midst.

2 **After several late nights burning out the fluorescent bulbs, you roll into the office bleary-eyed. As fate would have it, you bump into your perkiest colleague in the elevator. Do you fight through your exhaustion and try to engage him in conversation—or not?**

A. Two or three words are plenty.

If your colleague is already inside the cabin, a quick nod of your head in his direction and a sunny "Good morning" strike just the right balance between friendliness and indifference. The elevator is not the place to enter into any heavy-duty conversations. If your boss walks in, say, "Good morning, Satan," (or whatever his proper name is) and be sure to wave him off with a cheery, "Catch you later," or, "Until the staff meeting," if he disembarks first.

Are you trapped inside with the *Wicked Wag of the Watercooler*? Disarm her. A bland, "It's so nice to bump into you like this," may distract her just long enough for you to reach your destination *without* engaging in her favorite pastime. "Elevator talk" is misnamed. It's not about talking at all; it's really all about the tone. Always aim for cordial.

 If someone in an office elevator cracks a lame joke, do you have to laugh?

A. Yes, but it only has to be a mild chuckle, not a belly laugh.
Venture onto a particularly slow elevator with every stop pushed, and no doubt some would-be comedian will start referring to it as "the local." To this hackneyed attempt at humor, a mild chuckle is appropriate. Not everyone can be a Conan O'Brien or Ellen DeGeneres who, let's be honest, probably didn't start their celebrated careers by working at your company.

In crowded quarters, the less space per person, the more generous one must be with laughter. Carry this rule with you to all cubicles and gym showers.

Twelve Tacky Things to Never Ever Do in an Elevator (Even if You're 100 Percent Certain That No One Is Watching)

1. **Fix your lipstick.** You'll end up looking like Joan Rivers.
2. **Fiddle with your belt, fly, or jock strap.** The elevator may feel like a closet, but by the time you enter, you should be already dressed.
3. **Make a call.** Yes, your life is busy. Yes, we are undeniably impressed that you can't wait even ten seconds before emerging from the elevator

to make that critical phone call. We are like ants on the peanut butter and jelly sandwich that is your life, so enthralled are we with its fascinating details. Still, please remember that for us, there is no escape until the doors open. Wait until you disembark to pull out your cell.

4. **Check out your reflection in the mirrored doors.** You don't want to act like a lyric straight out of "You're So Vain."

5. **Comb your hair.** The rest of us won't appreciate having your hair castaways on our pinstriped suits, even if you're having a superlative hair day.

6. **Burp.** If Nature must have her way, bring your hand up to your mouth and say, "Excuse me!" (It also helps to look embarrassed.)

7. **Rifle through your briefcase.** Everyone will assume that you're neurotic (and not in an adorable, isn't-that-sweet, Woody Allen way). Embarrassing items could even pop out. *Oh, the horror.*

8. **Grope a friend.** You feel like no one's watching... so why not steal a kiss or a quick fondle? But even when "no one's watching," the building security guard *is* watching. Why expose him to an X-rated movie he never paid to see?

9. **Wear earbuds or headphones.** They muffle your ability to react properly or with propriety to those around you. The cornerstone of etiquette is consideration, and it's impossible to be considerate when you're in your own bubble singing aloud to the Beach Boys but sounding like an off-key Beastie Boy.

10. **Text.** If you're always wired, you'll miss out on many of life's most important interactions.

11. **Don't stare** . . . at someone's breasts, no matter how surgically enhanced they may be. Chances are, you're simply regarding such objects with the dispassionate scientific curiosity they merit, but it's far more polite to avert your eyes.

12. **Tap your foot and glower at the floor numbers impatiently.** We all have better places to be, Darling. Rise above.

> ## Who Knew?
> Ladies no longer walk first. For better or worse, women of the world have finally reached gender parity. Today, it's first person *at* the elevator door, first person out of the elevator—or every "man" for himself. However, if the person is elderly, always let him or her walk in front of you.

2. The Cube Farm

Welcome to *The Cube Farm*: that intricate rats' maze of cubicle half-walls which define the open space set aside for the office-challenged. In these parts, it's almost impossible to imagine there are any boundaries. Everywhere you look, workers are *prairie-dogging*, that is, standing up or hanging over a low-hung wall to chat with the person one cube over. You even hear a couple of workers carrying on a conversation between the cube walls—without bothering to pop up from their chairs. It's not as if the dog-eared walls muzzle sound. When having a door marks the line between the office "haves" and "have-nots" (and you don't happen to have one), how do you keep a cordial but respectful distance from your neighbors?

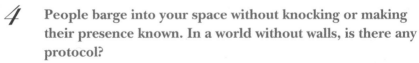 **People barge into your space without knocking or making their presence known. In a world without walls, is there any protocol?**

A. Precious little, but there are subtle ways to fight against the culture of interruption.

Position your computer so that while working on it, you also face the doorway. This will prevent unannounced intruders from frightening you as they charge into your space, causing you to leap six feet out of your chair. You really don't want to keep banging your head against the wall, even if it's only made of felt.

Want to discourage surprise visits? When someone pops in unannounced, keep your hands on your computer keyboard and start typing furiously. "I'd love to chat," you might say to the interloper, "but unfortunately, my report is due in an hour."

5 **In cube land, are you always "on call?"**

A. Yes—unfortunately.

It would be so considerate of your boss to give you some advance notice before descending into your cube. But don't count on it. He's from a different caste: one that grants surprise visitation privileges.

Make it your mission to anticipate his unannounced stopovers. You may not know his estimated time of arrival. But in a "world without walls," there are few landings that are genuinely a surprise. Keep your ear to the runway and you'll hear his approach long before he arrives.

When your boss cruises in like the stealth bomber, it's a good idea to be visible (and not whittling away precious company time on Facebook or Twitter). Strive to be present even when you're absent. Know that you'll be away for several hours? Leave a handwritten note near your computer or chair. "Meeting with a supplier from 10:30 to noon. Back later." (No need to also put the word out on Twitter.)

Knock Twice on the Invisible Door

The door is that thin line drawn on the industrial carpet between managers and underlings, full-time and part-time, or front office and back. Naturally, there are exceptions to be found, such as in a company that's experiencing electric growth or in one where no one has a door.

If you do have a door, chances are it means that you also have an office, and just as you would hate for someone to swoop into your office when your door was closed, you should ask permission to enter someone's cube. Since the door to the cube is completely invisible to the naked eye, make a show of knocking on the cube wall and say something cute, like "Knock, knock" or "Mind if I come in?"

6 **You feel like it's not only Big Brother who watches you, but Big Sister, the Seemingly Sweet Coworker Who Never Utters a Word, plus the HR Assistant Who Only Wears Black. When everyone in the Cube Farm is as inseparable as peas in pod, is there any way to create the illusion of privacy?**

A. Tap into your inner gardener.

There may be no real walls as far as the eye can see, but you can still erect your own personal sound barrier.

Create a wall of foliage by adding tall plants or trees to your cube. Worried they may die from overexposure to fluorescent light? Go green—with plants made from 100 percent plastic.

From a feng shui perspective, plastic greenery adds almost as much *chi* to your cube as the real thing; plus, plastic plants never need to be watered. A discreet sound machine may help block out some of the noise. (Lock it in your desk drawer at night to prevent any intrepid noisemakers from filching it.)

For Extra Credit

Mousy, felt-covered walls are superb conduits for conversation. Show some class by staying off speakerphone, dialing down the volume on all loudspeaker announcements, and taking any personal calls in a whisper.

3. *The Office Kitchenette*

You hate making decisions on weighty matters, and being forced to choose is spinning you into a midday crisis. On the one hand, things have been crazy busy and you need to keep pushing yourself. That tips the scales in favor of Option A-1. On the other hand, you already have too much on your plate—if you count the sixteen Jelly Bellies you scarfed at Greta's surprise baby shower an hour ago. That swings the proverbial pendulum over to Option B-1. At least B-1 can be subdivided into manageable, bite-sized chunks. A Snickers bar for lunch? Or a bag of Fritos? Your mind crunches over the dilemma, lost in a rhapsody of sweet versus salty. You finally opt for Fritos, knowing that your "sweet" fix will be alleviated by the bottle of Glacéau vitaminwater you so cleverly stored in the fridge earlier today.

Xeroxing Something? Copy This

At busy intersections, there is a "stop sign" protocol cars follow. At the bustling intersection near your company's Xerox machine, there is also a smart way to navigate traffic. If your document is long (i.e., over twenty pages), wave those with shorter documents ahead of you. If it's an enormous document and it's already underway, smile apologetically and give an estimate of the time you expect it will take: "Should be about five minutes," you can say. (Many companies have strict rules prohibiting the copying of personal items on their machines, but to date, *Xerox Police* isn't anyone's official title. If the personal document that you're copying is short enough, most managers will look the other way.)

---

7   How do you catch a thief? Your vitaminwater has disappeared for the second time in two weeks!

A. Step one: label your food.

Everyone should be able to recall the food they personally brought to the office, but why not aid those with faulty memories by declaring what's rightfully yours?

Buy a black Sharpie pen and use it to affix your name (first and last) to every item that you ever store in the fridge. This simple act is a polite way of telling a thief to lay off.

Even if your company has a laissez-faire attitude about refrigerated personal property, putting your moniker on your food sends an unmistakable message to a thief. It says, "Please rein in the urge to snag what isn't yours. This here is mine."

8   Your vitaminwater has been filched yet again, and you're beginning to take it personally. You carefully labeled it, but it still vanished. What now?

A. Write a note to the thief.

Put a message on the bottle. Bear in mind that others will be reading your communication with great interest, so even if tempted, you must keep the message expletive-free.

Affix your note to the bottle with some tape and a Post-it note in a zingy color. "This is the personal property of _____. Kindly stop helping yourself to it" is the no-frills version. Humorous threats about what might befall anyone who takes it upon himself to drink your vitaminwater are over-the-top (and might concern officemates about your sanity).

THE STRAIGHT SCOOP

Notes to thieves sometimes act as deterrents—although many workers claim that notes *without* any reinforcement from human resources (HR) rarely work. Crafting a note is a smart step to take anyway, because it focuses public attention on the larceny and demonstrates your reasonableness in the face of adversity (and thirst).

---

9 The office thief has ignored numerous missives taped to your bottles of vitaminwater, which all manage to get stolen before you've even had a sip. Isn't it time to kick this issue upstairs to the pleasant folks who are paid to deal with scoundrels?

A. Talk to someone in your HR department.

Stay calm and civil when you detail this barbaric behavior. Remember that while you have been the hapless victim of a petty crime for several weeks, this may be the *first time* that the HR manager has heard about it. As with any report on heinous actions, provide details and dates of all demented behavior.

(And don't forget that sometimes, leaving your food in the fridge for *too long* can grate on fellow workers. Pungent food, overly ripe fruit, and anything gooey or drippy should always be left at home.)

4. *Airplanes*

You were ecstatic when your boss first asked you to substitute for him at the Florida convention. Here was your once-in-a-lifetime opportunity to study palm trees up close, schmooze with industry tycoons, and reset your overworked body to "snooze" during what you had imagined would be an uneventful flight. Pity that your own plans are on a crash–collision course with those of the balding, red-faced man perched directly behind you in coach. He is using the lamest pick-up lines that you've ever heard to try to pique the interest of the jaded brunette in airtight jeans seated next to him. The plane isn't scheduled to land for over three and a half hours. Where are the parachutes stored, and is it okay to jump?

10 The man seated behind you on a plane is hell bent on jabbering to his neighbor for the entire flight. The plane is 100 percent full. What are your options?

A. Limited.

Unfortunately, it's very poor manners to tell someone that his manners are poor. This is known as the Great Etiquette Paradox™. You can't always correct someone or speak your mind if doing so will make you seem down-right rude.

Turn around to publicly scold the talkative twosome, and your manners automatically plummet ten thousand feet to their level.

Ask the flight attendant to suggest that the two passengers *please* simmer down, and they might hear you. In any event, doing so doesn't help you get you around the Great Etiquette Paradox.

If you say nothing but keep swinging your head around to hint that they are disrupting the peace, they will ignore you. Plus you'll come down with a wicked case of "rubber neck."

In the future, mentally prepare yourself for quiet time interruptus. Bring an iPod and sleep mask with you on all flights.

Matinee Manners

There are exceptions to the Great Etiquette Paradox, such as when two people directly behind you in a movie theater yammer about their love lives, whisper about the plot, or text non-stop. But in a movie theater, the "Law" is on your side. The rules are *explicitly stated* in the pre-movie promotional video. When you turn around to quiet these inconsiderate folks, you are merely asking them to cooperate, and you will find the rest of the room highly sympathetic, if not itching to defend your cause. On an airplane, however, there's no law against chatter.

---

11   **The woman seated next to you keeps hopping over your legs to get up. Is there any way to make her stop?**

A. You can offer to switch seats with her. Or suffer in silence.

On long flights, a few hops, skips, and jumps to the bathroom are to be expected, and if you're seated on the aisle, it's only polite to stand when your seatmate requests her freedom. If she seems to do this with the urgency of two hares in heat, do try to erase the smirk from your face. She's in enough discomfort without your adding to it by saying something humorous.

On Organizing Your Life into Tiny Compartments

The Transportation Security Administration (TSA) requires that all carry-on items in liquid, gel, or aerosol form must be three ounces each or less and fit inside a "quart-sized clear zipper bag." (Yes, this includes toothpaste gel.) Medications, baby formula, and bottles of breast milk are allowed in quantities exceeding three ounces, but you have to declare them for inspection. Basically, your bag is an open book. For the latest information, check out the TSA.gov website.

How Not to Pack Like a Terrorist

Here are some items best left at home (unless you want to be stuck in the airport for *a lot* longer):

1. Scissors
2. Knives
3. Knitting Needles
4. Metal Nail Files
5. Tweezers
6. Razor Blades
7. Guns
8. Toy Knives and Guns
9. Fake Passports
10. Bazookas
11. Manuals on Bomb-Making

12. Box Cutters
13. Ice Picks
14. Meat Cleavers
15. Any Item That Makes You Look Like an Ax Murderer

12 **Your company's travel agent botched the in-flight reservations. You're seated in the front of the cabin while your two officemates are all the way in the rear. Should you try to arrange a swap seat on your own?**

A. Don't play the middleman.

Try to befriend the flight attendant when you first board the plane. This will ensure better service. Don't exert any Herculean effort to do it. Just smile and appear friendly without being overly chatty.

Then, if you find yourself separated from your travel companions, politely ask your new best friend (the flight attendant) to intervene. It's less awkward than negotiating with several passengers to arrange a seat swap on your own.

What if a passenger asks if her five-year-old can switch seats with you? A polite fib provides the perfect alibi. "I would, but I suffer from Restless Leg Syndrome," you might offer, "and I really need the space for my legs."

Keeping the Skies Friendly

Many of the frustrations we feel when flying actually begin on the ground. The tragic events of September 11, 2001, lengthened the time we all spend in airports due to intense security. There's a hurry-up-and-wait aspect to even taking a shuttle.

If misery loves company, at least recognize that you're in excellent company with others who are suffering right along with you through interminable lines, delayed departures, and overcrowded flights. Below are some pointers that can make your airport-to-airport sojourn, however painful, a tad more cordial.

1. **There's no difference between you and the company CEO.** Everyone must remove his or her shoes before traipsing through the security gates, adding oodles of wait time to the endless lines (not to mention the pungent odors of smelly feet). However, if you anticipate that you will be trapped on line for a very long time, you won't feel quite as antsy when you hear the blue-haired couple ahead of you quarreling about whether the man really has to put his laptop in the plastic bin to be photographed and scanned. (The answer, incidentally, is that, yes, he does.)

2. **Build in the time it takes.** Flying domestically? Arrive at least two hours before departure time even if you're traveling with the world's most boring coworker. Get to the airport at least three hours ahead of scheduled takeoff for any international trip. When you shuffle through the metal detector, hang onto your boarding pass. If you don't have it on you, the agent will force you to wait for your bag to emerge from the X-ray machine so that you can fish out your pesky pass—thus holding up the line even more. (*Warning:* The hungry, cranky travelers waiting behind you may not take kindly to this. Today's enhanced security measures are designed to *prevent* incidents, not incite them.)

3. **Submit to the indignity.** Modern metal detectors are primed to beep at anything metallic, be it a piece of gold jewelry, a cell phone, or an underwire bra. What used to be termed "feeling up" seems to be the only way that female security guards can determine whether or not the female passengers among us pose a threat. Allow yourself to be scanned, frisked, and *womanhandled* by these officious people who are only doing their jobs, and try to stay jovial during the experience. Think of it as a breast exam where you don't have to pay a gynecologist.

4. **Pack light (or avoid it altogether).** If you don't check it, they can't lose it. Why not save yourself a whole suitcase's worth of agita?

5. **Nosh at the airport first.** Underwhelmed by the selection of eateries at your local airport? They are like *Daniel Boulud's finest* compared to what you can expect in-flight. With all airlines looking to shave costs, it's smart not to arrive on board ravenous.

6. **But, just in case you do have to wheedle, befriend the flight attendant.** She is more likely to squirrel away an extra snack for you if you resist the urge to carp at her just because the wings need to be defrosted, the runway is too crowded, or one solitary passenger hasn't checked in yet, delaying takeoff.

8. **Carry your bag in front of you as you walk down the aisle.** This lessens the likelihood that it will slam the unsuspecting shoulders of passengers who are already seated.

9. **Honor your air rights.** Know the personal storage space to which you're entitled, and don't try to expand on it. Store your bags in the overhead bin just above you or under the seat in front of you. Stow your jacket above your carry-on. Your jacket will swallow less room this way and prevent vengeful passengers from crumpling it with their baggage as they struggle for their fair share of space.

10. **Remain in your assigned seat until everyone has boarded.** Don't flout this rule, lest everyone else on the flight start screaming at you.

Claim Your Rightful Armrest

Many etiquette experts counsel, "Don't hog the armrests," as if that's a solution when space is at a premium. Advice not to use the armrests is unrealistic, given the size of the average American compared to the size of the average airline seat. It's like cramming a very large present into a tiny box: There is bound to be some spillage on both sides! Consequently, the first person on board *does* have the right to claim any shared armrests. Remember the wise adage, "You snooze, you lose."

5. *Office Supply Closets*

You recall the precise moment when your occupation morphed into your pre-occupation. That was the day when the adorable Accountant walked into your life, and ever since, your interest in all things financial has multiplied exponentially. The Accountant ("T.A.," for short) has such a way with numbers! You can't take your eyes off of them. Those assets are positively gripping. Chills zip down your spine as you picture your paramour accidentally knocking over the neatly stacked pens in the office supply closet. What a klutzy cutie! And even though you're aware that mixing business with pleasure may draw frowns from the higher-ups, you feel safe having this crush, because it's not as if the two of you work in the same department. But are you safe? Is a consensual affair between two people from completely different walks of life (well, from different floors anyway) a risk to your career, or isn't it?

13 **You know three intra-office couples at your firm who are not-so-secretly seeing each other. Where do companies draw the line?**

A. Time to peek inside your company handbook.
Today, love really is blind, and even companies with stringent sexual harassment rules sometimes turn a blind eye to consensual office relations. That said, before delving into deep breathing exercises with any of your local office hotties, it makes sense to peek into the company handbook to scope out its *intra-office f-policy*, otherwise known as "fraternization policy." (No, it doesn't stand for that other f-word. Can you please keep your mind on loftier matters?) Some companies strictly prohibit fraternization. Others have no issue with employees dating other employees who are at their level, but forbid supervisors and subordinates from dating each other.

14 **What is a "love contract?"**

A. It's a legal document that protects the company in the event of a breakup.

Love at the workplace is no longer confined to matters of the heart. Today it's all about covering the butt. Romantics may titter, but the lawyers are adamant. Certain companies coerce consenting partners in an office tryst to sign a "love contract"—a legal document stating that the affair is "consensual." (And you thought pre-nups were unromantic!) The *love contract* exists to prevent one partner from later accusing the other of sexual harassment in the event of a breakup.

15   **It's the stuff of urban legends: the secretary who marries the boss or two coworkers who end up tangoing to wedding bells. Don't you deserve your fair share of happiness, too?**

A. Even if your company is permissive, try to flash ahead to the bitter end.

Imagine that the affair has soured.

Will you and your paramour be able to resort to "business-as-usual?" How quickly?

Will there be any repercussions? If either of you has a vengeful streak, what started as lust could devolve into office finger pointing. You don't want to be a target in the Blame Game just because you and the Accountant's pleasure romp disintegrated.

After you, will there be others? How will you feel when the Accountant starts sharing his or her *ledger sheets* with someone else?

Is the person your superior? Your spoiled tryst could even spark negative performance reviews. (That's *office* performance, not *bedroom* performance.) Be honest: Is there anyone on the planet for whom it's worth taking all of these career risks?

That's a Wrap

1. If you are blessed with the gift of gab, never unwrap your gift in an elevator.

2. Every cubicle has a door—it just happens to be invisible. Don't forget to knock.

3. Filching other people's food from the company fridge is a potential reputation buster.

4. To achieve serenity in today's airports:
   - Arrive early.
   - Submit to taking off your shoes and being frisked.
   - Pack light.

5. Stay out of the office supply closet (unless you're going there strictly for supplies).

CHAPTER 2

You Always Have a Second Chance to Make a First Impression

Pundits tell us, "You never have a second chance to make a first impression." If that were true, we would meet a boss or client once, and if we failed to impress him or her, we'd have no choice but to immediately move on to another company. After all, in the cutthroat world of first impressions, there would be no second chances!

While the snapshot impression someone forms of you in a job interview may be indelible, in general, you have numerous chances to bolster the impression someone has of you at the workplace. That's because you're not at the office simply to make impressions; you're there to build relationships.

Meticulous attention to minor details colors the way that others view you. Do you run on time, or is your internal clock set to "unforgivably late?" Be honest: Do you have any idea who should be introduced first—your CEO or your client?

Would a rose by any other name smell as sweet? Possibly, but not if her name is Hyacinth! This chapter advocates different name–recall techniques than the Dale Carnegie method (much has changed in the world since 1936), plus subtle ways of teasing out people's names if you're completely at a loss.

You always have a second chance—and a third and a fourth—to make a first impression. This is your golden opportunity to learn how.

1. *The Importance of Punctuality (Or the Lack Thereof)*

To Murphy's Laws, you would like to add a few of your own: 1. The most important person at the meeting always arrives latest. 2. The moment you need the most important person to contribute to the meeting, he receives a phone call. 3. As a consequence, no real decisions are ever made at any meetings. 4. But it's essential to hold internal meetings anyway in order to organize the strange meanderings of your boss's mind.

And to the stragglers—those inconsiderate creatures who always manage to show up ten minutes late and leave five minutes early—you would simply like to say: Don't expect a glowing review from you on your 360-degree performance evaluations anytime soon! It's hard to run a serious brainstorming meeting when the only people who arrive on time are the seat-warmers eyeing the stale pretzels.

16 **You are hosting your first internal meeting when a couple of stragglers stroll in ten minutes late. Wow! It's so considerate of them to take time out of their busy day to grace your lowly meeting with their presence! Should you restart the meeting for their benefit or proceed?**

A. March forward.

The average internal meeting isn't like a great murder mystery where if one misses the first few minutes of the film one will remain clueless about the plot. Trust that most staffers are regular Sherlocks who will intuit the gist without your having to hit the "pause" and "rewind" buttons. Never feel obligated to pander to latecomers by replaying everything that's already transpired.

Restarting the meeting is chronically unfair to those who arrived on time. (The latecomers are the ones who deserve to be punished!)

For Extra Credit

Simply say to the stragglers, "Thanks for joining us. I'm afraid we have to keep plowing through the agenda, but if you have any questions, please feel free to ask them at the end."

The One and Only Ironclad Excuse to Explain Why You're Ten Minutes Late to an Internal Meeting (Don't Overuse It)

"I'm so sorry I'm late. My computer crashed."

17 **Your internal meeting is well underway when your boss wanders in half an hour late. (What a superb role model he is!) Should you stop the proceedings and bring him up to speed or continue the meeting, uninterrupted?**

A. Split the difference. (After all, he is the boss.)

Make your boss feel grateful that he stopped by rather than vexed that he's so late. Acknowledge his presence. Gently interrupt the staffer who's speaking and quickly recount the agenda items that have been covered, without dwelling on any of them.

Use an icebreaker, such as:

"Thanks for joining us, Stanley. Just to quickly recap, Ashley is our designated note-taker today. Thank you, Ashley. Danny, Petra, and Shelley reported on the upcoming *Hot Mama* marathon, Harry shared some of the MIS issues that continue to plague us, Hunter relayed how he nobly rose to the occasion during a recent client dispute, and we're just hearing now about Thomas's idea for a blog-a-thon that would put the product developers in touch with the customers." (Then keep fingers and toes crossed that Thomas doesn't restart his entire presentation just to impress the boss.)

18 **You are running a few minutes late to your first client meeting. Is there a five-minute grace period, or should you call and apologize the nanosecond that you realize you might be tardy?**

A. It's not so much when you call as what you say when you do.

Be forewarned: Your clients are likely to view even a short time delay as a capital offense.

Clients take special umbrage when you're late because they pay the bills. "We will be charged for these five minutes," clients think ruefully, "and we are not getting our money's worth."

That said, there are taxi strikes, snowstorms, exploding manhole covers, car accidents, bridge and tunnel collapses, traffic rerouting, train breakdowns, and air traffic delays. These legitimate excuses are considered just one step removed from "Acts of God," and thus are the *only* acceptable reasons for your tardiness.

Call the moment that you know you'll be late. (If you have a secretary who can call on your behalf to explain that the 747 you're on just ran out of fuel, necessitating an emergency landing nowhere near the correct airport, even better.)

For Extra Credit

When you arrive, apologize profusely, even if the delay could not have been averted. If love means "never having to say you're sorry," business means saying it all the time.

2. A Reintroduction to Introductions for the Rusty

Introductions are high-anxiety moments for you, transporting you back to an old world with which you are unfamiliar, except possibly through Edith Wharton novels. Are you supposed to introduce the most important person first or the least important person last? Do women get introduced to men or is it the other way around? And haven't the new "gender-bender" rules at the workplace turned the old maxims upside down? With the extraordinary degree of client contact accorded you, your boss no doubt expects you to be suave; pity that formal introductions make you feel like a rube in a cube. You look forward to the day when everyone will bend over backwards to present *you* first; so far, this has never happened. Adding to the angst is the fact that you're pretty certain you just spotted your former boss ducking behind the sprawling shrimp platter.

19 **You're chatting with your boss at a networking event when you spy your ex-boss. They have never met before. Who do you introduce first?**

   A. Your boss.
   B. Your ex-boss.
   C. Neither. Instead, you say something genial to your former boss, such as, "So nice to see you, Carl," and then let your current boss and ex-boss introduce themselves to each other.
   D. Neither. You dive into the hors d'oeuvres, hoping that your former boss won't notice you behind the crudités.

A. Answer A (Your boss.)

You always present the most important person first; in this example it would be your current boss. That means saying his name first: "Stanley Wibbick, I'd like you to meet Carl Jekyll. Carl was my boss at Jekyll & Hyde. Carl, Stanley is my boss at Kiss & Kowtow and the director of business development & strategic partnerships, worldwide."

There Are Only Ten Commandments. Introductions Aren't One of Them

Don't frame an introduction as a command. Never say, "Stanley Wibbick, shake hands with Carl Jekyll."

Some other goofs involve gushing, as in the phrase, "Stanley Wibbick, I'd like you to meet Carl Jekyll. Carl was the best boss I ever had until you, and now you're both vying for my love and adoration." Gushing makes people blush. Flush the gush from your introductions.

Introductions 101

1. **Name elders and high-ranking dignitaries first.** "Mrs. McGuiness, I'm pleased to introduce you to my cube mate, Chris Jenkins. Chris, this is Mrs. McGuiness, our company librarian."
2. **In social situations, men are introduced *to* women.** "Mrs. McGuiness, I'd like to present Mr. Jekyll." In business, however, the gender rule has disappeared. Poof! In these quarters, equality now reins supreme, and "Mr. Jekyll, I'd like to present Mrs. McGuiness" works nicely too.
3. **If you torture someone's name during an introduction, stop and interrupt yourself.** "I'm afraid I inadvertently mispronounced your name, *Dufus*—I mean *Rufus*. Would you kindly say it again, so that I'll get it right next time?"
4. **If you are seated when someone standing introduces himself, stand up.** This is not only polished, polite, and pedigreed, it has the advantage of putting you both on the same level so that you can establish eye contact. Your chiropractor will charge you for fewer neck adjustments. That's a win-win-win.

20 You arrive at a networking event alone and don't know a soul in the room. How do you swallow your jitters so that you can bravely approach a group of people, and, then, what do you say by way of introduction?

A. How do you do?

A friendly smile and a proffered handshake conquer all. Simply say hello and state your name. The person will probably respond by telling you her name and saying what a pleasure it is to meet you. At that point, you might want to pipe in with a request for information or pose a question about the evening's events: "I've never been to a Gurus of Greatness meeting before. Do you know if dinner is held during the presentations or afterwards?" Other questions might center around the Gurus' featured speakers, choice of food, or venue. Don't be shy. Resolve to be the guru of sparkling, pre-dinner gab even if you know no one.

How to Receive a Compliment

A simple "thank you" will do. Nothing could be easier, yet a lot of people find it surprisingly difficult to accept a compliment. So let's practice this together:

Person A: You look great!

You: Thank you.

Person B: Your presentation rocked!

You: Thank you!

Person C: What an amazing job you did.

You: Thank you.

Don't brush off the compliment as if it were lint on a sweater or shirk it off with your body language. If appropriate, sometimes you can add a tiny compliment of your own to the conversation and then lob it back to your admirer like a professional tennis player. For example, when someone tells you that you did a spectacular job on a project, you can say, "Thank you. And I return the compliment. I can't tell you how much I learned from your seminar."

You never want to flatter gratuitously. Only respond to a compliment with one of your own if warranted.

---

21 **While negotiating the frozen tundra during one of the coldest winters in recent history, you bump into a client. Do you leave your gloves on, or remove the right glove to shake hands?**

A. In the dead of winter, leave your gloves on.

Isn't it amazing? Etiquette gives you so many tools that you need to succeed and yet asks so little in return. It does not ask you to risk frostbite or a nasty germ transfer by removing your gloves.

However, on a sublime spring day, it *is* more polite to remove your right glove to shake your client's hand. Do this, and the forecast for your relationship will be seventy degrees and sunny, irrespective of the actual weather.

Kiss, Hug, or Shake Hands?

When it comes to greetings, it's hard to top the handshake here in America. It's friendly, professional, and establishes human contact—all within three seconds.

Don't shrug off the hug if you and a client share a close bond, but let him initiate the gesture. (Imagine how undignified it would be to aim for a hug and have your client awkwardly stick out his hand to fend you off!)

Air kissing—an ironic joke between close friends who would prefer not to smudge their lipstick—does not promote professionalism. Of course if your client air kisses you, there's no reason *not* to return the air kiss. (Try not to say, "Kiss, kiss," when you do it, though, or you may get the kiss off!)

A real kiss on the cheek is rare, especially today, when sexual harassment lawsuits abound. But there are numerous occasions when nothing whatsoever is meant by it, and no offense should be taken.

After a particularly successful new product launch, commercial shoot, or press conference, exuberance runs like adrenalin. If spirits are running high and a client happens to kiss you on the cheek in jubilation, there's no harm in kissing him back on the cheek. (In fact, you *should*, lest he find you cheeky.)

To avoid banging heads or, God forbid, noses, make a beeline with your lips for your client's right cheek.

3. *What's in a Name? Only Everything*

People should not be allowed to stand in clumps, cliques, or coteries at conferences. It's disadvantageous to outsiders, such as yourself. Everyone in the clique already knows one another and they bandy each other's names with aplomb. Meanwhile, you feel like the new kid at school, having to memorize a bunch of strangers' names all at once. For the record, you also find variety to be overrated. There should be only *one name* allowed per alphabetical letter. How are you supposed to keep the Mikes, Marks, and Mitches straight from the Milts, Matts, and Mickies? (The Marys, Maries, and Marges are no better, and add the word "Ann" to a name and you're completely befuddled.) The cliques that band together at these conferences are like a confederacy designed to make you look like a dunce!

 You have total face recall but brutal name recall. What tricks are there for conquering this peculiar brand of forgetfulness?

A. Think of clever ways to repeat the person's name three times during the conversation.

Imagine being able to latch onto a new person's name with perfect recall, instead of having it evaporate from your brain the moment you hear it.

Today is a beautiful day to start that habit.

All habits involve adopting new behavior and figuring out novel ways to make it "stick." This requires repetition over time. So start by repeating the new person's name three times. The first time is easy:

"It's so nice to meet you, Mark," you can say.

The second time requires some tact, but it's not difficult. Look for an opportunity to weave the name "Mark" into the ensuing conversation:

"Mark, how many times have you attended the Gurus of Greatness conference? This is my first."

Excellent job! Now you'll just need to drop the name "Mark" into the dialogue one more time. This can be surprisingly painless. Simply ask for his business card:

"I was wondering if we might exchange business cards, Mark, so that we can debrief about the Gurus of Greatness conference next week sometime? I'd love to hear your thoughts on it once all of the meetings are over."

Name Trick

As you leave the conference, commit Mark's features to your long-term memory bank. When you're alone, jot down a brief physical description of him on the back of his business card. The description should be minimal—you aim merely for a memory jog down the road, at some unspecified date. For example, your description of Mark could read: BROWN HAIR, MID-40's, GLASSES, 5'7. Later, input this information into your Blackberry or Palm Pre and import it into your computer contact base under "notes." Best to keep all physical descriptions ultra-short and objective.

23 Repeating someone's name numerous times when you first meet him makes you sound like a used car salesman! Is there a less clunky way to commit his name to memory?

A. Create two mental files and code them alphabetically.

When a new person first introduces himself to you, quickly decide if he has a common name or an uncommon one. For example, John, Mark, Thomas, and Robert are fairly common names for men. Mary, Ann, Catherine, and Jennifer are common names for women.

If it's a common name, say to yourself, "Common name, initial ___" (and fill in the blank with the first letter of the person's name). Later, when you try to recall the name, this simple shortcut may help spark your memory. You might remind yourself, "I filed that person's name under 'Common name, letter J for John.'"

If the name is uncommon, this technique will still work but it will be aided by repeating the person's name in the conversation once or twice as well.

Never forget to ask for someone's business card. Seeing his name emblazoned on that tiny white billboard is the best memory boost of all!

24 You tried the "common" and "uncommon" file folder trick but found that it only helps you recall common names. How are you supposed to remember uncommon names?

A. Practice mental associations.

A mental association is a rhyme, verbal trick, or photographic recall technique that can help you remember the names of new people.

Let's suppose that you meet a man named Paulo whose breath is torrid. You might try rhyming his name with a popular breath mint and say to yourself, "That *Paulo* could really use a *Mentos.*" Or you might think, "Remind me not to powwow with Paulo without buying him a bottle of Scope."

Or picture that you meet a woman named Janet. Her skin is jaundiced-looking and sickly. You might write yourself a mental note, "The words

'Janet' and 'jaundiced' both start with the letters 'ja.' Janet is the jaundiced-looking one."

Or imagine that you meet a man named Brutus who is real comedian (in his own mind, only). He cracks three jokes a minute. You might think, "Brutus sounds like a Roman name." And you only wish that friends, Romans, and countrymen would lend you their ears so you wouldn't have to listen to another one of Brutus's brutal jokes with your own ears!

Why This Technique Works

You are training your eye to be like a writer's by creating mental pictures that you associate with each new person whom you meet. Pair a physical characteristic with each new name to create a mind-picture and future memory building block that you can return to later. The observations need not be negative to work brilliantly. Someone named Stella might have long, tapered fingers like a stenographer's. Or she might remind you of the Tennessee Williams' character "Stella" in *A Streetcar Named Desire*. Or she might make you think of the Latin word "stella" for star because she's a corporate superstar. Picture yourself filling in a crossword puzzle. The answer is "Stella." What clues might there be to help you recollect this person's name?

Don't Strain Your Brain

Why struggle to remember two names when you only have to recall one? Except in excessively formal situations, most business people expect others to call them by their first names. When meeting several new people at the same time, concentrate on memorizing their first names, and realize that, in time, you'll come to know their last names as well.

---

4. *Pressing the Right Buttons in an Elevator Pitch*

As fate would have it, Satan stops you as you're flying out of the elevator. "Have a minute?" he asks, all innocence and charm. You nod, alert but wary. He never wants to chat before 3:00 PM and it's only nine-thirty in the morning. You've studied his migratory patterns as if he were an arctic tern. "I'd like to hear your elevator pitch," he says, with false brightness. *Huh?* You turn around and glance at the rapidly closing escape hatch, er, elevator, mystified. *You don't pitch elevators, you ride them.* Something about his fiery eyes and standup cowlick makes it difficult to frame a proper question. "Let me get right on that!" you say, in a loud, peppy voice reminiscent of *Alvin and the Chipmunks.* "I can see right through you," your boss says with a smirk. "You have no idea what an elevator pitch is, do you?"

25 Help! What is an elevator pitch?

A. A cute name for a very short but persuasive pitch for a new product, service, or project.

William Shakespeare once wrote, "Brevity is the soul of wit." It's also the essence of the elevator pitch, named for the length of time it takes to ride from the lobby up to a potential investor's office on the top floor of an office building.

Elevator pitches are about two minutes long and explain a new concept in a succinct manner that builds the case and whets investors' appetites to pour money into a project. However, cute name aside, it's actually *atrocious* etiquette to deliver a pitch in an elevator!

Who Knew?

The term "elevator pitch" is typically used to suggest an entrepreneur pitching an idea to a venture capital firm or an "angel" investor. But many other professionals use short pitches to communicate quickly and sell ideas, including project managers, salespeople, literary agents, realtors, policy makers, job hunters, and executive recruiters.

26 What is the key ingredient of an elevator pitch?

A. A great idea, succinctly explained.

An elevator pitch needs to be terse but tantalizing.

First, explain the problem that you're trying to solve. Then, show how your venture will provide an elegant solution. Make sure that your speech is easy to understand and intriguing enough for the listener to invite you back to give a longer, more fleshed-out presentation. Don't be afraid to ask for the "ask," which is a future appointment.

Some Bullet Points to Highlight in an Elevator Pitch in Rapid-Fire Succession . . .

- Industry
- Deal size
- What the transaction will accomplish

And One Point to Minimize

- "I have got this very accomplished friend with an amazing track record…" Yeah, yeah. Heard it. Been there.

---

27 How should you structure an elevator pitch?

A. The same way you'd construct a very tight essay.

Open with a compelling question or quick anecdote that leads the prospect to ask a question.

Then build the body of your case. Explain how your product will answer the question.

Describe the value proposition. Why is the product the smartest, most efficient, or most cost effective? What will it do for buyers? What will it do for investors? (Hint: Making them richer than God is always appreciated.)

Finally, close. Reiterate why your product will fulfill an urgent need—and ask for an appointment to describe it in more detail.

5. *Starting Over: How to Erase a Gruesome First Impression*

You showboated, peacocked, and talked a blue streak with the client at the conference a few nights ago. Now you'd like to request that your boss send you to remedial client relations school, but realize there is no such thing. Conversing with a client, listening to a customer: These are the things they still don't teach at Harvard Business School! On a scale of one to ten, you calculate that your conversational diarrhea gaffe was at least a fifteen, but you are unsure how to rectify it. Do you write a letter of apology or simply go buy yourself a muzzle so that next time you'll shut up and listen harder? What would the ghost of Emily Post advise, and is she asleep at the keyboard today? She hasn't returned any of your emails!

28   **You talked about yourself non-stop during the cocktail hour with the client, and then continued to set the record for longest monologue during dinner. Do you apologize for being the world's biggest narcissist or just bury your head in the sand and pretend the whole sorry conversation never took place?**

A. Get over yourself.
You might try to leave a short, self-deprecating voicemail. Or you can trust that you behaved appropriately.

Perhaps you seemed more vulnerable than you would have liked or showed more of your "real self" than usual. But sometimes vulnerability can be a charming trait, and clients glimpse it so rarely that they often appreciate it!

Go with your instinct. If the client spent four hours by your side, chances are he wasn't bored out of his mind. He could have left you at any time to go talk to someone else. Unless you were holding him captive in a dungeon, of course.

THE STRAIGHT SCOOP

If you really fear that you bent your client's ear against his will, a simple apology mixed with a teaspoon of heartfelt humility should suffice. Then, top it off with a soupçon of flattery: "I'm sorry if I held you hostage the other night at the sales conference. You are such a terrific listener and so much fun to chat with, and I really didn't mean to monopolize you."

Conversation Killers

Great conversationalists carry a list of fail-safe phrases in their heads that will spur dialogue. Some are flattering: "You look terrific! That trip must have really agreed with you." Others are straightforward requests for information. "Do you know where the dinner will be held tonight?" Still others are open-ended questions intended to launch the receiver into an extended discourse. "Did you find the speech informative?"

Here are some phrases to *banish* from your vocabulary:

1. **To an unattached, pregnant female**—"Who's the father?"
2. **To men and women over a certain age**—"How old are you?" Or its cousin question: "What year did you graduate from college?"
3. **To a woman who has lost a lot of weight since the last time you saw her**—"Are you ill?"
4. **To anyone frail or elderly**—"I can't hear you. Speak up!"
5. **To anyone**—"You look exhausted." Or the equally observant, "You look pale."
6. **To anyone back from the hairdresser**—"What in the world have you done to your hair? It looks purple!"
7. **To anyone who's been mysteriously absent and reemerges with tighter skin or a shorter nose**—"Honey, can you tell me the name of your doctor?"

29 In the cold light of day you realize that your client was trying to discuss business while you waxed prolific on movies, sports, and Siberian huskies, of all topics. Is there any way to take back that moment?

A. It's not so much what you talk about, but the degree to which you reveal yourself that matters.

Don't spend a lot of time rehashing what didn't feel quite right about the conversation. It just burns energy better spent on solving a client issue or building the business.

But going forward, try to analyze whether your client is an introvert or an extrovert, and figure out what you are. It could be the key to why the two of you aren't quite clicking. But don't worry: that can change!

There is a concept in psychology called the "Johari window." Some people are introverted and reveal little. Their Johari windows are shut tight. Others are extroverted and reveal a great deal. Their Johari windows stay open even when it's pouring outside. To some degree, your ability to communicate depends on how well you can align your style to those with whom you interact. Are you hobnobbing with an introvert? Strive to be more tight-lipped. If you're fraternizing with a raging extrovert, time to open up your Johari window and let it all hang out.

Given a choice, most people gravitate to others who are like them.[1]

Through the Looking Glass

Are you coming across as likable and empathetic, or petty, territorial, and narcissistic? Practice simple techniques that allow you to see yourself as others do, such as taking photographs of yourself, listening to your outgoing message the way an outsider might, and playing back your voicemail messages to double-check them for tone. Don't be afraid to make minor tweaks. You are a work in progress.

30   In hindsight, the topic was neither black nor white. Your client said black. You said white. Then, inexplicably, your client changed his mind and said white. But by then you realized that he had been right the first time. "No, it's black," you said. Clearly it's a gray area, but by now, things have gotten rather heated. Is there any way to back down?

A. Thank your client for a spirited debate, and tell him that you learned a great deal from his insights.

"The customer is always right," you learned, and so is the client, even when he's dead wrong.

Right or wrong, *insisting* that he's wrong isn't the right thing to do—as far as your company is concerned. Everyone is entitled to his opinion of course, but clients are a little more so.

Stay detached from your own opinions, and you'll find it easier to tolerate other people's (even when their opinions are wrong-headed and twisted). Use "I feel" and "I think" statements rather than accusatory "You" statements.

"It seems to me that the Bull Moose Party had its chance" is less inflammatory than, "You're wrong! The Bull Moose Party blew it! And don't get me started on TR's failed attempt to regain the presidency. It's a hot button issue even now!" (Of course, you shouldn't be discussing politics in the first place. Tsk, tsk.)

At the end of the debate, say something designed to pacify: "Well, we may not see eye to eye, but you made some astute points and I learned more about Teddy Roosevelt tonight than I ever did in American History 101! You had some fascinating insights. I really appreciate having you as my client and I'm thrilled that we're working together. I think we make a dynamite team."

When Words Matter

An "I feel" statement does not necessarily have to use the words "I feel."

It's an admission that the matter is subjective. You happen to view the issue in *this* particular way, but the matter is open to interpretation.

Anecdotal evidence suggests that women prefer to use the actual words "I feel," while some men believe that "I feel" isn't nearly as persuasive as "I think." Here are some other ways to convey the same idea:

- "In my opinion"
- "In my estimation"
- "The way I see it"
- "I believe"
- "I know not everyone will see it the say way, but"
- "It seems to me that"

Agreeing to Disagree Is Not a Copout

Working with people closely sometimes strips away the mask we wear to venture into the outside world. Under the guise might be some unpleasant qualities better left covered, such as stubbornness, an insufferable inability to back down, or even a regional narrow-mindedness. Your real friends probably won't hold it against you, but some clients will *not* take kindly to it.

When you find yourself in the midst of a heated debate, take a giant banana step backwards away from the cliff and ask yourself, "Is it really worth it to me to sacrifice the entire client relationship over this idiotic, miniscule point?"

The answer will certainly be "No."

Then, smile at your client and deliberately cut short the discussion. "Let's simply agree to disagree," you can say. If that sounds too curt, you can soften the sentiment even more by saying, "Let's agree to differ," or, "May this be the largest disagreement we ever have."

Seat-Warmer? Schmoozer? Superstar? Getting a Grip on What Your Handshake Says about You

Men used to extend their open right hands to prove they weren't carrying weapons. The practice dates back to ancient Egypt and Babylon, if not even earlier.

Women were late to catch up to their male counterparts. Then again, back in the old days, women bore children more often than weaponry. But women have been making up for lost time ever since, and today, either sex can extend a hand first (or bear weapons).

The best handshake is firm, but not vice-like, and lasts for three seconds. Keep vigorous hand pumping to a minimum unless you are at a health club. Release your hold as soon as you feel the other person relax his hand.

What's in a shake? Consult the handy handshake horoscope below.

1. **Limp, fish-like handshake**—You are a seat-warmer with few new ideas. You and your handshake are only going through the motions.

2. **Pump, pump, pump handshake**—You are a schmoozer with an overinflated sense of self-importance. People extend their hands to you but wish those hands *were* bearing weapons!

3. **A sure clasp (like a person grasping a tennis racket with a forehand grip)**—You are a go-getter who will move far in your career. Others look to you for your leadership, guidance, and inspiration.

That's a Wrap

1. Never disrupt a productive meeting for a straggler.

2. The most important person is named first; the less important person is presented *to* him.

3. When remembering the names of new people, experiment with repetition, rhyme, and the creation of mind-pictures until you find a technique that works for you.

4. Although real elevator pitches often target wealthy "angel" investors, the elevator pitch is often used to describe other types of sales spiels used by many types of professionals.

5. Occasionally it's a good idea to have a spirited debate with a client because it reveals your vulnerable side. Just keep tabs on when the discussion is about to rage out of control so that you can work to pull it back to a more civil discourse.

CHAPTER 3

Every Line
Has a Silver Lining

Interminable lines and jostling crowds of strangers bring out the worst in us, stripping away the thin veneer of civility that we reserve for those whom we know and like. But while the mass may lack class, this chapter explores how to bring class to the mass.

Long lines challenge our sense of self-worth and make us feel under-appreciated. "How will others ever value our time," we can't help asking, "if we are willing to fritter it away, standing on this long, slow ribbon to nowhere?"

On the other hand, the absence of special treatment makes each line a great democratizing force. Whether you are rich or poor, a billionaire or beggar, in a time crunch or on vacation with nothing but time to kill, you and the others in the chain are all subject to the same rules.

"First come, first served" is law number one. Law number two: no cutting. You can choose to let someone go ahead of you at your discretion, but you are never obligated to give up your status of being served first, if indeed that's when you arrived. Saving someone a place in line will be tolerated— albeit grudgingly. If traveling with others, you may want to roam together as a band.

Lastly, you are not the entertainment. If a stranger in line chooses to engage you in conversation and you're open to it, by all means indulge. But you needn't feel compelled to!

1. *"Excuse Me, but I Hailed That Cab!"*

The competition is out in full force today. On one corner an eagle-beaked old lady, looking fiercely territorial, wields an iron walker. Across the street from her, a harried mom sporting obese purple curlers tries to calm a screaming infant. Kitty corner from her lurks a clot of rowdy teenagers. All three groups wait for cabs, which at rush hour can feel like waiting for Godot. Inconveniently, it has started to rain big sloppy drops that weren't forecast, so none of the cab-waiters sports an umbrella. Things could get ugly, and you're not just talking about your hair. Should you cut off the old lady's access to the first cab that belts by you or genially offer to trade places with her? Is it age before beauty? Or getting back to the office for the 4:00 PM staff meeting? Decisions, decisions.

31 **You relay your destination to your cab driver, and ask him to take a certain route. To your consternation, he starts cursing you out in multiple languages, only half of which you understand. In this battle of the routes, who's right?**

A. You are.

The rider has the right to direct the route. You wouldn't necessarily know it by the way some cabbies react to direction, but you do. So you need not feel guilty about behaving like a "backseat driver."

There are several ways that you can politely insist. You can tell the driver that you've taken this route to your office every day for years and are convinced that traffic will be light. You can also appeal to the driver's sympathy: "If I don't get to the meeting by 4:00 PM, my boss will go nuts," you can implore. But be prepared. Sometimes, your pleas will fall on deaf ears.

Is your driver ignoring your request? Screaming at you *and* ignoring your request? Squawking into his cell phone, screaming at you, *and* ignoring your request? Take it out of his tip.

If your preferred route isn't chosen and the ride ends up costing more as a result, you have the right to forego the tip (or at least severely skimp on it).

Don't Whistle for a Cab (Unless You're a Doorman)
Whistling for a cab is déclassé. Hailing one is considered more genteel. To hail a taxi, simply raise your right arm. You needn't flail about,
flash some leg, or scream unless at least six different groups of people
have leapt in front of you to steal a cab that was rightfully yours. Have
faith that the driver has eyes and can see you.

32   **You're taking a taxi with three superiors from the office. You:**
A. Get in first, and slide all the way over. (You've heard of
apple-polishing. This is seat-polishing.)
B. Get in second, so that you can take the uncomfortable
middle seat.
C. Get in third.
D. Get in fourth so that you sit up front with the driver.

A. Answer D (Get in fourth so that you sit up front with the driver.)
The answer depends on how many people are taking the cab and their
hierarchical rank in comparison to yours. The question asked was about
taking the cab with *three* superiors.

If traveling with *more than two* bosses, offer to sit in the front of the cab
with the driver (and fantasize about the day in the not-too-distant future
when *you'll* be Boss).

However, if traveling *with two bosses or fewer,* enter the cab first and slide
across the seat to the far side to make way for your superiors (unless one of
them kvetches about sitting in the middle).

Since there is more room in the front than in the back, occasionally,
heavyset people prefer to sit up front. If one of your superiors offers, by all
means let him.

The New "Flat" Corporate Ladder

What if you work in a so-called "flat" organization where there is no hierarchy? In that case, determine which person enters the cab first according to his guesstimated salary. The person who makes the least offers to sit with the driver when traveling with three people who earn more money. (This shouldn't blossom into a talking point. Just think about it and act accordingly. Are you still at a loss? Length of service to the company is often another indicator of seniority. Newbies sit with the driver.)

Rest assured, there is *always* some sort of a hierarchy. The structure at most companies is as flat as the Earth.

Time for Some Serious Seatbelt Tightening

If you predate the time when wearing a seatbelt was mandatory, this rule may be as difficult to remember as all nine digits of your social security number. But every year, there are several thousand accidents involving cabs, many traveling at ten miles per hour or less. It doesn't sound scary until you recall the plastic sheathing that often barely separates the riders from the driver. Even an accident at a relatively low speed can send you crashing into that hard, un-crushable, inflexible plastic windowpane. It gives new meaning to the term "plastic surgery." Ouch!

33 **You are thoroughly bewildered whenever work sends you to a city on the zone system. Where were these maps drawn—in the ozone? How on Earth are you supposed to know whether the price you're paying is fair?**

A. Ask a local expert: the driver.

Avoid sticker shock. Verify the price with the driver *before* he puts the pedal to the metal and the price zooms off into the stratosphere. If the price sounds too steep, keep the following in mind:

Note which zone you are starting from and which one you are heading to. (It's always a good idea to know where you are and where you're going.)

Remember that additional charges are not the same as "hidden charges." There could be a perfectly legitimate "rush hour surcharge" or a "luggage charge" tacked on for trips to and from the airport. There is also an extra charge for each additional passenger.

Review the zone map posted inside the cab. Calculate your fare based on the number of zones traversed. Does it more or less match what the driver predicted the ride would cost? Excellent!

Always tip for good service. Tipping ranges between 10 and 15 percent.

The New Math of Tipping

In a *metered* cab, there are two basic ways to calculate the tip: the mathematical method and the rounding-up method.

The mathematical method takes a 20 percent tip as standard, unless the driver quarrels with you, illegally smokes, or refuses to take the route you suggest. (*Like that ever happens.*) But unless you're planning to report him, you should still tip him 15 percent. A 25 percent tip is de rigueur if the driver lifted your luggage or helped you in and out of the vehicle.

The rounding-up method simply rounds up to the nearest dollar, but it still acknowledges that a 20 percent tip is standard. Therefore, a cab fare of $5.40 would be rounded up to $7 not $6.

This just in from a real-life cab driver: More women prefer the mathematical method and more men prefer the rounding-up method. Why? One real-life etiquette author posits it may be due to the fact that most guys hate metallic objects jangling around *down there.*

The Most Embarrassing Thing That Ever Happened to Me in a Cab

Bedecked in my navy blue worsted wool mini skirt and robin blue ostrich cowboy boots, I fastened my seatbelt, as always. But this time when the cab drew up to my destination, the seatbelt refused to pop open.

The seatbelt and I wrestled with each other for several moments. It prevailed.

As my eenie weenie mini skirt slid up a dangerous inch, I posed the dilemma to the cabbie, who at first thought I must be joking.

"Are we on Candid Camera?" he said.

"No, I'm serious."

"A reality TV show then? America . . . such a funny country!"

His bronze face crinkled into accordion folds as he let out a huge chuckle at my expense—literally—the meter kept running. Then, recognizing that I might never disengage without his help, the driver hopped out of the front to aid in my unbinding. A New York moment.

While the two of us tugged at the seatbelt and my skirt skedaddled up my thigh into erotica territory (of the *highest literary quality*, I assure you), I had an epiphany: Staples!

I directed the driver to the closest store location, five blocks away, stuffed twenty dollars into his outstretched palm, and ordered him to buy a large pair of orange-handled scissors. Wielding this life-saving item with finesse, he snipped the seatbelt open, and I rewarded him with *a twenty-dollar tip*, a hefty price for my freedom, but worth it.

Manners Moral: Should a cab driver go out of his way to help you out of a bind, be sure to tip him handsomely.

---

2. *The Commute through Purgatory*

You feared they'd find out about your dalliance and broadcast it on You-Tube. Surely, they'd wonder why you were hanging out in the wrong elevator bank every morning, and with an Accountant, no less. But your merry band of coworkers turned out to be oblivious to your ill-fated love among the elevator banks. They didn't foil it—you blame its demise entirely on the commute. Together, you and the hot, but geographically undesirable, Accountant experimented with trains, buses, and automobiles until they sucked the lifeblood out of your rapport with tedious reroutes and delays. Your impatience flared. The Accountant played "chicken" with one auto merging into his lane too many. And, after a bitter quarrel about the true meaning of the HOV lane, your relationship quickly commuted from the asset side of romance to the debit side.

 34 **Is a man supposed to give his seat to a woman or is that straphanger standby something no one stands by any longer?**

A. Are you sitting down? Good. Stay there.

It's every man for himself and every woman for herself—assuming that the men and women on the train are all perfectly capable of taking care of themselves. But chances are, not everyone on your train or subway this morning will be.

If you spot an elderly man or woman in your caboose, rise and relinquish your seat to this person. It's also polite to offer your seat to pregnant women, and anyone, male or female, who seems excessively burdened—not with the meaning of life—but with a suitcase, shopping bag, or small child.

What if you need to stay seated because you're still polishing a report that's due in an hour? Practice thinking about what needs to be changed while you're standing up.

Being able to think on your feet is a valuable skill that will stead you well in business.

35 **What are the rules regarding texting while driving?**

A. Don't become a statistic.

As fate would have it, text has a lethal subtext: Texting behind the wheel is as dangerous as driving drunk.

Six thousand people die each year and half a million are injured in crashes due to distracted driving. (Hmmm. What are the drivers distracted by? Text "TEXT" to I-D-I-O-T if you have any guesses.)

Kick this pernicious habit. Your car is not your office.

Texting and Driving Don't Mix

To her great credit, Oprah Winfrey asked viewers of her show to take a pledge to turn their cars into "no cell zones." Oprah said that texting behind the wheel was the equivalent of having "four drinks and driving."

According to the Federal Motor Carrier Safety Administration (FMCSA), drivers who text take their eyes off the road for an average of 4.6 seconds for every 6 seconds while texting. At 55 miles per hour, this means that the driver is traveling the length of a football field, including the end zones, without looking at the road.[2]

Driving while talking on the phone can be just as deadly. A University of Toronto study found that a driver talking on a cell phone is *four times more likely* to get into an accident. In a census of police-reported fatal accidents involving cell phone use occurring in the United States, a third of those who were engaged in conversation were using mounted phones of the "hands-free variety." [3]

A survey of Maryland motorists discovered that drivers who used cell phones were more likely to drive while drowsy, travel 20 mph over the speed limit, drive aggressively, run a stop sign, drive after having multiple drinks, and engage in other behaviors that place them at risk for a traffic crash.[4]

---

36 **Is the left lane of an escalator "the passing lane," and if so, why doesn't anyone enforce it at your train station?**

A. You can be The Enforcer.

"Etiquette enforcement." It sounds like a hard, lonely job where the rewards are few and far between. But you don't have to be a tough guy, a wise guy, or even be a guy to be The Enforcer. All you have to say is, "Excuse me, please."

Ask politely enough and you can move mountains (well, people anyway). That said, if everyone departing from a train is saddled with baggage, they have no choice but to drag it onto that skinny escalator right next to them. And while you may be able to convince one or two people to skedaddle out of your way, chances are you won't be able to persuade every last person on a teeming escalator to accommodate you.

Conversely, you could decide to ride the escalator today and ignore Time's inexorable march forward. How long will that ride take out of your day? Perhaps five minutes, tops? Today, you could decide *not* to risk an apoplectic attack worrying about how long it will take to ascend from the station's bowels to the exit—especially since you know that it pretty much *always* takes five minutes.

Flash ahead to the end of your life. Lying on your deathbed, will it really matter if you spend those five extra minutes today refining the chart on page 47 of your report? Perhaps—but not if stressing out about it shaves two years from your lifespan.

As the expression says, "Don't sweat the small stuff."

3. *How Not to Have a Cow at the Cash Machine*

As the singer Meatloaf never crooned, "Two out of five is bad." Only two out of five ATMs are working today. And that's just pitiful. At one of the only two functional ATMs, a couple loiters, bickering about how much cash they need for their weekend getaway. At the second machine, a doddering man appears confused as to his whereabouts. Your heart reaches out to him, but your feet don't. You would *never* sacrifice your hard-earned spot on line! Peering inside the bank just behind the ATM vestibule, you discern another long line slouching towards Kalamazoo, or the teller windows, anyway. You recheck your wallet, just to make certain that you really are down to your last $3. You are spending your entire lunch hour at the ATM machine. Is your life glamorous, or what?

37 The techie from the MIS department rode the elevator downstairs with you, walked one foot ahead of you for three blocks, and then opened the heavy door of the bank—only to let it unceremoniously slam in your face. Who holds the door for whom these days?

A. Someone should hold the door for you if he's five feet ahead of you or less.

You can thank the Women's Liberation movement. Or you can blame it if you prefer. But today, whoever arrives at the door first needs to hold it open for the person behind him. This cuts across all gender lines and is true for men and women, men who look like women, and women who look like men.

We are all equal when it comes to holding the door! So if you arrive first, open the door and *keep holding it open* for the person behind you.

However, if there is someone *far* behind you—over ten feet—then, holding the door for her exacts a heavy burden. It could force her to hurry up and run to the door. This is a case where both people are being far too polite for their own good!

To prevent this incredibly awkward situation, *do not hold the door* for anyone who can't reach the door within thirty seconds without performing a marathon sprint.

38 If an ATM vestibule is empty, is it correct to let the door close behind you?

A. It's not just correct, it's mandatory!

Don't let a potential hoodlum "piggyback" onto your ATM card by allowing him to follow so closely on your heels that he doesn't need to pull out his own ATM card to be let inside.

Empty ATM vestibules can be magnets for thieves, muggers, and other unsavory characters. Take precautions. Try to extract your money during peak hours when there is pedestrian traffic milling around. If you *must* use an ATM after hours and the vestibule is empty, enter and exit with minimal fuss. Don't check your balance or perform any unnecessary ATM functions. Swipe your card, remove it, and withdraw your cash quickly.

A Clean, Well-Lit Room

When selecting an ATM machine, what are the three most important considerations? Location, location, location.

Make sure that the ATM you choose is in a well-lit locale. After sundown, ATMs in heavily trafficked supermarkets are safer than ATMs in the barren vestibules of empty banks.

If there is anyone who looks suspicious, tune into your *E.S.P.A.Y.P.* (Extra Sensory Perception About Yucky People) and leave the vicinity immediately.

Never enter an ATM vestibule at night if you will be the only one there! Ninety-six percent of ATM crime occurs when there is only one person at the ATM machine.[5]

 A lady struggles to squeeze her enormous shopping bag through the revolving door of a bank and once inside, the bag bursts. Should you help her pick up its contents?

A. Absolutely, positively not.

Transfers and withdrawals at ATM machines are high-security operations. It's essential to give anyone engaged in these activities as much space as humanly possible. This takes precedence over helping a random stranger in distress. There's also a sliver of a chance that the woman is a con artist trying to prey on your goodwill.

Don't get distracted from the task at hand. Get in. Get your money. And get out.

4. *When in Starbucks, Do as the Starbuckians Do*

The frappuccino machines whir; the overhead lights dim. Toasted coffee smells waft and cling to the air, forming a fog above the patrons that, for many, mirrors what's going on inside their heads. Twenty strung-out customers await their mid-morning fix. The long line lurches and then comes to a tepid standstill. Every person on the chain gang is either texting or calling someone from a wireless device to alert them that—newsflash!—they have now arrived at Starbucks. Standing there, patiently waiting, you feel unknown, unidentified, anonymous, and faceless. Who cares how you behave? Who's watching? Indeed, who minds if you trip over someone or bang into his elbows on the way to the napkin dispenser?

40   **If no one is there to monitor your behavior, does it really matter whether it's exemplary or poor?**

A. Yes—unlike the proverbial tree falling in the forest with no one around to hear it.

Are you tempted to cut in line? Or, worse, steal someone else's latte just so that you can escape faster? Ask yourself what the Starbuckian experience would be like if everyone cut in line or pilfered drinks that weren't their own. It would be like the wild, wild west and we'd all need to be gunslingers defending our drinks against the bad guys!

The next time you feel the urge to edge out the little old lady or the ebullient sixth graders in front of you, imagine yourself challenging one of them to a duel over a grande latte, and instead smile and say, "After you."

Who Knew?

Manners matter, whether or not they are observed. Manners are the unenforced standards of conduct that show someone to be cultured, polite, and civil. Manners defer to the common good over individual gain.

THE STRAIGHT SCOOP

What do you do if someone cuts ahead of you? You can politely remind her that you were there first, or you can sing Elvis Costello's lyrics inside your head, "Oh I used to be disgusted/And now I try to be amused." Are you with a colleague when the line–cutting incident occurs? Simply ignore it. Snippy comments about the rudeness of others will boomerang back and make you look unprofessional, catty, and mean.

---

41 You always ask for "small," "medium," and "large" whenever you're in Starbucks because their system makes no sense. "Tall" sounds like it's "medium" rather than small. What's wrong with being clear?

A. When in Starbucks . . .

Your comprehension of the English language is on par with a linguist's, but perhaps inadvertently, you're being rude to the people standing in that long, lurching line behind you.

Every time that you request a "medium," the server behind the counter will feel compelled to correct you. "You mean grande?" she'll ask, all pie-eyed and innocent.

"Why, yes," you'll snicker. "I meant to say 'Grande,'" you'll claim, even though (c'mon, admit it) you actually meant "medium."

"Oh, okay," the server will say as if she's never played this game before. "One grande skim cappuccino!" she'll scream to the drink crew in the back.

Cappuccino in hand, chances are you'll think nothing more about the incident, but your exchange with the server just added 2.5 seconds to everyone else's wait in line behind you. Moreover, if you're with a potential client, being a pain in the butt in public may alert him to the fact that you'd be even more of one in private! Most people don't want to work with difficult, picayune sorts.

How to Get around Planet Starbucks

1. **Learn Starbuckese.** Size matters. So does vocabulary. Small = *Tall*, Medium = *Grande*, Large = *Venti*.

2. **Know your order.** It's faster to say, "Venti skim cappuccino no foam" than to say "Uh, you know, I'd like to order a large, no make that a venti, latte, no, I think I'll have a cappuccino after all, and can you go easy on the milk?"

3. **Don't vie for special treatment.** While anecdotal evidence suggests that flirting with the staff *will* succeed in getting you your order sooner, it's horribly impolite to others suffering on the same interminable line, others who perhaps feel too grouchy to flirt this morning. Perhaps they had a fight with a spouse the night before. Being more socially adept does *not* entitle you to skip out of the store after only five minutes when they have to wait fifteen. Etiquette is not about getting to the head of the line faster. Etiquette is about making the process of *standing* in line more tolerable. Remember that. Etiquette is not results-oriented. It's all about the process.

4. **Don't flash your cash.** But have your money ready.

5. **Examine the footprint of the Starbucks when you first enter.** If it's spacious, you may collect your drink and food first if you wish, then circle back to pick up your napkin and other accoutrements on your way out. But if it's a tiny Starbucks, your ingrained behavior may need to change. If the napkin stand is located too close to the line of people waiting to place their order, it's probably smarter to pick up your napkin and straw first, either as you join the line or even beforehand. The architect Ludwig Mies van der Rohe once famously remarked, "God is in the details." So is navigating your morning sojourn to Starbucks.

42   **Every morning you wait on line at Starbucks, as serene as a yogi in meditation. But you can't help noticing that some people behind you in line get served their drinks before you do. What's going on?**

A. They are regulars and you aren't.

The system at Starbucks is "first come, first served" except where regulars are concerned. Once the person behind the counter recognizes you and "knows" your drink, she will automatically make it for you, regardless of the call order for the rest of the patrons.

It may be unjust to everyone trapped behind you on that long, crawling line. But if you want to get out of that store faster, you will have no choice but to become a regular.

Think of it as the "frequent buyers' loophole" of Starbucks etiquette. If the servers whisk you out of the store faster because you're a regular customer, then you're just following protocol. But if you showboat and flirt as a way of escaping faster, then you're exhibiting abominable manners.

5.   *The Bar Where No One Knows Your Name*

It's been a hard day's night. After taking the dog and pony show all the way to San Diego, your team has been informed that you don't have a chance at winning the business. You want to retreat to your hotel room to try to glue the shattered pieces of your ego back together, Humpty-Dumpty style. But others on the team feel that a drink or two (or three or four) might lift spirits. A plan is hatched for everyone to reconvene in one hour at a well-lit Caribbean bar a half mile due south from the hotel. Considering that the boss will probably fire all of you for your team's lousy performance anyway, you opt in. After all, you might need these people for references in the very near future! The bar is crowded and noisy when you arrive, and you feel like the bartender is deliberately ignoring your whole posse.

Bartenders Have Eyes in the Backs of Their Heads

Never fear, the bartender sees you! It is unnecessary to tap your fingers or yelp or even drill your eyes into the back of the bartender's head in the hopes that somehow he'll feel them and turn around to serve you. Trust that the bartender knows you are there and will attend to you the moment that he's done serving the others who actually arrived first.

---

43   **What's the fastest way to a bartender's heart?**

A. Here's a tip.

Live large. And tip generously.

The tip is the same amount at a bar as at a restaurant—between 15-20 percent.

However unless you're running a tab at a bar, be sure to tip drink by drink. When using cash, always round your tip up to the nearest dollar. Carrying around a tip sheet can be très tacky, so here's a "cheat sheet" that you can carry in your head.

Let's suppose that your glass of wine costs $12.00. Move the decimal point over one space to the left. The result is $1.20. That would be a 10 percent tip (which is too low). Now, double the amount. A 20 percent tip would be $2.40. That's a bit high. So you would pick a number in between, which in this case, is $2.00, or 16.66 percent (rounded up, it's 17 percent). Leave $2.00 for each glass of wine.

By the way, there's no reason not to leave the correct tip. Ultimately, your company will pick up the tab.

--- **THE STRAIGHT SCOOP** ---

In a restaurant, it's completely kosher to calculate the tip based on *the cost of the meal alone*. Yet, out of sheer laziness or chronic math phobia, most people use the total plus tax. Depending on which state you happen to be in, sometimes doubling the sales tax or even tripling it is a quick way to arrive at the tip or at least usher you into the right neighborhood. Then you can add a few dollars, or subtract, to make the tip amount more precise.

44   **You never know what to call the bartender. Any suggestions?**

A. "Bartender."

In a recent anecdotal poll, 99.9 percent of bartenders surveyed hated being called *Honey, Darling, Lovey, Miss, Pal, Sir,* and especially *Buddy.* The bartender does not view you as his buddy, unless you happen to be roommates with the fellow. He regards you as a temporary houseguest in his own home. If you behave yourself, which, above all else, means being generous with tips, you are welcome to come back and stay every night if you'd like, and he may even honor your return with a free drink.

If you are disruptive by, for example, hitting on the other houseguests (especially if they happen to be married and sitting with their spouses) or by bringing in colleagues who insist on playing drinking games after midnight, you might be allowed to come back, but don't expect the bartender to trundle out the welcome mat.

If you overstay your welcome by refusing to leave once the lights have been extinguished, you will be escorted from the premises. If you violate the law by smoking cigarettes, anticipate a stern reprimand (unless the bartender also smokes, in which case he may ask to bum one of your cigarettes, or unless the bar is French).

When you first enter a bar, ask yourself if it's the type of establishment that you may want to frequent. If it is, start off your relationship with the bartender with a generous smile and a big, Santa Claus-sized tip.

For Extra Credit

If you tip handsomely enough, most bartenders will pour you a free one on the house. Should that happen, it's only fair to grace the bartender with an even more generous tip.

45 Is it ever appropriate to tip over 20 percent?

A. Yes—when you have treated the bartender like your personal shrink, a work mentor, or your bodyguard.

Long after your buddies leave, you unburden yourself to the bartender. You share your hopes and fears with this perfect stranger. You tell him about the online dating service you once tried where your date was into poultry sacrifice. It still gives you the heebie-jeebies. At midnight, you confess that you've killed every plant you ever owned and feel like a serial Kentia palm murderer. Then you detail how your team botched the most recent assignment and speculate that at least three heads will roll. Visions of headless bodies dance through your head as you order another piña colada and locate "The Piña Colada Song" in the jukebox.

An hour later, you suddenly notice that the bartender has a *beeea-autiful* set of ears and a most *gener-ooouous* hand with liquor. His advice wasn't bad either, that which you can remember. He deserves more than a normal tip! Hey, Satan, this one's on you!

Start with 20 percent and add several dollars to it.

Good. Now, add a few dollars more.

Faster Than a Speeding Rumor

When you're on the road, a local watering hole is the ideal oasis to savor an alcoholic libation. But be cagey about engaging in character assassination in a public place. If you must vent in public about a boss, invent a nickname for him, such as "He Who Must Be Obeyed" and take care not to let the name of your company slip.

That's a Wrap

1. Hailing a cab works on a "first come, first served" basis, even if it's cold outside and you're in a rush.
2. Elderly men and women need to sit down even more than you do, so relinquish your seat to them with a smile.
3. The normal rules of courtesy *do not apply* when your own security could be in jeopardy—such as when you're in an empty ATM vestibule after hours.
4. Becoming a regular patron will rescue you from some lines faster.
5. The quickest way to a bartender's heart is through a generous tip, whether or not you know him.

CHAPTER 4

Meetings 'Round the Great Oval Table

Meetings spawn meetings.

No wonder meetings give meetings a bad name.

Status meetings. Work meetings. Staff meetings. Team meetings. Client meetings. Ad hoc meetings. Management meetings. Kickoff meetings. Pitch meetings. Monthly meetings. Monday morning quarterback sessions. Thursday afternoon huddles. Sales conferences. Debriefs. Customer calls.

Honestly, we have got to stop meeting like this!

The barrage of meetings is a dastardly thief of time. Yet by viewing the time spent in meetings a bit differently, you may be able to make them work for you.

We glean so much information about each other without the words being said. And meetings—even the dreadful sort that drag on for hours where absolutely nothing is accomplished—help us fine-tune these impressions. Start thinking of meetings as your chance to bolster others' impressions of you.

Are you horribly bored? Hide it. Are you irate? Do your best to seem even-tempered. Comport yourself with dignity during these bull sessions, and eventually, you'll move into a position where you are running them. If getting promoted is the only way to make the meetings at your office productive, then really, you have no choice but to shoot for the moon.

1. Never Underestimate the Importance of an Agenda—Transparent or Opaque

You've heard of a meeting of the minds. This is more like a meeting of the mouths. Your boss makes a point. Someone counterpoints. A third points out that we all have clients to service and fires to quell, so could we please resolve this quickly? A fourth pipes in, defending the boss's point of view (usually a junior, or one of the interns). Three or four participants surreptitiously check their smartphones, far too important to be drawn into the controversy. Heads bent, they dash off mission critical texts: YES, HONEY. I'LL BE HOME AT SIX. DO BUY POT ROAST. An hour later, the filibuster draws to its inexorable close. Your boss suggests that since absolutely nothing has been resolved, you all have no choice but to set another meeting.

46 **What agenda? Your boss never seems to have one, and the meetings drag on for hours!**

A. Ask to be put on the agenda.

There's nothing hidden about it. Your only agenda is to *have* an agenda.

Is that so wrong? Of course not. But if you're waiting for your boss to wake up one morning and say, "Wow! I should have had an agenda!" you are looking for management in all the wrong places. You will need to show him the beauty of a well-crafted agenda without drawing attention to the fact that there has never been one at your company before.

Circle around to your boss several days before the next internal head-banger and specifically ask if you can discuss your project during the meeting. Give him a puncture-proof reason why your assignment will benefit from some undivided group attention. If he approves your request, craft an agenda (just for your portion of the meeting). Make the agenda visually appealing, perhaps with three or four bullet points.

As the meeting draws near, print out your agenda, and ask your boss for his final "blessing." (This request should make him feel like a very important dignitary.) Convey that you intend to hand out the printed agenda at the meeting unless he strenuously objects.

Now, imagine that the meeting is a pilot study on the value of agendas. Do your part to increase the likelihood that the meeting will run smoothly. Will there be any allies of yours in the room? Tell them in advance that your project will be discussed, and gather their input so you can factor it in *before* the meeting starts.

If, for any reason, your boss approves of you speaking in the meeting but doesn't wish the agenda to be distributed, follow his lead.

Before you ever become a general, you have to prove that you're a good soldier.

 47   Everyone else seems to get heard at the meetings but you. How can you get your day in court, er, at the next meeting?

A. Raise your hand.

Is it your project? Get yourself on the agenda in advance if possible. That's your best guarantee of having a "voice" at the meeting.

Is it someone else's project? Let him have his five minutes of fame. Don't be one of those people who thrill to the sound of their own voices! If you have no ownership rights to the project, then really, your voice doesn't "count," and those who toiled long and hard on the assignment probably won't appreciate hearing your opinion (unless it agrees with their own, of course).

But if it is *your* project that's being discussed and you can't seem to get a word in edgewise, raise your hand. Look the meeting organizer in the eye and lift your arm. Hopefully, he'll acknowledge you, and then you'll take the spotlight as everyone in the room simultaneously pivots in your direction to stare at you, wondering what could be important enough for you to go out on a limb.

If that fails, stand up. In that brief pause when everyone quits talking for just a second to imagine how you could possibly be leaving when it's *your* project that's under the microscope, you will finally find an attentive audience keen to hear your thoughts!

For Extra Credit

Eloquence is a learned trait. If you know for a fact that you'll be called upon to speak in the meeting, rehearse your speech. Ideally, you want to seem spontaneous rather than studied and practiced. But as Olympic figure skaters know, it takes an enormous amount of advance preparation and effort to look effortless!

To More Productive Meetings

As compliments go, "You run a tight meeting" is on par with "You have outstanding leadership ability." It may not be strictly true, since running a meeting that begins and ends on time is more of a display of managerial agility than of any leadership prowess, but it still makes *VIH's* (Very Important Honchos) perk up and take notice. Ideally, you would like every meeting to be time well spent. If it's your meeting, follow the steps below to make sure the "face time" doesn't devolve into a faceoff. (If it's someone else's meeting, try leaving this book open on your desk and see if he picks up the hint.)

1. **Timing is everything.** Monday morning quarterback meetings at 9:00 AM are a good idea. Meetings on Friday afternoons—when everyone's thoughts have turned to beer and guacamole—are chronically unpopular, unless you're willing to bring Margaritaville to the conference room.
2. **Have everyone confirm their attendance.** It's not too much to ask.
3. **Develop an agenda that will allow for a short but productive brainstorm.** Do internal meetings generally last for fifty minutes? Pare down the waiting-for-the-meeting-to-begin time and the yada yada yada, and you can shave your meeting time to thirty-five minutes.

4. **Send a reminder notice.** If your office uses a program such as Microsoft Outlook, it will automatically place the meeting on the calendar and shoot attendees a reminder minutes beforehand.

5. **A few days before the powwow, ask key players if they have any issues they would like to raise.** Tell everyone to keep his or her speeches and presentations to *under* five minutes.

6. **Draw a hard line with the gaggle of stragglers.** Relentlessly proceed with your meeting in spite of any latecomers. Then return the favor: Never a straggler be.

7. **Announce the rules.** Pretend you're Henry Martyn Robert, better known as the guy who wrote *Robert's Rules of Order* during the 19th century. Bullet the agenda items that you expect to cover.

8. **Orchestrate the meeting.** This way each person with an agenda item can raise it without interruption.

9. **Assign a scribe to take notes.** You need to run the meeting and can't multitask.

10. **Leave time at the end for Q&A.**

11. **Cut the meeting off at the appointed thirty-five minute mark.** Better to leave everyone wishing the bull session had lasted a bit longer than in pain from hemorrhoids caused by an endless meeting!

12. **Follow up.** If there are unanswered questions, assign a mini team to the project and set up a time for those members to meet. They can report back to the group at large at a later date.

48 What's the fastest way to table an issue at a meeting?

A. Suggest that the issue be resolved offline.

There are many sage reasons to do this. If the meeting seems to be stretching to eternity for no reason, you can suggest tabling the rest of the agenda.

If there is one issue that draws heat from the people sitting around the conference room table, putting off the discussion protects the table from spontaneously bursting into flames and gives tempers a chance to dampen.

If group discussion of one issue devolves into a drawn-out dialogue between just two of the participants, you might suggest that they find a time to fence with each other about it *without* the benefit of an audience and present a solution to the group the next time around.

Most team members respect tight agendas and meetings that begin and end within ten minutes of when they're supposed to.

Keep your meetings crisp and moving.

Who Knew?

At meetings, people sometimes cut off discussion by saying, "Let's continue that conversation offline." It's a curious malapropism, as clearly, the "offline" meeting will simply be another in-person, face-to-face meeting that doesn't involve the computer.

Today, "offline" is a new synonym for "in person." You heard it here first!

Pseudo Parliamentary Procedure 101

Companies, even those with supposedly "flat" hierarchical structures, should not be confused with democracies.

This is why you'd be well advised to *never* suggest taking a vote as a way to resolve an issue—unless the matter is of the most trivial importance.

You can call a vote on whether to have doughnuts or bagels at the Friday morning staff meeting if you wish, but only if you're willing to bring them!

---

2. *Breaking Through Devious, Deranged, and Dastardly Personalities*

You don't get it. You simply can't fathom why the whole team has to meet in conference rooms when you can all hear each other perfectly clearly through the felt walls in the Cube Farm. *Hail, hail, the gang's all here,* your boss bellows with enthusiasm. But you are all attached like pearls on a necklace anyway. What, you wonder, is the real agenda behind your boss's agenda-free meetings? Are they simply a way for the pinstripes to make sure the plaid shirts are still working at the company? One of those pinstripes has started to drive you crazy, adding to your considerable ambivalence about attending the meetings in the first place. Clearly, this bloviator believes meetings are for *saying* smart things instead of *doing* anything smart. And the only way he ever feels smart is by putting you down. So by now, he must feel like a frickin' genius!

 There is a new man on your team who tries to bully you into silence. The moment you open your mouth to speak, he interrupts you. What can you do to make him stop?

A. Realize that he's trying to put you down. And do what you can to prop yourself up.

First, understand the psychology behind his constant interruptions. He's trying to undermine you to gain status. He perceives that by putting you down, it somehow makes him look smarter.

If he is your exact equal, you might try acknowledging his need to interrupt with either a quick segue or even a light joke, as long as you can do so and get back to your point.

The segue approach: "Ah, well, I see that not everyone in the room agrees with my take on this, and I'm looking forward to hearing David's point of view *after* I finish what I am getting at." (Then, once finished, politely ask David to comment.)

The light joke approach: "I honestly applaud your passion for this project, David. And I know you don't mean to interrupt, but let me just quickly finish by saying..."

Both the segue and light joke tacks will be more effective if you can deliver them with a "smile" in your voice.

50   **You fear that disagreeing with someone will be perceived as belligerent. Is there a polite way to get your point across?**

A. Pedal softly, but be direct.

Think before you speak, and if necessary, jot down a note or two about the points you wish to express long *before* you open your mouth. Then translate your key arguments into what psychologists call "I feel" language.

Look at your opponent and calmly say, "I feel that pursuing this path may be a mistake." Back up your assertion with any research or hard evidence you may have: "In the last focus group, we learned that customers in their mid-fifties hate being referred to as 'seniors' because in their minds, they are still young and vibrant. Yet our list doesn't allow us to segment by people's age. I worry that we may inadvertently insult a good portion of our market with this approach." Next, propose a novel solution: "Instead of calling the promotion, 'Senior Special,' let's call it something that makes everyone feel young again, like 'Spring Fling' or 'March Madness.'"

> *Why This Technique Works*

You're disagreeing with someone in neutral language that won't automatically put him on the defensive. Instead of using negatively charged trigger phrases such as "You're wrong" or "Are you nuts? Clearly this won't work!," you're softening your language so that your listener might actually have a shot at hearing it. You are also positioning your disagreement in subjective terms by using phrases such as "I feel that" and "I worry," which acknowledge that you are expressing an opinion rather than a concrete fact. Finally, the solution that you propose is eminently reasonable.

That's So Not Funny: Why Sarcasm Leaves a Bitter Aftertaste

Sarcasm is a humorous comment based on expressing the polar opposite of what you mean.

A coworker three cubicles down from you conducts a meeting with a potential new business prospect over speakerphone. You have no reason to be involved with that particular pitch, yet you can't help overhearing the entire meeting through the flimsy cubicle walls. Static emerges from his phone in erratic gunfire bursts. Once the conference call ends, you swing by your coworker's cube.

"Thanks for sharing your meeting with the entire office," you say. "I really learned a lot!" Your coworker apologizes.

A colleague stumbles into the office one Thursday morning wearing blue jeans instead of "business casual" work attire that is the required uniform at your company.

"Thanks for dressing up," you say.

A coworker stops you and comments on how deadly the meeting was. "Oh, really?" you zing back as if you hadn't noticed. He laughs, and the two of you have formed a bond. You're both in on the cosmic joke—for the moment.

But let's suppose that a few days later, that coworker overhears you making a sarcastic comment to someone else on staff.

"Love the new do!" you chirp to the Receptionist who looks like she's the diva of bedhead.

Suddenly, instead of thinking of you as the office clown, your coworker begins to suspect that you've got a nasty streak. And he is not alone.

If you find your sarcasm skills flowering with unusual frequency, keep in mind that this shrub comes with thorns—you risk coming across as mean-spirited if you use sarcasm too often.

While sarcasm can be your best defense against a coworker who constantly tries to belittle you, it can also work against you if you use it so often that everyone on the team secretly thinks you're a jerk.

Resolve not to be one of those post-modern jokesters who view the world as if all speech, actions, and thoughts must be inserted between ironic quotes.

Watercooler Wisdom

"Human nature is so constituted that if we take absolutely no notice of anger or abuse, the person indulging in it will soon weary of it and stop." —Mohandas Gandhi

51 **Your boss diligently thanks workers for their contributions to a project in public, but for some unknown reason all of the clients assume that he's the one who's propping up the whole department. How can you get the credit you deserve?**

A. Imitate what he does and thank the people who helped you on the project.

To some extent, your job is to make your boss look good. You're being paid to follow his directions and employ your special talents in service of the greater team. Think of him as the coach. In sports, coaches always get credit for the wins and blame for the losses of their teams. Anything brilliant that anyone on the team ever does will make your boss look absolutely phenomenal.

But if you want to get more credit and lift morale, start thinking of yourself as the team captain. You can't promote yourself if it's not true, but you can certainly begin crediting others on your team for their efforts. This will make them feel highly regarded and make you look as if you have leadership capabilities.

Oddly enough, credit tends to trickle up in organizations. Start taking advantage of Trickle Up Theory™ no matter what level you happen to be at right now. Instead of worrying about the credit that you're *not* receiving, start seeking ways to give others the credit they deserve. Chances are, your leadership will eventually be recognized. And in the interim, everyone on the team will love working with you.

The benefits of tooting other people's horns can't be overestimated.

Thank You. No, Thank *You.*

Every day is Thanksgiving. Well, maybe not, but try to seek opportunities to thank people on staff before the holiday rolls around and everyone is at home, stuffing his and her face with marshmellowed yams.

Are you hosting a meeting? Thank people twice—once at the start for taking the time out of their busy schedules and once at the close of the fabulous confab for their input. Studies show that employees appreciate morale-boosting pats on the back almost as much as raises. So trust in the power of positive thanking.

Then, you can thank the Academy and your parents for having you.

---

3. *Tom, Dick, or Hilda? Decoding the Pecking Order*

You have never seen so many clients clumped together in one tiny, sterile room. There are thousands of them. Granted, that's a slight exaggeration, but there are at least ten. And, to a person, they are all wearing blue suits. It's like a sea of blue! The faces swim before you, only distinguished by their ties and scarves. How is it possible that all of these terribly important people can find time in their jampacked schedules to meet in person on something so mind-bogglingly trivial? Isn't that what teleconferencing is for? You quickly shake hands with the clients: seven men and three women. (Or is it four women? It's hard to tell under that moustache). Then you sink into a chair made of 100 percent tan leatherette. If someone offered you a million dollars at this very moment to rank the clients, from most important to least, you would be just as impoverished as you are today.

 You know what the clients' titles are but have no idea what the titles mean in terms of pecking order. What's the cleverest way to find out?

A. Watch how the clients treat each other.

Beware of title inflation. It can make the humblest secretary sound like she is a vice president and a vice president sound like he's Grand Poohbah. Meanwhile, someone else in the room may have the Grand Poohbah's ear, or it's equally possible that no one does. (The Poohbah says, "Bah humbug," to all ideas that aren't his own.)

Attend as many meetings as possible and pay special attention to how the clients behave towards each other. Much can be gleaned by simple observation.

Through both verbal and unspoken cues, the rank and file of an organization often betray who is the top dog, who is the middle dog, and who isn't yet worthy of a bone.

In some companies, the tradition is that the *lowest-ranking person* in the room cites his opinion first. In others, it could be the *highest-ranking* person. Do the other clients nod vigorously when this person speaks? Or do they trample on what he says with the weight and girth of their own opinions? Is there one person with whom all the others seem to agree? Are any of them taking notes? (Notetakers are never the most important players in a room.)

When you are back in your office, pull out your clients' business cards and compare your own observations with their titles. Doing so will help you shed light on the real pecking order.

THE STRAIGHT SCOOP

When you first call on a client, leave your business card with him. Chances are, he will give you his card as well. (Most executives receive a huge batch of business cards and are dying to give them away to as many people as humanly possible.) If he does not give you his card, don't take offense. He probably has a perfectly reasonable excuse, like his box of business cards happens to be doubling as a doorstop.

Cheat Pad

You may not be able to memorize a lot of new names quickly, but you can certainly set up a smart name "cheat sheet" during any meeting you ever have with any new people. When you first sit down at the table, remove a pad of paper and devote the top quarter of the page on the right-hand side to capturing people's names. It's helpful to jot down the names in the same order in which people are seated. Mentally circle around the table, and write down the names, moving from left to right (clockwise). If George, Jake, Julie, and Jillian are all seated together, left to right, then write down their names in that order. If George is seated next to someone whose name you can't recall, skip a space in your list. So it would read:

George

_____

Julie

Jillian

This way, if you happen to discover Jake's name later in the meeting, you can place him in the correct order on your cheat sheet.

53 Employees at your company march shoulder to shoulder with their opposite numbers on the client side. People at your level are supposed to interact only with those clients at their exact level. Is there any way around that? Your counterpart is a complete nincompoop!

A. No. Just roll with the punches.

Try to figure out what the underlying problem is and work around it.

Is he disorganized? Design a schedule of polite memory jogs and jingles for him so that he'll remember to follow through on any necessary approvals.

Is he powerless at his company? Ask him what you can do to help see the project through. Don't step on any toes or trip on any coattails, but inquire if he might want your team to come back to present *with him* to his upper management. If he needs any backup, you've got plenty of reinforcements.

Is he a waffler? Help him streamline the scope of the project. Beyond that, offer to help him weed out any ideas or approaches he doesn't like. If he really can't make up his mind, you can always suggest focus group research, which will delay the real decision even longer but may make him *feel* as if he's accomplishing something vital.

Is he terrified of his own shadow? Don't take him outdoors on Groundhog Day, but *do take him* out for lunches and dinners as much as your corporate budget will allow. It's important to befriend this fellow. He may not be a rocket scientist, but he also hasn't made scores of internal enemies. It's likely that he will be in the organization for a long time and rise to great heights!

Visit with Your Eyes

It's impolite to stare, but it's also rude not to acknowledge. Don't lock onto anyone's eyes, but spend time visiting with each client at the table with your eyes. Train your eyes on a client's face for one or two seconds and then move your eyes onto the next client's face. Let your eyes linger a little longer on any client who is speaking rather than on anyone who's taking notes. You often don't know who the most important person in the room will turn out to be, so you can't afford to ignore anyone.

54 **Are there any rules about business cards? It seems like we've entered the era of "anything goes."**

A. You will never go awry following the old rules.

Rolodexes may be beyond out, but business cards are not going out of fashion anytime soon. And these days, there's renewed interest in how much information to cram onto these tiny placards.

What with the office landline number, fax number, website, Twitter account, direct dial, cell, and your own Blackberry number, contact information has mushroomed into a novel that's the length of Leo Tolstoy's *War and Peace* without any of the hairpin plot twists.

If it's your charge to design a business card, consider what its primary purpose will be and whether its recipients will truly need to be able to reach you 24/7. If they don't, you may want to eliminate some of the contact information in favor of more precious white space. This will make your business card look crisper, snazzier, and more visually gripping.

The standard business card size is 3.5 inches by 2 inches and has a land-scape (horizontal) orientation. Think twice before deviating from this size, because it was designed to fit conveniently in most wallets.

Think three times before turning your business card into a folded "tent" or mini brochure! We are all inundated with marketingese. Your business card should have a "tell me" feel to it, not to be confused with a "sell me" gestalt—even if you're a salesperson.

Unless there's a special branding or marketing reason to do otherwise, the background color of the card should be white, off-white, or ivory to enhance legibility. The type needs to be one color and in the same font unless there is a company logo, which likely has its own typeface.

Navy, gray, burgundy, and black are perennially popular colors for type, but they may not be appropriate if your company has a youthful, cutting-edge reputation. The business card should capture the corporate culture of your company, be it conservative, old line, and institutional or hip, modern, and wired.

Sometimes a small design element on the card breaks the color scheme, and either this design element or the type or both can be embossed (i.e., raised) for a more elegant, luxurious feel.

As a general rule, the person's name—with the title just beneath it—is centered. The company name and address are often (but not always) nestled in the left lower corner while the phone number, fax, and email address are in the right lower corner.

4. *Why Women Take More Notes than Men and Why They Should Stop*

In school you were graded on your regurgitation skills. And your ability to spit back facts, figures, and historical data with the precision of a video camera earned you high marks. But in business, everyone is graded on a completely different set of criteria—such as the ability to soothe ruffled client feathers (clients are birds, you know), cheerlead one's underlings to greatness, and get behind a set of sky-high projections that were concocted by someone who must have been very *high* indeed. No one blinks if you can't reiterate what anyone else said verbatim. So why does the new woman on the team seem to be writing down *every single phrase* that you've uttered during your presentation? Your oratory skills are good, but they're not *that* good!

55 A woman on your team takes copious notes during everyone's presentations. Meanwhile, you never pull out your pen and notepad. Who's right?

A. You are.

Note well: Taking notes is rarely a good notion.

When teammates present ideas, it's only courteous to listen. If you only listen with your ears, you will receive only half of the information conveyed. Active listening uses two senses—sight and sound. It's only fair to the person speaking to listen with your whole body, and that's impossible to do when you're looking down, taking notes. Pivot your body towards the speaker and sit up straight. This shows him that you're paying attention.

Watch the presentation closely. Do you have any questions? Scribble them quickly, but don't try to capture his entire presentation in shorthand. He can always forward the presentation to you after the meeting if you really need it. So show your support by opening both your eyes and ears to the wisdom he imparts.

56 Should you ever take notes during a job interview?

A. Never. Don't act like a court stenographer.

Note taking is a telltale sign of being a junior. Even if you *are* a junior, you never want act like one!

Taking notes betrays a lack of confidence in your ability to remember what your interviewer is saying. Whatever you may gain in terms of accurately recalling every detail you will lose, both in terms of "face time" and eye contact.

Your eyes are cast down, staring at your paper instead of peering into your interviewer's eyes. Plus if he wants to convey anything remotely confidential about the team, morale, current situation, present or past management—he can't! (He's too worried that you'll write it down.)

Don't try to simulate the demeanor of an obedient student. It's so much savvier to look like a leader in training!

57 Do you have any recourse if your client or customer takes notes?

A. Not really, no.

You can't change anyone's behavior unless the person really *wants* to change it. This is not just one of the key tenets behind etiquette; it's a great philosophy to keep in mind whenever you encounter humans.

You can light up the room with a joke or some charming banter so that your client will look up at you when you first begin speaking. And you can make your talk so riveting that he'll have no choice but to glance up at you occasionally. But you can never ask him to "please put the damned pen down" or to stop taking notes: These requests will make him feel like a fish out of water. And towards what end? Your request goes counter to his corporate culture, which may reduce his willingness to do business with you. Oh no!

If you find yourself presenting to a note-taker, take solace in the fact that at least every single word of your presentation is being documented! You won't have to send him the tape-recorded version later.

5.   *Getting Past the Definite Maybe*

If deciding not to decide is a decision, then your client is superb at it. Meanwhile, you can't decide if he's commitmentphobic, passive-aggressive, aggressive-passive, or just plain lazy. You want to tell him that *no* decision should ever take this long, and that he should just trust his instincts. Unfortunately, the *one* instinct that he seems to possess in spades is to draw out this process for as long as humanly possible. He has strung you and your team along for four months, three weeks, and 67.2 hours! When someone who's essential to your success won't say either "yes" or "no," how do you make it comfortable for him to turn a definite maybe into a "definitely?"

58   **Your client promised to review the presentation three weeks ago. But every time you check in with him, he has forty-seven items on his to-do list to check off first. SCREECH! That's the sound of momentum braking to a dead halt. How can you break the impasse?**

A.   **Offer to meet him in person on his turf.**

Emails, phone calls, and texting all lose their effectiveness with the bleating sounds of constant repetition. Your client may mean to follow through, but after he's received two emails from you posing the identical question, the third one is bound to strike him as nagging. And while most people may tolerate nagging from a significant other or spouse, that's only helpful if you're *married* to the client!

You need to give him a meaty reason to come to the table that's incontrovertible: lunch.

Offer to meet him in a spot that's convenient *only* for him, such as at a delicious eatery that's spitting distance from his office (not literally, spitting is poor etiquette).

Sweeten the deal by adding an element of "fun" to your suggested meeting, if possible. Instead of having the subject of your email promise something that's as drab as dishwater, such as "Checking in on the status of the GHI project," craft a line that shows some spunk, such as "There is such a thing as a free lunch!" Then offer to take him to his favorite lunch hideaway to discuss his idea on the project.

Why This Technique Works

Congratulations! You've turned your frustration with his delay into a tangible benefit for you both. Your client now has an incentive to review the project while you can finally stop needling him and actually move the project forward. Plus the lunch really is free, assuming, of course, that you can expense it.

The Seamy Underbelly of Delay

Delay on a client's part is not always due to indecision or waffling. He may be stretching out the process to allow a competitor the time he needs put in a bid that will undercut yours. This is questionable etiquette on his part. But you can rise above it. Come up with some new information as a reason to meet in person. Then, surface any outstanding issues one-on-one to see if they can be resolved. At that time, ask if he is exploring other options.

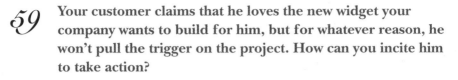

59 Your customer claims that he loves the new widget your company wants to build for him, but for whatever reason, he won't pull the trigger on the project. How can you incite him to take action?

A. Show him how buying your widget will make him look like a genius to his management team.

What's in it for him, you need to ask yourself. Glory! Accolades! Super-stardom! Your customer needs to perceive that, in addition to all of its other virtues for the end-customers, your product will make him shine in front of his superiors. (However, be cagey about the way you phrase it. He may be reluctant to admit that he's motivated by anything other than what's best for the company.)

When you put his needs first, he's far more likely to arrive at the decision you wish.

The Three R's of Getting to the Next Step

You've had a productive meeting and now you just want your client to sign on the dotted line. But your client is not about to sign his life away on such short notice. Can you help him take a mini step in the right direction? You can, and you should. Otherwise, that first meeting will simply beget more meetings and probably even more meetings after that! Meeting reduction is a beautiful thing. This can sometimes be achieved by espousing clarity.

1. **Rephrase.** At the end of a meeting, quickly sum up the scope of what was covered. "This was a great meeting, Wyatt. Today we covered A, B, and C." Then ask for agreement. "If we do all three, is that a list?"

2. **Reiterate.** Restate any pressing homework that your company must do or any research that your client needs to investigate before you both meet again. "So, in terms of our next move, I'm going to go back to the

> troops and ask them to brainstorm on D while you'll talk to your boss about that persnickety E issue." Set a date to discuss issues D and E.
>
> 3.   **Repeat.** Commit steps one and two to a conference report or letter once you get back to the office and gently re-emphasize the agreed upon next steps and the deadline.

60   You believe that your client is less likely to concede when you ask him for something than when others do. He had a close relationship with your former boss, but that person is no longer with the company. You suspect that your client stalls because he just doesn't like you all that much. Suggestions?

A.   Make sure that it's not a matter of his preferred working style versus yours.

"Don't take things personally," you always hear. "It's just business." That's a great maxim to keep in mind when it happens to be true. But sometimes, a person's preferred working style *can* interfere with his or her ability to get work done. Make sure that you're not one of those people!

Do you strongly favor early morning calls? That may not work if your client is a late riser. Do you vastly prefer email to any calls? You may be missing vital signals that your client would rather discuss the matter via phone. Are your emails a study in formality from a bygone era? That may impress some clients and customers but turn off others.

Flexibility is one strong predictor of success. If you have clients, you will need to tease out what their preferred personal working styles are and then force yourself to adapt, because *their* preferences always take precedence over *yours*!

If you are not sure what your client's preferred working style is, there's no harm in asking him. "Do you prefer emails or calls?" you might ask sometime when you're not pulling out a hair from your head, carefully wrapping it around your finger, and then snapping it in two while you wait for him to get back to you.

Remember always: Great selling is in the asking. If you want to sell, don't tell. Ask instead.

That's a Wrap

1. Sometimes, asking to be put on the meeting agenda can actually inspire your boss to craft one.
2. When disagreeing with someone, use neutral "I feel" language, and back up your assertion with hard research if possible.
3. Titles on business cards are an indication of one's power and stature within a firm, but watching people in action is also a valid test.
4. No one, male or female, should ever take copious notes during a presentation when it's so easy to request a copy of the presentation deck.
5. Don't automatically assume that the friction between you and a client is due to personality differences. The tension could be caused by a distinct difference in preferred working styles, in which case you will need to adjust yours.

CHAPTER 5

When in Rome . . .

It's a small world, we're told. And in some ways, that's true. Travel to most major cities and you can't help but notice that the same stores now exist everywhere. On an upscale cul-de-sac, Milan doesn't look all that different from Beverly Hills. Oh, look. There's the Armani store, Cartier, Tiffany's, and even Starbucks. Maybe if the dollar is strong, you can pick up an Hermes watch from Hermes in Madrid that's even less than what you'd pay for it in New York City. The world is our shopping mall.

Stroll around the corner and you can hear Madonna and Taylor Swift belting out the latest pop tunes from a merchant's radio. Buy a Coke. Snap some photos with your cell phone camera.

It's just like home, but with better architecture.

Some believe that the impact of globalization, including the unprecedented spread of the Internet across the International Date Line and consciousness, has almost eliminated the need to brush up on cultural distinctions. But business traveler beware: Those differences cut deep.

Cultural attitudes, behaviors, and beliefs run like the fault lines of an earthquake throughout different nations. Tread carefully. Learn how to navigate the terrain and never assume that things work just the same way "over there" as they do here. This chapter will serve as an introduction to some of the cultural diversity you'll discover in the big, beautiful world out there. For further study, you'll find recommended resources in the Bibliography.

1. *The Myth of the Ugly American*

You are not loud. You are not fat. And, when you look at yourself in your full-length mirror at home, you do believe you're rather fetching. And yet, when Satan informs you that you're being sent abroad for a quick due diligence trip spanning six countries on three continents, you experience crippling fear. The myth of the ugly American looms large in your mind, even if you don't wear shorts or slop ketchup all over filet mignon. Will you be perceived as a member of your Latin American client's affinity circle? Will you be able to greet your Japanese counterparts with humility but without embarrassing yourself? Will you feel upbeat and confident even when you're down under in Australia? With some advance planning and a quick refresher course, it's eminently possible.

61 **What are the top three mistakes that Americans make while trying to conduct business abroad?**

A. Gestures, gestures, gestures.

Not every American custom translates well when you're halfway across the world. In the United States, smiling often sends the recipient a positive, happy signal. But in some cultures, a benign smile can be misinterpreted. In some Latin cultures, a smile is meant to convey "excuse me," or the word "please." And in some Asian cultures, smiling is reserved only for informal occasions. You aren't supposed to smile during a formal introduction, so please, wipe that look of glee off your face.

Another bugaboo for Americans abroad is eye contact. In some Asian cultures, it's actually considered a sign of respect to *avoid* looking at someone directly in the eye. Even the British have been known not to look at each other when they speak. Here's *not* looking at you, kid.

The thumbs up sign, which in America means "Great going!" or "Great job!", is a gesture of disrespect throughout Australia and countless other destinations. (FYI: It's definitely not a good idea to hitchhike in these places by sticking your thumb up.)

Some American Gestures that May Be Misunderstood Abroad

We tend to think of gestures as being "beyond language." Nothing could be further from the truth. Most gestures do not have universal meanings. They have specific meanings with different nuances from culture to culture.

Several American presidents learned this the hard way while traveling to foreign cultures. These U.S. presidents flashed gestures that were interpreted one way in the United States but whose meanings did not translate the same way in the country visited. And you can be sure that this presidential ignorance did not reflect well on the highest "office" in the land!

But with a little advance homework, you can avoid that humiliation at your office. Here are just a few of the gestures to pay attention to when you're traveling. But there is no substitute for reading up on the specific country where you will be doing business. Be sure to ask your business associates and friends about their own experiences as well.

1. **Thumbs-up Sign (sticking the thumb up while the palm remains closed).** The thumbs-up sign can be a real thumbs down. In Australia, the thumbs-up sign shows disrespect. In Nigeria, it's a sign of derision. It's considered hideously offensive throughout the Middle East. But leave it to the French to have a completely different interpretation. In France, it means "okay." Okay? Meanwhile, in the United Kingdom and Russia it signals approval, much like the American interpretation.

2. **Okay Sign (thumb and forefinger forming a circle).** In Norway, it's an insult. In Guatemala and Russia, it's obscene. In Brazil, it's as lewd as a hand gesture involving a middle finger. In Spain, it's just plain gauche. But leave it to the French once again to weigh in with their own interpretation! In France, it means "zero," or "zed." Viva la France!

3. **Smiling.** You always want to put your best face forward, but believe it or not, smiling is not always universally appreciated. Never smile while being formally introduced in Japan. In Greece, smiling sometimes indicates the person is angry. (Greeks smile both when they're happy and when they're upset.)

4. **Nodding.** In Bulgaria, a nod means "no," while shaking your head from side to side means "yes."

5. **Chin Flick (stroking fingertips under chin and thrusting them forward).** It's a sign of contempt in Italy.

6. **Fidgeting (toe tapping, knee jiggling, etc.).** Avoid fidgeting in Ecuador as it's considered terribly distracting.

7. **Gesturing with your left hand.** The left hand is considered unclean in the Arab world because of what it might have touched. Never shake hands, eat, or present an object with your left hand. Use your right hand instead. (Yes, even if you're left-handed.)

8. **Serious Canoodling.** Be especially careful about public displays of affection in Thailand, Turkey, Malaysia, and Singapore. Honestly, it's not such a brilliant idea in America, either.

THE STRAIGHT SCOOP

In Japan, the bow is the traditional greeting. When someone bows to greet you, observe closely. How low did he go? If you are greeting an equal, bow to the same depth as you have been bowed to and quickly lower your eyes. Keep your palms pressed flat against your thighs. Believe it or not, President Obama got this wrong when he greeted the Emperor of Japan in November 2009. Obama bowed down too low, setting off a windstorm of conservative commentary. Furthermore, he bowed while shaking the Emperor Akihito's hand, another no-no. Bows are not meant to accompany physical contact.[6]

 Is it true that a handshake can be misinterpreted?

A. A handshake initiates physical contact that's not always appreciated.

Study up on the country you're visiting before you automatically stick out your hand. Many Asians, including Japanese, have learned to accept the American handshake as a friendly greeting. But in Japan, the bow is still customary.

When in Japan, remember that limp is the new power shake. Don't pump your hand or grip the other person's hand too tightly. A limp hand-shake shows your Asian clients both humility and respect.

As a general rule, there is less physical contact in Japan than in America. Keep a polite distance.

63 **When two people are discussing business, how far apart should they stand?**
A. 10 feet. (Or even further—if one of them hasn't showered.)
B. 7 feet.
C. 6 feet.
D. 3 feet.

A. Answer D. (3 feet—in America.)
Chances are, no one will be standing next to you with a ruler, but as a general guideline, three feet is the standard distance in the United States. But check local customs before conducting business in a foreign country. In Singapore, people stand approximately 2 to 3 feet apart. In India, people stand a bit farther apart, between 3 and 3 ½ feet. In the Ukraine and Russia, the distance is approximately 2 feet. In Argentina, Brazil, Ecuador, Peru, and Venezuela, the distance is closer, as it is in Mexico. (Is someone standing so close that you can practically feel him breathing down your neck? Do not back away as it may cause the other person to step forward in an attempt to close the gap.) An American's personal space is greater than that of an Arab or a Russian but smaller than that of someone British.

2.   Why Time Is Not Necessarily Money Everywhere on the Planet

The Rolling Stones were wrong. Time is not on your side. In fact, once you pass the International Date Line, you feel like you stepped inside a Time Machine where time stands still or is quite possibly moving backwards. Here all of your projects are frozen in time. Back in the States, your boss keeps sending you cheerily persistent memos—"Tell us your progress!," "Don't forget to keep us in the loop!," "Want to join Monday's status call?" But the problem is that you have nothing to report. You arrived with agendas, deadlines, and a project timeline. Pity it's all Greek to your Japanese clients. Meanwhile, you've had more sushi with your clients than you can shake a chopstick at and almost feel like you're part of their extended family.

64 Are Americans considered too impatient by the rest of the world?

A. It depends on the country.
Some business people from other cultures are put off by the abrupt, "get-down-to-business" attitude for which Americans are famous.

In the United States, time is money. But in some cultures, it's considered beyond rude to brush all else aside in the dogged pursuit of filthy lucre, even at a business meeting! If you are traveling in the Middle East or Asia, reset your internal clock and get used to conducting business at a much more leisurely pace. Gaining your clients' trust is more important than completing any particular transaction.

By all accounts, the Chinese will sometimes deliberately stall negotiations well beyond your deadline to gain an edge. They may try to renegotiate on the final day or angle for a better deal even after the contract is signed.

Learn to adapt to other cultures and alternative customs and you will be far more successful and feel less frustrated.

High-Context vs. Low-Context Cultures (in Context)

An anthropologist named Edward Hall coined the terms "high context" and "low context" to describe the attributes of certain cultures.

The United States, Canada, Germany, Switzerland, and the Scandinavian countries are low-context cultures. Their business people tend to send unambiguous messages: "What you see is what you get." When it comes to getting things done, time is of the essence, and it's bordering on negligent to let it go to waste. This leads to more straightforward, transaction-oriented business meetings.

High-context cultures rely more on nonverbal communication, indirect verbal signals, and implicit meanings. Developing trust between the individuals is critical before *any* business can be done. Getting from point A to point B can be a long and winding road, and you probably won't even get in the car together unless someone who the driver really trusts introduces you. Would you get in a car with a total stranger?

High-context cultures include Asian countries, such as China, Japan, and Korea; some European countries, such as Spain and Greece; Turkey; the entire Arab world; plus Latin America and Africa. (That's a lot of places to write off because you don't understand how business gets done or because their business leaders find you unconscionably rude.)

People from high-context cultures view people from low-context cultures as too brash and impatient. People from low-context cultures see those from high-context cultures as glib about deadlines. No matter which side of the divide you find yourself on, take some time to learn how the other half works.

 **Punctuality: Is it a plus?**

A. Foreigners are expected to be on time for meetings, pretty much no matter what.

Be on time, but don't fret if your counterpart isn't.

In Ecuador and Columbia, you are expected to be punctual. But those whom you're meeting have a 15–20 minute grace period. (Fifteen to twenty

minutes late *is* being on time as far as they're concerned.) In other countries, such as Portugal and Russia, the delay could be even longer. Don't be
surprised if your host is a half hour late.

In Egypt and Saudi Arabia, you will need to show up on time. But your
counterpart may be late or may not show at all! In Greece as well, it's only
courteous for you to show up at the appointed hour. But don't be shocked
or dismayed if the other party keeps you waiting. In Honduras and India,
it's the same policy. In Italy, you should plan to be on time. But there is an
understood rule that important people arrive late (so your client may well
show up later than you).

Don't let it unravel you. Adopt an Existentialist way of viewing the
world. Tell yourself, "Whatever is, is."

THE STRAIGHT SCOOP

Always anticipate delays and factor them into your schedule for getting things done.

---

66 In America, timeliness is of the essence. Are there cultures
that treat punctuality as seriously as the United States does?

A. Always check local customs before hopping on a plane.

In China, being late or cancelling a business meeting could derail the
entire transaction. The Finns don't take kindly to it either. The Swiss run
their meetings on time and with the precision of a Swiss timepiece.

But recognize that change happens at the speed of business and make
it your mission to brush up on protocols before you leave for that country.
Ask friends and colleagues about their experiences in a particular locale.
Check out travel blogs. And invest in travel guides to the country and the
area where you'll be staying.

Too much is at stake to get it wrong and the rules can sometimes be
subtle.

3. We've Come a Long Way, Baby. Or Have We?

In Latin America, your client came on to you. When you pushed him
away, he looked at you as if you had dropped down from another planet—

America. "I thought you were interested," he said, all saucer-eyed and emotionally damaged. "You agreed to eat dinner with me—ALONE!" Of course you did . . . he was the *only person* you knew in that part of the world. And now that one-and-only person is very annoyed with you. "Plus, you sat in the front seat of my car!" he said. *Wow, you harlot, you.* In Egypt, you felt so uncomfortable eating dinner by yourself that you bunked up with room service in your hotel room every night for a week. You've traveled an awfully long way to discover that your sex really hasn't come all that far, after all.

67 Do American women traveling abroad need to take any special precautions?

A. Better safe.

In Egypt, a woman dining by herself could be viewed as morally degenerate. It's not recommended in Latin America either where the trade winds of feminism haven't blown. There, women should not dine alone! Also, be careful about sending the wrong signal. Don't go out to dinner with a Latin American male without another companion in tow. Going out with a man alone will be misinterpreted, as will sitting in the front seat of his car and drinking more than one glass of wine.

No matter where your itinerary happens to take you, read blogs and plenty of guides about that particular destination so that you develop a feel about cultural norms before you arrive. Rome wasn't built in a day, and it certainly won't be changed by a foreigner on a business trip—ever.

Who Knew?

In the United States women and men are equals. Today, there are just as many women as men in the workforce, and while there is still a salary differential, even that gap is closing. Stories in the media tell us that more women than men graduate from college, and that starting fairly young, girls get higher grades than guys. All of these facts contribute to an environment where no one blinks an eye if a woman in the United

States—business traveler or not—chooses to dine alone. That's not always the case in other cultures. (See Question 67.)

68 Are female travelers more susceptible to theft?

A. Yes.
When traveling on foreign soil, perception is reality, and the perception is that women are still the weaker sex. This makes American women walking targets in certain cities. A beggar in Naples may try to prey on your sympathy by "petting" your hair (while trying to sneak his other hand in your pocket). In Rio, you could be asked to part with your money, even on the beach.

Don't send out "rich American tourist" vibes. Keep costly handbags, cameras, and smartphones hidden. Don't flash cash or model extravagant baubles.

Lock your valuables in the hotel safe. Wear a money belt when strolling the streets. Ask the front desk of your hotel if there's a particular neighborhood to avoid and mark it on your map.

Make sure the bellman checks all areas in your room when he first lets you in to guarantee that you are the only one inside. Stay alert as you approach your room. Check door locks and window locks, especially if the room has a spiffy feature such as a balcony. Be certain that there is no other access to the room except via the front door and double-lock it.

A Woman Alone

1. **Put a lock on it.** Keep your watch squirreled away in the hotel safe. The safes downstairs in the lobby are industrial-strength and should be used for anything valuable that you don't wear daily. Depending on the

country, you may need to lock your Passport in your room safe. Rumor has it that stolen passports fetch well over $10,000.

2. **Never rely on the kindness of strangers.** Don't be a Blanche Dubois. Study up on your surroundings so that you can remain confident and poised while traveling instead of feeling scared and helpless.

3. **Geolocate your next destination.** Planning to take a train to the next stop on your itinerary? Make it a point to tool down to the station before the day of your departure just to identify how much time you'll need to build in when you *have* to arrive by a certain hour.

4. **Be the mistress of your own domain.** Don't let others broadcast your whereabouts. If the clerk calls out your room number to the bellman when you first check in, discreetly tell him that you'll need another room and to be quiet about it.

5. **Follow local dress mores.** Don't wear anything that's wildly different than what the local women wear. Blending in is vastly preferable to standing out.

6. **Dial down your outsider status.** Wearing shirts, shorts, and baseball caps that scream "I am a tourist" alerts pickpockets to your vulnerability. Carrying a large map is another dead giveaway.

7. **Don't be camera happy.** Take pictures, but keep it snappy.

8. **Don't leave home without an international calling plan.** If you get lost, call your hotel for directions to a local cab stand or the American Express office.

9. **Retain your optimism.** Traveling abroad has its share of challenges, but when you know that you can rely on yourself you become a good traveler. Tell yourself that whatever happens, you'll be able to figure it out.

How should a single woman traveling alone handle invitations from a man?

A. Make sure that he understands just what you're RSVPing to.

If you're straight, single, and traveling alone and *never* once talk to a male stranger, you will miss out on half of life's fun, so by all means do it, but be clear about your intentions.

In some countries, if you're alone, a man may automatically assume that you're available. If you don't want him to think that and he ventures too close for comfort, tell him "no" in the local language, firmly but politely. Should he persist, ask someone who's sitting nearby if you can join him for a while.

If you agree to have dinner with a mysterious stranger, eat in your hotel dining room. Charge your meal to your room to avoid any miscommunication about the date's conclusion. You don't want to be the parfait with the cherry on top. (Even if the cherry is only a euphemism.)

Should you choose to get together again, stay in the public eye. Meet in a public place, and tell him that you're traveling with fifteen business colleagues. Better yet, bring some of them along to meet him. Announce that you must be back at ten o'clock sharp because you have a most important meeting the following day.

———————————————— THE STRAIGHT SCOOP ————————————————

Visitors are not expected to mimic the natives, only to be respectful of their customs in terms that are internationally understood. Mastering some polite phrases is always appreciated, as is an apologetic admission if you do not speak the native tongue.

4. The Not Freudian Slip

"Actions speak louder than words," you've always heard, but naturally, you took it for a cliché. But if you've learned anything during this trip it's that your actions screamed something to your Japanese client that you never intended, and then no one had the fortitude to explain what you did that was so darned insulting! You were completely perplexed until one of your junior associates (who wasn't even at the meeting) heard the play-by-play during your conference call back to the States. "So then I stuck the client's business card in the back pocket of my pants," you recounted, "and for some reason, the room fell silent." Your associate then explained that no doubt your client felt miffed that you held his business card in such low regard. You've been apologizing for the business-card-in-your-back-pocket blunder ever since!

 Your meeting seemed to be going so well until you crossed your arms. What's up with that?

A. Crossing your arms is one of those no-no's.

Don't beat yourself up about it. But consider it a lesson well learned.

Crossing your arms is considered very rude in Finland and Turkey.

That shouldn't come as a huge shock. It doesn't go over that well even in America.

On the Defensive? Some Cultures Find it Offensive.

In Argentina, putting your hands on your hips is considered unspeakably rude. In India, standing tall with your hands on your hips is perceived as overly aggressive and will diminish you in your clients' eyes. In Malaysia and Singapore, this posture is also not appreciated.

---

71 The singer Alanis Morissette sang "Hand in My Pocket." But when you inadvertently put one hand in your pocket at the Belgian business meeting, the client stared at you as if you had cooties. What should you have done differently?

A. Kept your hands on the desk.

Never talk to a Belgian with one hand in your pocket. It's considered horribly rude.

Keeping your hands in your pocket is also not appreciated in the Czech Republic, Finland, Switzerland, or Turkey. In Norway, talking with your hands in your pockets is considered too casual to be taken seriously.

They don't even approve of it in Britain.

 72 **Paul Simon crooned about "Diamonds on the Soles of Her Shoes." But you've heard that showing your soles is bad form in numerous countries. True or false?**

A. True.

In Belarus, it's gauche to sit with your feet propped up on a table. In the Czech Republic, never put your feet up on anything higher than a footstool. In Egypt, you'd be well advised to keep both feet firmly planted on the ground. Never show the bottom of your foot to anyone. Follow the same decorum in Israel. In Finland, never rest your ankle on your knee. In India, Singapore, Malaysia, and Turkey, feet are considered unclean. Don't point yours toward anyone. In Indonesia, do not show the soles of your feet or shoes. Feet should never be rested on tables or desks. You can cross your legs at the knee, but don't put your ankle on your knee. (But in Canada, sitting with your feet propped up on chairs or desks is just fine. Oh, Canada!)

─────────────── **THE STRAIGHT SCOOP** ───────────────

How do you apologize if you make a gaffe during an international business trip? Simple. You apologize. And then, you apologize again. And then it's high time to apologize again. In high-context cultures, extensive apologies are the norm. Acknowledge your mistake. Ask for forgiveness. And redouble your efforts to learn from the error so that you won't have to keep apologizing for it. Hopefully, this will help smooth the way for an improved outcome the next time around.

5. Out on a Limb—Taking the Next Step When There Are None

You put the "t" in transaction. (Otherwise, the word is "ransaction," which, to your knowledge, doesn't mean anything.) The meetings went well—at least *you* think they did—but you're unclear about any next steps. Unless, oh please say it isn't so, you're supposed to plan *another* series of meetings exactly like the ones you've just had. Realizing that this may well be the case when dealing with clients and counterparts from high-context cultures, you spend the rest of the flight home fantasizing about all of the tourist destinations you didn't have a chance to catch on this trip. There was that Japanese tea house in Tokyo . . . the historical district in Honduras... and that world-class design center in Milan.

 The deal is progressing slower than a tortoise. Can you bring a hare with you the next time to get a jump on it? Are you allowed to bring new players to future meetings to help speed things along?

A. It's probably a bad idea.

If the clients are taking longer than you'd like to acclimate to you, introducing new players into the mix, mid-negotiation, could have catastrophic consequences. However, before you visit with your clients again, you might take stock of what went well and what didn't and see if you might do better on the follow-up trip. Following are some points to consider:

1. Did you do enough scout work in advance? Did you unearth the common bonds between you and your clients? These "bonds" could be people who you know in common, interests that you share, or greater affinity circles that you belong to (such as being alumni from the same college or members of the same organization). Just because you failed to do the proper amount of homework before you left does not prevent you from doing it now. In the words of the famous Nike campaign, "Just do it."

2. Did you bring your own translator? In countries where you don't speak the language, bringing a translator can be enormously advantageous—even if your client speaks English. Let's suppose that you're in Hong Kong. The meeting seems to be going well. That is, until your client turns to someone else in the room and their conversation in Cantonese lasts for ten whole minutes. Even if your client is gracious enough to summarize the gist of it, you're going to feel like you missed something significant unless you have your own translator.

3. Did you make any gasp-worthy gaffes during the trip? If so, it never hurts to re-apologize.

4. Were you appreciative enough for the hospitality that you were shown on the trip? If not, now is the time to express your gratitude.

5. Don't let petty territorialism between the departments in your company prevent you from learning all you need to know. Take advantage of any institutional knowledge that your company has collected about these clients. Find the last person in the organization who visited with them and make an appointment to sit down with him and compare notes. The relationship that your company has with this client is probably well-documented. Now is the time to peer into to those conference call notes so that you can compare and contrast.

Who Knew?

The affinity circle shapes how most business is conducted in Latin America. Picture a target on a wall with various circles that all share a center. One's nuclear family may occupy the innermost circle. In the next largest circle might be one's extended family.

Moving outwards, a larger circle might include work colleagues, members from a club or church, and school chums. Another even larger circle might encompass people from a community or an institution with which you are affiliated. You might even share an affinity with someone you've never met who is technically outside of your sphere if he or she happens to share your patron saint!

---

74 What is the single most important criterion for reaching the next step with your foreign client?

A. Trust.

And there's only one minor problem: The trust needs to happen first.

Without the trust, there won't be a next step.

So if it takes multiple dinners, museum trips, golf outings, trips to the theater, and scads of money sunk on international travel costs, you need to invest in the relationship.

You may need to plan on spending half a year on the other side of globe instead of half an afternoon. And it's you who will need to acclimate.

Resources

Business councils and chambers of commerce can be invaluable liaisons to new connections overseas. Make it a point to speak to the commercial attaches at the local consulate for the country you're visiting. Go in person and suit up. Foreign government officials manning embassies in the United States can also be an excellent source of information and business contacts while providing the cultural briefings and the education you need to do business in their specific countries.[7]

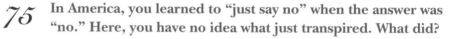 In America, you learned to "just say no" when the answer was "no." Here, you have no idea what just transpired. What did?

A. Learn to read the tea leaves.

In some cultures, not every little nuance will be spelled out. The Japanese, for example, never say "no." In this most gracious culture, no one wants to offend. However, if you listen closely, you can intuit the answer. Your clients may say something vague, such as, "Perhaps not at this time."

First, take away the word "perhaps."

Next, remove the words "at this time."

What are you left with? The word "not." And you can't spell "not" without the word "no."

"Perhaps not at this time" is just an excruciatingly polite way of saying "no."

That's a Wrap

1. Some body language speaks louder than words. Make sure your body isn't screaming something that you would never utter with your lips.
2. Patience is a virtue when dealing with clients and counterparts from high-context cultures. And punctuality (on your end, anyway) is mandatory.
3. Women traveling in machismo cultures face a special set of challenges and need to make a special effort to communicate their intentions clearly.
4. If you make a mistake, acknowledge the error and apologize for it profusely. Then apologize again.
5. It takes time to build enough trust for some clients to close a deal. Attempting to hurry the process may backfire.

CHAPTER 6

Pounding the Pavement with Panache

There's only one thing worse than working for the man. And that's finding yourself in a situation where you are no longer working for the man!

If only you had had the wisdom to work with the new administration instead of rebelling against it, you probably would have never found yourself in this undignified position—each morning consumed with making phone call after phone call just to find a brand-new job working for the man!

It's humiliating to make so many calls, even with introductions. Can't we just make avatars of ourselves and dispatch them into the big, cruel world instead of us?

Avatars don't weep, do they?

Whenever you find yourself grappling with whether to call someone (yet again!) to meet in person, it's helpful to remember that most jobs are obtained through "weak links," that is, connections of connections. And in general, these connections are still made the old-fashioned way (i.e., in person and via phone).

These connections can help you unveil a job—and land it—long before a position is ever advertised in the open market or on the electronic job boards. You could be working while hundreds are still competing online, just for a chance at an interview. It is possible to pound the pavement with verve. Don't be shy. But also recognize that there is a thin line between being enthusiastic and an over-eager pain, and take care to never cross it.

1. *The Trials and Tribulations of Inheriting a New Boss*

To all those Pollyannas who always claim "change is good," you have a message: Change is bad. And you have no intention of adapting to it. You are not a chameleon! If you were, your parents would have been chameleons, and they are both human beings, thank you, yes, even your mother. While you were abroad, the "change advocates" at your firm came and turned everything upside down, creating a new multi-headed Hydra of a reporting structure. Now you're saddled with a brand new boss and a whole new and unnecessary layer between you and Satan. Upon reading the announcement in the company bulletin (*so nice of them to tell you in person*), your face flushes scarlet. Why, why, why you ask—pounding your fist against your desk—couldn't they have promoted you? Ingrates!

76 In your absence, they promoted your exact equal at the company to be the boss of you. Should you be worried?

A. **Yes, very.**

If your company sent you abroad during the time that the decision was being made, they also sent you an unmistakable message. The message was, "Deal with it." There could be numerous reasons why the other person was promoted instead of you. She could have a gift for pacifying clients or have lobbied harder for a promotion. She could have had a personal growth plan in place for years that your company finally decided to honor. In any event, you'll never know unless you make strides to find out. (And no one will ever tell you the cold, hard truth if it seems like you can't handle it.)

Wait three business days until you've had a chance to simmer down. Then, go find the person who made the decision and debrief with him about it.

Endeavor to spot the "silver lining" in the situation even if you have to squint hard to see it. This could be the very entrée that you need to sit down with Satan and map out a plan for your own development. Feel free to express your disappointment, but don't mope. Calmly explain that you wish *you* had been promoted. Quickly detail your rationale for why you feel you were overlooked. And then try to extract a commitment: When *does* he anticipate that you will be ready for more responsibility? What steps do you need to take right now to fulfill that promise?

A few days later, check in with your former rival, otherwise known as your new boss. (Aargh!) Congratulate her (even if your heart is breaking) and promise that you'll support her in her efforts to pull the team together.

For Extra Credit

At moments like this, imagine that you are a figure skater in the winter Olympics who just took a bad tumble in front of the judges. You may feel temporarily off-balance and bruised, but with the proper moves you can regain your poise and equilibrium.

---

77 A new boss from a competing organization sweeps in like a tsunami. To leave or stick it out? That is the question.

A. Stay put. That is the answer.

Tsunamis leave much wreckage in their wake, and it's conceivable that you could be one of the unfortunate victims. But it's also equally likely that other people will be swept away during the tempest, clearing the way for your own promotion.

Never leave a company voluntarily just because someone new has arrived. You could win this person's admiration and be gainfully employed for the next ten years!

─────────────────── THE STRAIGHT SCOOP ───────────────────

Whenever a new boss arrives, it's a good strategy to treat your old job as if it's a brand new job. Recognize that years of glowing performance reviews may not save you. (In fact, they might actually frighten a new boss who's insecure.) Stay late. Work hard. And arrive early. Then repeat for best results.

Why It Pays to Pay Your Dues All Over Again

It could be your fifth year in the company. Assignments that used to consume you for days are now brushed off in a few short hours. You are a model of efficiency! Why should you behave exactly like a junior all over again, just to impress a new boss?

1. **It gives you a chance to spy.** This is your opportunity to scope out the new boss's habits, rhythms, and daily rituals. Is she a paranoid nut, a genius on par with Einstein, or a moron from outer space? You'll never know unless you hang around long enough to observe her in action.

2. **It provides a once-in-a-lifetime opportunity to befriend the "new kid."** Even though she's your boss, there will be *plenty* of things that she doesn't know. Where's the watercooler? Where does one obtain office supplies? Where's the conference room, again? You can be her Sherpa, guiding her through her first few weeks on the job.

3. **It positions you as part of the solution.** Sales are poor, billings are down, and there's no new business. "Let's kick out the old management!" someone screams, "They're responsible for this mess!" "Rah, rah!" others concur. If you are too high and mighty to stick around after hours, someone who *is* putting in a lot of overtime may try to hint that you're part of the problem. But if you *are* around, the new boss might solicit your opinion about what actually needs to be changed. And then you become part of the solution.

78   **Your old job feels like a brand new job but with fewer responsibilities. What recourse is there?**

A. Little, if any.

You don't want to be a legal beagle about it. You are not a dog! Still, a passing familiarity with employment law isn't such a bad thing when you're working for others. Employment at most companies is "at will" (theirs, not yours). There. Now you're an expert.

"At will" employment means that you're free to leave the company for any reason, but the company is also free to let you go for any reason. Extreme truculence based on the fact that you now have a new boss you can't stand, for example, would be the only justification required to cut you loose. Unless you have a contract, you do not have a ton of legal recourse.

2. *Congratulations, You're Fired*

Your new boss asks for the PowerPoint presentation to be in blue. As an experiment, you print it out in green. When she starts seeing red, you don't turn yellow. Instead, you set out to prove to her why green is the color of choice. After all, isn't green "in" these days due to self-sustaining efforts from New York to San Francisco? You're smarter, sharper, and more pivotal to the success of this company than any of your predecessors. God knows how they ever managed without you, but you don't. And apparently, neither does your boss, because in the twelfth hour she finally changes her mind and green lights the presentation's new kelly green color. You're pink with pride at victory. Or so you think.

79 **Must you follow your new boss's directives, even when you're convinced beyond the shadow of a doubt that she's wrong?**

A. Pick your battles.

When a new boss walks in the door on day one, you are starting with 100 points. That's an A-plus. Debate with her about something trivial, such as the color of a PowerPoint presentation, and that automatically deducts three points from your impeccable grade point average. Nitpick with her a few more times on trivial matters without a spiffy new business win to help raise your score again, and suddenly your boss will regard you as being in the 85-point range, or only a B-player.

No one ever considers her own ideas mediocre, only other people's. So stop outshining your senior before she banishes you from the kingdom.

80 **The personality conflicts with your new boss have escalated. You're not even sure why it is that the two of you always quarrel. You believe that she's "staging fights" with you expressly for the higher-ups to overhear. What steps should you take?**

A. Figure out if it's a culture clash, a clash of personalities, or a clash of ideals.

There could be many reasons why your new boss stages mock feuds with you. Maybe at her last company, she amassed all of her power by challenging lowly staffers. There are plenty of companies where "alpha chimpanzee standoffs" are the norm: this could be where she learned her modus operandi. If so, you may need to make a show of fighting her back openly if only to prove that you're not frightened of her.

A personality clash is a bit easier to deal with. Make an appointment to sit down with your nemesis. Tell her that you intend to patch up your differences. Explain why you believe it's in *both* of your best interests to coexist peacefully. Then ask if there's some behavior of yours that "sets her off." If the answer is "yes," promise her that you'll tone it down. (And then force yourself to actually work on it.)

A clash of ideals can be challenging, because no matter what actions are taken the underlying core disagreement will always be there festering like a stealth germ. Let's suppose that she's process-oriented while you're transaction-oriented. Chances are, you will never "report in" enough for her liking. You just want to roll up your shirtsleeves and get things done without kowtowing to the burdensome bureaucracy.

Nevertheless, if you have to wrap a piece of red tape around your wrist as a reminder you *will* now have to work on your kowtowing skills. You can start by emailing her a progress report on all of your projects today!

Sparring with her may feel like the clash of the Titans, but unless you do something dramatic, your prospects are likely to sink faster than the Titanic.

81   **One morning, your new boss summons you into a conference room. An HR person that you've never seen before is seated at the table with her. "I'm really sorry to tell you this," your new boss says, "but things aren't working out. You should pack up your bags and go." Uh-oh. Now what?**

A. Fight for an office, fight for severance, and fight for fairness.
It's likely that you will experience shock so it may take all of your internal resources to remain calm. But you must stay poised even though you feel as if the industrial carpet has been pulled out from under you.

Your first step is to ask the HR person if you can *stay* in your physical office to take advantage of the company resources, such as the phone and copying machine.

If your cut is part of a general layoff, the answer may be "yes" because your company will have the extra office space to spare.

In etiquette parlance, you are asking the company to extend you this simple courtesy after your many years of tireless devotion.

Once you secure a physical office, see a lawyer. Have him comb through your severance package to make sure it's fair. Even if it is, there is still usually a little "wiggle room" for employees who successfully make the case as to why they deserve more than the standard package. Some reasonable arguments include: your length of service to the company, your loyalty, your excellent track record until the new boss came on, and the fact that, these days, you can expect to be out of work for at least nine months. (Bolster the last claim with the most current research you can find on the topic. You can start with the U.S. Department of Labor website or keep tabs on the statistics by reading *The New York Times*.) If you have received any glowing emails from clients or former bosses, now is the moment to surface them. Circle back to the HR person and your ex-boss with a "paper trail" that will help you defend your exemplary track record.

Finally, shake the plum tree of your contacts. Visit with each and every person who you are planning to use for a reference. Let them know how much you loved working for the company and how much fun you had. Ask each of your contacts for *five* of his contacts.

Be sure to stay placid during these many interactions. It may be emotionally draining to appear calm when inside you're a tangle of nerves. But outwardly, your composure *must* remain intact. The impression that you make during these conversations will stay with people for years.

Remember: You never have a second chance to make a *last* impression.

Why This Technique Works

It's always easier to find a job when you already have one. And even though you no longer have yours, you still have the *trappings* of the job—the physical office, the company landline, and possibly even an assistant to help you put together your job-hunting materials. By remaining on company turf, you also maintain access to the very people with whom you were working only yesterday. If the company "overfires" (as so many do) and happens to need an extra pair of hands, you're on premises to freelance and help solve their personnel shortage. Above all, you still have a place to go every morning so you are less likely to feel as if your dignity has been stripped away from you.

Conduct Two Audits

Audits bring to mind visions of the taxman banging on your door. Shoo the bogeyman out of your head and get down to business.

First, conduct a financial audit. Sit down and review how much money you have. Don't forget to factor in the unemployment money that you will receive plus any severance. Calculate if you will have enough income to tide you through the next year. It may be rougher out there on the tarmac than you had feared.

Start thinking now about any lifestyle modifications you may need to take as a precaution. Should you fire your maid? Take on an additional roommate temporarily? Cancel your upcoming vacation?

Next, conduct a serious "career audit." This sounds frightening, but it only involves being able to answer one question honestly. Simply ask yourself: "Is this truly my chosen career path?"

If the answer is "yes," that's great news because finding a job will be considerably easier. You can focus all of your efforts on your contacts and "contacts of contacts." But if you have any nagging doubts, this is the moment to open yourself up to investigate new opportunities.

Is your field drying up? Are all of the jobs being outsourced to other continents? If so, you may need to brainstorm with yourself on new ways to repackage your skills to make the case for a career jump.

Big or Small?

Small businesses comprise approximately 97.7 percent of all employers and create 75 percent of the jobs in the United States If you have left a big company and are targeting a smaller one, think of how to leverage your "big brand expertise" in ways that will be palatable to a small company. Do you want to migrate from a small company to a larger one? Consider how well your "small company experience" will translate. For starters, you're probably used to doing more tasks. That flexibility may be a handy skill to have these days at a larger company—particularly if it has experienced recent layoffs.

3. *Finding Nirvana from a Pink Slip*

You haven't had time to feel the pain. Directly after you were cut, your colleagues threw you a sendoff party. And your close friends have been treating you to drinks and appetizers ever since! It's not like you can afford to go anywhere on your own anymore. After hearing numerous pep talks about how this was the probably "the best thing that ever happened to you," you are almost beginning to believe the hype. Maybe there *will* be a silver lining, and, in the words of Joni Mitchell, someday you'll be able to "look at clouds from both sides." Right now, however, you see only a big bunch of hideous gray storm clouds on the horizon that remind you of elephants coming to trample you. On this afternoon's agenda: You have to practice for an upcoming job interview, rewrite your résumé for the third time, and get thee to Happy Hour on time. Freedom's just another word for nothing left to lose.

82   You were fired. How do you explain that in a job interview?

A. Closely align your story with that of your former company's.

Imagine for a moment that you are William Safire, one of the foremost authorities on the English language. Before you script yourself to answer this question, ask yourself: "Was I really fired?" If the answer is "yes," then, you will need to craft a strategy for explaining it. But if the answer is "no,"— there were tons of other employees who received pink slips on the very same day—that's called a *layoff,* and the strategy for discussing it is mark-edly different.

Being *fired* means that you, alone, were canned. You might have been fired due to your performance or because of your personality. In general, "personality" is a better reason to cite. You may have clashed with one person but gotten along swimmingly with everyone else. Personality reasons are also subjective whereas performance reasons are considered more objective. (However, if a new boss upended the criteria for performance, mentioning it can be a superb strategy since almost everyone can empathize with this exasperating situation.)

Whether you were fired or laid off, it's critical that your story *match* that of your former employer's. Fields are small; some are shrinking by the nanosecond. Your interviewer could request a list of references and then turn around and call someone from the company who was never even on your list!

You don't want to be eliminated from consideration simply because you claimed that you were "laid off" when you were really fired. All circumstances can be explained, just as long as you know what the real reasons were that led to your leaving (and are honest about them).

─────────────── THE STRAIGHT SCOOP ───────────────

There are four generations of workers competing for jobs today: the traditionalists (they remember World War II which ended in 1945), the Boomers (they were born between 1946 and 1964), Generation X (the post–Boomer generation), and the Millennials (sometimes referred to as "Generation Y"). If you are on the older end of the spectrum, you will need to make the case for why your *experience* is an asset. If you're on the younger side, be prepared to prove that you are a *quick study.*

83   So technically, you suppose that you were laid off. Is there any "magic" to the way you discuss it in an interview?

A. Calculate the percentage of employees who were laid off versus the number. Then pick the best story to tell.

Your interviewer asks you how many people "got the ax." If the company was large, cite the actual number (e.g. "fifty people"). If you worked at a small company, it's usually smarter to talk in terms of percentages (e.g., 25 percent) because it will sound like more people were beheaded.

If you can add a little color to the tale, it might lead to a more successful exchange. Don't be a Drama Queen about it, but think about ways to add a narrative element your experience. You don't have to compare it to the Spanish Inquisition for your story to be memorable and resonate with your interviewer. Simply speak the truth: "There were rumors that the layoff was going to be severe, but no one imagined for a moment that it would actually affect fifty people. As you are probably aware, this was the third and worst layoff that the company had in the past year."

| *Why This Technique Works* |

By mentioning previous layoffs that you managed to survive, you demonstrate that you were considered a valuable player at your company. You've also answered the question in an eloquent manner, proving that you possess both objectivity and public speaking ability—two skills that interviewers often look for in candidates.

84   **You have no clue whether you were fired or laid off. Your new boss didn't use either of those terms when she relayed the sorry news. Suggestions?**

A. Try to uncover the truth before you walk out the door for the last time.

Many bosses deserve a "D" for how they cut ties with their own employees. Seeking to numb the pain of termination, these bosses use language that's deliberately vague. For example, a boss may say something like, "Due to our lackluster third quarter results, I have no choice but to let you go." It sounds like a layoff. But is it?

Adding to the confusion is the fact that choices *are* made, even within layoff scenarios. It's not as if bosses stick a round target on the wall, affix employees' photos to it, close their eyes, and throw a dart! Sometimes, performance issues *do* impact who gets cut and who doesn't.

If you have no idea whether you were fired or laid off, try to raise the subject with your former boss *before* you walk out of your office building for the very last time. While the truth sometimes hurts, knowing it will help you craft a more intelligent reply to your interviewer's question. If you have already left the company, you can also try picking up the phone to discuss it with your former boss, although you may find her surprisingly difficult to reach. Once employees leave, they become ephemeral and ghost-like and sometimes layoff survivors have difficulty remembering to return their calls. Nevertheless, persistence pays. When you reach your ex-boss, frame the question in the most amicable manner possible with the verbal script that follows:

"Thank you for taking my call. I really appreciate it. Listen, I've started to pound the pavement and some interviewers heard about the massive company layoff and have been asking me if I was one of the victims. I've been telling them I was, and I'm just double-checking that fact with you in case any of them give you a jingle. By the way, I hope everything is going smoothly in my absence. I really miss you and the team!"

What Do Interviewers Really Want, Anyway?

Going on an interview is like a speed date. By the end of a meeting that lasts but forty minutes, the interviewer will decide whether she wants to see you every day for the foreseeable future. (Well, five days a week anyway.)

You can make the decision easy for her or you can make it difficult. Generally, if you emphasize these skill sets, she'll find it easier to commit to you.

1. **Problem-solving skills.** Don't just claim that you know how to solve problems. Bring case studies with you that demonstrate you do.
2. **People skills.** These may be a bit harder to prove, if in fact you were fired due to a personality conflict. But strong, positive references should help assuage any doubts. Also, remember that the *interview itself* is a true test of your people skills. If you relate to your interviewer, she can't help but admire your facility with people.
3. **Closure skills.** Emphasize your ability to accomplish miraculous feats through your intelligence, perseverance, excellent judgment, and ingenuity.

Are You an A-Personality or a B-Personality? That Depends. What's Your Interviewer?

According to Wikipedia, since the early 1950s, the Type A and Type B personality theory has been widely popularized, but also widely criticized for its scientific shortcomings.[8]

That caveat aside, most laypeople agree that Type A individuals can be described as impatient, time-conscious, concerned about their status, highly competitive, ambitious, and aggressive. Wikipedia claims that Type A people are often disliked by Type B personalities for "the way they are always rushing."

By contrast, Type B individuals can be depicted as patient, relaxed, easygoing, and generally lacking any sense of urgency. Wikipedia claims that Type Bs often seem to be "apathetic and disengaged."

If you are an A-personality, strive to pretend that you are a B-personality (at least for the interview). The chemistry will be better whether the person interviewing you is an A or a B. Plus you won't come off as one of those super-aggressive, pushy types determined to take charge of the interview even at the expense of seeming horribly rude!

Conversely, if you are a B-personality, you may want to put on your A-personality game face during interviews so that it seems as if you are serious about getting the job. By striving for the rarest of personality types, that is type A-B, you'll temper some of the extremes and come across as balanced and serious-minded, without appearing to be overly aggressive.

4. On Being an Excruciatingly Polite Pain in the Butt

You feel like everyone should be fired at least once in their lives simply to learn what they *should* have been doing while they were employed. All of your problems with your former "new" boss have vanished as you've had to approach her on a number of dicey situations—help with references, help with data mining, and help with obtaining a better severance package. It's amazing! She's such a sweetheart! If only you had been able to see *this* side of her while you were still under her wing, you're certain she wouldn't have pushed you out of the nest so quickly (and without a nest egg). Today she even promised that you could camp out in your old office for another three months! If you weren't unemployed, poverty-stricken, and on the cusp of starvation, you'd be absolutely ecstatic.

For Extra Credit

Turn your job search into everyone's pet project. Don't just ask for favors; request feedback. Most colleagues will feel flattered when you solicit their advice. And who knows? Feeling like they can help on your job quest may even assuage some of the guilt they feel about surviving the cut when you didn't. Take advantage of their guilt fest to ask for critiques of your resume as well as your other job-hunting materials. You never have to follow your colleagues' counsel, but asking for their opinions invests them more in your search and helps keep you top of mind should they hear of any openings. Always thank coworkers for their input; but of course, don't pester them for assistance too often!

---

85 After years of loyal service to your company, you were given zero notice and told to get out within two working days. How do you broach this in a job interview?

A. You don't.

Instead, put on your rose-colored glasses and think back to the "honeymoon period" when you loved your job. Share everything you learned from the glorious experience!

Get into the habit of *good-mouthing* your former boss. Describe something specific that you picked up from him. There are numerous ways to credit people with your professional development, and a job interview is the ideal venue to recognize their contributions, however belatedly.

Did your former boss teach you how to read a spreadsheet or hone your problem-solving ability? Did he encourage you to become a more gifted speaker? Under his tutelage, did you learn how to organize your day or blossom into a better salesperson?

Be the most gracious interviewee, and you will snag another job more speedily. Who wouldn't want this eloquent person—who has only the kindest things to say about others—working at his organization?

The Halo Effect

Social psychologists investigate how people arrive at important judgments about other people. It turns out that there is a sort of shortcut that we all use. And yet most of us are unaware of it.

The shortcut is called "the halo effect." Basically, if we consider a person gifted in one category, then we are likely to make a similar evaluation about her in other related categories. For example, if someone is extremely like-able, we might also credit her with being smart, good looking, and eminently qualified for the job.

Back in the 1920s, Edward Thorndike discovered that when officers were asked to rate their charges in terms of intelligence, physique, character, and leadership, there was a high cross-correlation.[9] People have trouble thinking of other individuals in mixed terms; we seem to see each person as roughly "all good" or "all bad" across numerous categories of measurement.

Use this knowledge to create a "halo" around yourself. Work on becoming more likeable—and it will improve the scores interviewers give you in all other related categories.

─────────────────── THE STRAIGHT SCOOP ───────────────────

The decision to hire someone is usually made within the first two minutes of meeting the candidate. That doesn't give you a whole lot of time to impress your interviewer with your intelligence, conversational ease, or ideas. You need to look the part and, assuming that your interviewer approves of you "on sight," try very hard not to unravel that great first impression by what you say later during the meeting!

86 You had a spectacular interview and now need to follow up. Email? Snail mail? Or phone message? What's the best way to leave your competition in the dust (politely and with the utmost respect, of course)?

A. Don't think in terms of one method of communication. Design a follow-up communications campaign.

Hopefully, in your in-person meeting, you gleaned an important insight about the corporate culture. If the culture seemed traditional, then a hand written note, sent via snail mail, is appropriate. But if the ambience struck you as casual, there are many cogent reasons to send your thank-you note via email.

If your email service provider allows it, code your email so that you can figure out when your recipient opens it. That's useful data to have (and information you'll never know if you send a handwritten note). If the interviewer happens to be really nice, she may even hit the email back to you, saying how lovely it was to meet you. This is the ideal situation, because now you're in a dialogue with her rather than a monologue.

Send your first communication within twenty-four hours of your meeting. Also, follow up with your headhunter immediately. Describe your impressions of the meeting and ask her to call your interviewer that day and report back to you. Once she does, keep meticulous notes of anything interesting that your headhunter confides.

You will now need to plot, with the precision of a Marketing Guru, how many times to follow up with this prospect, what to say in each communication, and above all, how to keep the momentum moving.

If you choose to call, think carefully about whether you actually *want* the person to pick up (or whether it's less intrusive to just leave a chipper message when you know she won't be around). Eagerness and enthusiasm are always appreciated; the whiff of desperation is deadly; and too much eagerness quickly rots into desperation.

What the Japanese Can Teach Us about Reading Someone's Business Card

When you receive someone's business card, read it carefully, almost as if it's a very short novel. The person who hands it to you is the protagonist. Be sure to say something that acknowledges the hero of the story. "Lucinda Evans, thank you for your business card. And I see here that you are a senior vice president of the largest division in the company. That's a great testament to you."

Newsflash

Emails petitioning prospective employers to hire you quickly turn rancid. That's why you need to conjure up new ways to keep your email communications fresh. One technique is to add a "news element" to them.

Did you read an intriguing article about your prospect's company? Why not send her a link? Then add a tiny bit of gloss to it, if appropriate. "I read this article about your company in *Business Week* and wondered if you had seen it. The writer seems to feel that the XYZ company has a brilliant future, and here's hoping that I will be part of it!"

87 **How many times is it appropriate to give an interviewer a friendly reminder nudge before you should just give up?**

A. It depends on the job, the corporate culture, and whether you're using an executive recruiter.

As a general rule, you should plan on reaching out more than once and less than seven times to the same individual. Of course, much depends on the length of the company's search, how many people the interviewer needs to meet before arriving at a decision, and whether a real, live, open job actually exists at present. If the company is merely "thinking" of hiring someone down the road, you could have considerably more interactions with that same individual. All the more reason to invest serious amounts of time to fine-tuning your message!

Multiple job interviews at a company may genuinely aid your communications campaign, because after you've followed up with everyone once, you can vary your approach with the different individuals. One person may be more of a "snail mail" type: perhaps she's more formal or strikes you as more of a traditionalist. Another person may have more of an "email personality." Tune into your intuition and trust it.

Always assume that the various people on a team will consult with each other about your case. Strongly resist the urge to barrage them all with communiqués at the same time! Spread out your communications, and give prospects time to breathe before you tap them again.

5. *Staying on Their Radar*

Your company let you go on a Thursday afternoon. After negotiating to stay in your physical office, seeing a lawyer, obtaining a better severance package, and arranging for unemployment compensation, you went on a flurry of job interviews. Now you're in phase II of the interview process—the phase where nothing seems to happen, day after day. The weeks sprawl on, and while you struggle to make the task of *looking* for a job feel like a real job, you find yourself leaving your office earlier and earlier each day to catch some of the afternoon talk shows. How do you wean yourself from

Oprah, Dr. Phil, and Tyra when they feel like they are the only "friends" who are truly there for you? How can you stay top of mind without driving your interviewers berserk? And, how do you keep plugging away at this gargantuan task, day after day, without checking yourself into the loony bin?

 Your interviewer told you that they'd make a decision in two weeks. That was eight weeks ago. How do you know if you are over-communicating your desire to work at a company?

A. They will tell you. But by the time they do, it will be too late.
It's crucial to communicate with a company *just* often enough to stay on their radar without communicating anxiety. It's a cruel irony that those who are desperately seeking employment do not get it.

Do you have bills to pay? Is your landlord one nanosecond away from kicking you out for not paying your rent? Are you about to take a job serving at a local eatery to make ends meet? Never reveal *any* of these sorry details to a prospect at a company, or you will not receive the offer!

As a general guideline for the timing of your communications campaign, write to your interviewer and contact your headhunter on day one. Then wait at least a week before crafting an email that officially inquires about any next steps. If that missive doesn't spur your interviewer to action, draft your next email communication—but don't send it for two weeks. Then wait two more weeks before communicating again (and this time, consider using a medium other than email). A phone call may be necessary or even a handwritten letter.

Feel free to communicate with your headhunter much more often. She will earn her commission *only* once she places you so she should feel enthusiastic about contacting the prospect on your behalf. Realize that your follow-up communications campaign will proceed—both separately and as a coordinated effort—alongside your headhunter's. Also, importantly, if you know for a fact that she already talked to your prospect during a particular week, consider *skipping a cycle* in your communications campaign. Sometimes adding a bit of unpredictability to your communications can work in your favor. Plus it's really your *headhunter's job* to bug the companies who are looking to hire candidates. Circumstances may have forced you to act like a headhunter on your own behalf, but nagging a company too often can feel downright demeaning (and work against you).

THE STRAIGHT SCOOP

Ask for "next steps" when you leave an interview and follow them slavishly. If your interviewer tells you that you'll hear from her "in seven days" and you don't, write to her in *exactly* seven business days. (That would be seven business days after your initial Thank You email to her.) Never write to any interviewers over a weekend or at odd hours in the morning. It looks desperate!

 You met with five different people at the company, and all of the interviews went smoothly. How do you follow up and what do you say?

A.   Use each conversation as a springboard for what to write.
When you first get home from your appointment, devote an hour or two to quiet contemplation. Take out a notebook (or use your computer if you prefer) and capture everything that you can remember about each conversation. Try to recall the talk *verbatim* and write down every word that was spoken. This document will really help you as weeks slip by and the details of one conversation melt, higgledy-piggledy, into one another.

Then review your notes. Was there something asked in the interview that you failed to answer fully enough? Use this as content for your follow-up communications.

Email

Dear Marcia:

I want to tell you how lovely it was to finally meet you in person after hearing John Merchant sing your praises these many years! Thank you for sitting down with me for such an informative interview. I think it's no secret that I would love to work for you, and towards that end, I wanted to follow up on one of the questions you asked me during our talk. You asked if I had any experience with foreign clients. As fate would have it, I spent three months last year with our clients in Tokyo, Sydney, and Costa Rica, a sign, I believe, that my company had faith in my ability to close deals during some pretty challenging circumstances. I did end up negotiating deals in both Tokyo and Sydney and have heard through reliable sources that the Costa Rican deal is finally closing now. Very much looking forward to finding out if there might be a spot for me at XYZ.

Cordially,

90 You suspect your headhunter is avoiding your calls. How can you force a return call?

A. Switch media.

There are only two reasons why your headhunter would shun a phone call from you. She either doesn't know the answer to your question yet or she feels overwhelmed by all of the communication from you! If you sense it's the latter, force yourself to cease and desist. Back away from your landline!

Give it a few days before you hound her again, and when you do, consider shooting her an email instead of picking up the phone. In truth, you don't really need to talk to her. You just need her to give you a simple status report, covering:

1. Are you still in the running at the XYZ company?

2. Have they stopped interviewing other candidates?

3. How does your prognosis look?

4. When (oh when) will they make a decision?

This can all be covered in email.

Chances are excellent that once your headhunter has any news to relay, she will hunt you down like a bloodhound! It's fairly safe to assume that she has nothing to report—yet.

That's a Wrap

1. If your exact equal is promoted over you, try to view it as an opportunity to open a dialogue about your own career development.
2. When clashing with your direct supervisor, it's smart to figure out the underlying disagreement behind all of the verbal sparring.
3. Decode whether you were "terminated" or "laid off" and why—so that you can devise an intelligent job-interviewing strategy to explain it.
4. The follow-up communications campaign continues *until* you land the job. But don't over-communicate, lest you come off as overanxious for employment, and thus, unemployable.
5. Sometimes an unanswered question makes the perfect topic for your follow-up correspondence.

CHAPTER

Secret Meetings

In some companies, clandestine meetings are anathema. In other companies, closed-door tête-à-têtes are the only way that any business gets done. After all of the filibusters, side conversations, and posturing in the open meetings, a small, select group of decision makers clusters together, collectively sharpens their pencils, and gets down to the task of filling in the blanks, dotting the i's, crossing the t's, negotiating the contracts, refining the content material, and approving any work that goes forward.

If you are privy to these meetings, you need to respect why the doors are closed. Confidentiality is of paramount importance, and breaking it is considered an act of high treason.

Many companies swing like a metronome between an unprecedented degree of reticence and extraordinary openness depending on whose names happen to be on the door at any given time. Small companies sometimes mirror the personality of the top CEO or owner. If his Johari window is open, so is the company's. If his Johari window is closed, the executives around him can be rather tight-lipped indeed.

When the cloak-and-dagger ambience spills into the politics of personality and you sense bands of people gossiping about each other behind shuttered doors, then there is often a deliberate movement away from covertness during the next administration.

Regardless, from your standpoint, a closed door always means to keep the content of any conversations held therein private.

1.   *Loose Lips Sink Ships (and Accounts)*

You can take a secret to a grave (and have on numerous occasions). So it's easy for you to respect other people's confidentiality requirements. Granted, sometimes you may feel like shouting, "Oh, please! Who am I going to tell?" and, "Get over yourself. Do you honestly think anyone cares?" But you have no philosophical objection to keeping a tight lid on the proverbial "Pandora's Box" of corporate secrets, product launches, and strategies. If there is a confidentiality agreement, you are keen to sign it. You are neither a blabbering brook nor an open book and have never worn a corporate secret on a T-shirt. Better mum than dumb, you always say.

 91 Your job-hunting buddy hails from the same field and uses the same headhunter as you. You're convinced that the two of you might be competing for the same job. Are you obliged to tell your friend?

A.   Certainly not.

All's fair in love, war, and the competition for that scarce commodity known as a job. Today, you can expect to compete with at least ten people for an open position, and your competitors may span four generations. Consider yourself lucky that you know one of the candidates. Now, there are only nine more to trounce!

92 You inadvertently obtain some damning information about a company while interviewing for a job. Should you share the ill-gotten rumor or keep it to yourself?

A.   Consider it an insight: one there is no need to share.

Your interviewer shouldn't be unlocking any closets during the interview and allowing the skeletons free run of the facility.

But, just as rascals sometimes abuse the interview process to tease out confidential information about their company's competitors from naïve candidates all too willing to spill, occasionally a naïve interviewer will let a secret out during an appointment with an outsider.

Did she just let it slip that the CEO would be forced to resign due to some recent ethics violations? Oops! That *was* a blooper of epic proportions.

Write it off to her naïveté and resolve not to pass on the sordid rumor.

─────────────────────────── THE STRAIGHT SCOOP ───────────────────────────

You may want to refuse a job at a certain company if someone alerts you about some improper managerial behavior that's surfaced. Or you might draw the exact opposite conclusion. You may figure that now that the transgression has been exposed, the company will go to extraordinary lengths to clean itself up in an effort to repair its damaged reputation. For all you know, it could be the dawning of the age of transparency! But no matter what you personally decide, it's *never* a good idea for you to share any lurid company gossip (unless you ply your wares in the yellow journalism trade).

──

93 An interviewer inquires if you have any plans to attend business school in the near future. You are planning to apply in two year or three years. Must you reveal it?

A. Spin it.

Now here's a secret worth knowing: Everyone interviews as if they are seeking workers who will stay at their firms forever, while statistically nothing could be further from the truth!

Most people stay in a position for a couple of years and move on. Or they are "moved along"—due to a merger, acquisition, buyout, or bankruptcy. We are all a transient population of migrant workers!

Under the circumstances, it's perfectly legitimate to relay that you may apply to business school in a few years, but you're "99 percent certain you'll choose one that will allow you to go at night." The implication is that there will be no break in your service to the company.

2. *Send Lawyers, Guns, and Money*

To quote Justice Sandra Day O'Connor, "There is no shortage of lawyers . . . In fact, there may be more lawyers than people." Before you lost your job, you never had the privilege of meeting with even one lawyer. Now, during your copious free time, you have already met with three. First, a labor lawyer reviewed your severance package (no loopholes, darn!). Next, you met with an estate lawyer to review your parents' will. (It seemed like the only way you'd earn any money in this lifetime.) Now, by sheer coincidence, you have been asked to meet with your former company's in-house counsel to review some materials for one of your former clients. Your life has devolved into a series of endless waits in chambers as airless as King Tut's tomb! You chafe in the one and only three-piece suit that you happen to own and feel that, at any minute, you will mummify.

—————————————————————— THE STRAIGHT SCOOP ——————————————————————

When meeting with lawyers, it is imperative to dress as if you were attending a funeral, or another somber event. (If you're *paying* the lawyers for their services, that shouldn't be all that challenging.) Wear a conservative suit in a muted color, such as charcoal gray, black, or navy. Women should wear low heels and stockings. Men need to wear ties.

---

94   Great news! Your old firm called and asked if you are available for freelance. Clearly, they can't live without you! Should you take it?

A. Absolutely.

In a downsizing, most companies over-fire. As the dismal third quarter results filter in and the actual sales/billings/money flowing in is so much less than the rosy projections at the beginning of the fiscal year, widespread panic ensues. Doors shutter close as executives lobby for months about who should stay and who must go. Anyone privy to these grim meetings never wants to experience this agonizing process again, so there is a tendency to behead a few more people than is strictly necessary from a financial standpoint.

When your former company asks you to freelance for them, it's practically an admission that they made a mistake in cutting you. Take advantage of their corporate guilt to negotiate a fair (and hopefully higher) price for your services! Factor in that, as a consultant, you won't receive any health insurance, so the money you charge as a day rate will need to be enough to protect you from the unexpected.

In any other job interview you take, mention the fact that you are currently freelancing at your former company and watch the stigma of having been laid off vanish into thin air!

95 Hallelujah! Your old company wants to rehire you, but in a different department and for less money. What should your negotiating strategy be?

A. If they won't give you money, negotiate for a better title.

Titles are the world's cheapest perks. They look snazzy on a business card, impress friends at parties, and position you as a bigwig to clients. Titles: You've got to love 'em!

When negotiating for a title, remember they are free to the company. So always ask for the biggest title that you can possibly maneuver. Were you an associate before? Ask to be anointed senior associate. Were you a vice president? Ask to be crowned senior vice president. (Titles such as vice president and senior are *especially* easy for a company to dispense: there are tons of them, sometimes to the point of meaninglessness.) Depending on your field, "Director" also has a very posh ring to it.

Less Is More When It Comes to Titles

When negotiating for a title, remember that one substantive title is better than a whole batch of mediocre/measly/marginal titles strung together with a series of slash marks!

---

96 **Your former company wants to rehire you without a contract again. Fool you once, shame on them. Fool you twice, shame on you. How can you make the case that, this time around, you deserve a contract?**

A. Talk about your need for job security.

You can declare that you loved your job. You can swear that your company loyalty was unparalleled. You can share the waves of shock you experienced when you were cut and convey that you would dearly appreciate having more built-in job security this time around. But recognize that you may not yet have reached the level where your company normally accords contracts, so you may encounter a wall of resistance!

If you don't prevail, don't beat yourself up about it. Companies can wiggle out of ironclad contracts with the ease of a Houdini. So in reality you're not really losing all that much by not having one.

Feel proud that, at least, the contract discussion is "out there." It may take multiple rounds of spirited negotiation for you to wrangle a contract down the line, but at least you've opened the dialogue.

It Ain't Over till the Offer Is Accepted

Offers are made and sometimes they are rescinded. When you get an offer:

1. **Don't take forever to think it over.** You can take the weekend; don't take a whole week.
2. **Questions?** Air them with your headhunter first, if one is involved. She may be able to procure a phone appointment with your future employer so that you can resolve any outstanding issues smoothly and within a day or so.
3. **Show your enthusiasm.** When you accept the job, agree to a reasonable start date. If you are employed, or committed through a date due to freelance or a consulting project, then your start date

can be in two weeks. If you are unemployed, your start date should be considerably sooner. Take a week off to shake the job-hunting angst out of your system, but then START!

3. *Closed-Door Huddles*

You were only away for a few months, but in one fell swoop the corporate culture seems to have changed diametrically. It's as if a stiff wind blew through the hallways, suddenly slamming everyone's doors shut. And now you feel like each office door has an invisible "DO NOT DISTURB" sign on it. The odd thing is that there aren't even any new players to account for the new KGB-like aura, unless you count yourself being back on staff. And, out of adherence to the old Cube Farm culture, you would prefer to keep your new temporary door open. When secrecy is the defining characteristic of the office culture, should you try to stay hunkered down and out of sight, or is there a provocative reason to buck the trend?

97 At long last, you've finally broken into the "inner circle." You know who's moving up, who's moving out, and who will be stuck in the Cube Farm for eternity. But you're worried that the closed door of your temporary office may make others on the team feel paranoid. Is that a legitimate concern?

A. Keep all doors open, except during an emergency.

Open doors inspire trust and a spirit of camaraderie. Closed doors inspire distrust and waves of paranoia. And considering that moods are contagious, you'd probably rather have cheer circling through the hallways than its opposite.

Keep your door open and people will respect you more (even if they can only be found behind closed doors).

Your office technically has an "open door" policy where anyone can walk into the most senior person's office and unburden himself. You and your new supervisor don't see eye to eye on a lot of issues. Can you go over her head to air your concerns with her boss?

A. Not without massively negative repercussions.

Going over your manager's head will only exacerbate the original problem.

She will feel irked that you didn't trust her enough to try to solve the issue without third-party assistance and terribly wounded that you "kicked the problem upstairs" to her boss's level. Quite correctly, she will feel that you've disrespected her.

Is this really the way that you want your manager to feel about you? And toward what end? It's *extremely* unlikely that her boss will have *any* new insights to share or a brilliant solution to this particular problem. (Honestly, you have a better chance of winning the lottery.)

So in effect, you've succeeded in getting your direct supervisor rankled for no productive purpose whatsoever!

The Open Door Policy vs. Keeping Your Door Open

The open door policy should not be confused with keeping your door open. Always keep your door open unless you have a loud visitor or are conducting a meeting or a conference call in your office that will disturb others.

In theory, an open door policy allows employees of any rank access to the most senior managers. An employee might have a question about company policy, research results, target markets, marketing, social media outreach—anything—and then stroll into the office of a manager many levels above him to discuss it. This type of input is beneficial for top managers to hear and is the sort of information they'd pick up by the time-tested "management by walking around" method, anyway.

However, too often workers use the "open door policy" to *avoid* voicing a concern they have about working with their direct supervisor. They take great pains to go around her and approach her boss instead.

While some egocentric senior managers may love hearing from under-lings laboring many rungs under them, the manager really should *redirect the employee to discuss his issue with his supervisor first.* If the senior manager tries to step in and solve the problem, he's doing his part to sup-port a dysfunctional atmosphere where the chain of command is absolutely meaningless. Instead, he should try to monitor that the problem is being addressed by the only two people impacted.

"Did you manage to solve that issue with Carla?" he can ask the lower-level employee, "And did she respond to your satisfaction?"

Problem Solved

Senior managers need to take the long view when it comes to per-sonality frictions. If a low-level employee has a nitpick with his direct supervisor, it will help the supervisor's problem-solving skills if she is allowed to address it with the employee one-on-one, rather than having the senior manager assert himself into the quarrel. By redi-recting the employee to talk to his supervisor, it also honors the chain of command instead of breaking it.

---

99 One person on your team keeps her door closed all the time. Should you ask her to open it once in a while to let the air circulate?

A. Only if she directly reports to you.

It may feel like she's starting a countercultural revolution, especially if everyone else's doors are open. But one person cannot a corporate culture change (unless it's the CEO).

There is no need to criticize your teammate for trying to get some peace and quiet.

If her need for privacy disturbs someone higher up on the totem pole, let him address it with her directly.

Keeping doors open is a good idea, but it's not mandatory.

Where Would You Rather Work?

Given a choice, would you rather work at a company where the doors are open or closed?

Open Doors	Closed Doors
1. Communicate trust	1. Communicate secrecy
2. Indicate guilelessness	2. Indicate you're hiding something
3. Foster openness	3. Foster paranoia
4. Nurture camaraderie	4. Nurture lone wolves
5. Communicate "no news"	5. Communicate "bad news"
6. Say "business as usual"	6. Say "business interruptus"
7. Show you're accessible	7. Show you're inaccessible, except to a select few

---

4. *Salary Negotiations When Everyone Around You Is Losing His Job*

No doubt about it, Satan is a grump. Recently, you said "good morning" to him and you're pretty sure he mumbled, "All mornings are terrible until I say otherwise." He stared through you with his black, marbleized eyes, making you quickly rethink your plan to implore him for a raise. But several productive months have passed; your accounts are all bubbling; and you feel like it's high time for a little remuneration—especially since you came back on staff at a reduced compensation. You may be able to survive on a pauper's stipend that barely keeps you in plaid shirts, but your evil landlord isn't into rent rollbacks!

100 **With all of the layoffs happening at your company, you're actually frightened to ask for a legitimate raise. How can you overcome your fear?**

A. Start an accomplishment log.

If you want a raise you are not alone. Everyone always wants a raise!

If you deserve a raise, you are in excellent company. We all deserve raises!

The real question is, how can you make the case that you deserve a raise?

Has your performance exceeded expectations? Did your exemplary work result in either increased profits or substantial cost savings? Did you secure a new piece of business or prevent one from leaving? Did you successfully extend your customer base? Or expand the brand in a memorable way?

Put it on paper. Start an accomplishment log with dates, achievements, and any accolades received from clients, customers, vendors, or internal supervisors along the way. If you have glowing emails about your performance, bring them in with you as backup.

Does your boss agree that you're a superstar but claim that he just can't part with the money right now due to other considerations? Set up a planned date for the two of you to sit down in six months to readdress the topic.

For Extra Credit

If your boss rejects your request, don't take it personally. Just ask him what you need to do to turn his "no" into a "yes" next time. And resolve to follow through. If he murmurs about the pitiful state of the economy, you may want to ask for something that's easier for him to obtain for you than a raise, such as paid tuition or even stock options. Can the company perk you with transportation to and from the office? The one thing you *don't* want to request is more vacation time. (If the economy is being used as a catch-all excuse to put off your raise, asking for more vacation time sends the wrong message.)

101   Instead of a raise, you wouldn't mind working four days a week for your current salary. How can you broach the topic?

A. To see if a four-day work week is in your future, take a cold hard look at your company's Mommy Track.

These days, the four-day work week isn't just reserved for Mommies. It's also reserved for Daddies and anyone who is on the "Furlough Track." Numerous companies have started furloughs as a way of avoiding layoffs and keeping more of their employees on staff. But that's a top-down decision: one that will be embraced by management.

When you approach your company about a four-day work week, you need to consider how asking for this will reflect on you. Is the culture at your company cutthroat or more laid back and easygoing? The most reliable indicator of how you'll be viewed is by studying how others in your company are treated when they opt for four-day work weeks. Some companies are not as flexible about their flextime as you might hope.

You Can't Fight City Hall

While there are laws in place to protect against "parental status discrimination," you really don't want to get into a lawsuit with your employer if you can help it. A smarter tactic is to find a job where workers telecommute one day a week or where flexible hours are embraced.

---

102 You feel like management gave raises to all of the people who couldn't care less about the company while sticking it to those who really care. Is there a solution?

A. Yes. Keep your mouth closed about it, unless asked.

They reward people who work hard but inefficiently.

They reward people who stay late but whose output isn't Earth-shattering.

They reward martyrs, whiners, complainers, and kvetchers.

They reward back-stabbers, glad-handers, and schmoozers.

But the people who just get their work done quietly—and without drawing attention to it—they're *not* rewarded!

You're free to think that management has it all wrong and has no idea what it's doing. Just don't broadcast your thoughts, because management really has no interest in hearing them until *you're* in management.

Why This Technique Works

"The squeaky wheel gets the grease," you always hear. And in the short term, that philosophy often does succeed. Complainers and whiners annoy bosses into giving them raises. Irritated by the constant barrage of begging, bleating, and horn-tooting, a boss will sometimes relent. However, those raises carry a cost. Secretly, the boss resents doling out any rewards that he doesn't see fit to bequeath. Later, when the business cycle moves into a down cycle and the boss is reviewing people to cut, the complainers are at the top of his list. "Not only do these folks grumble all the time, they are too expensive," he thinks. As a general rule, never lambast management. You can politely ask for a raise. But don't compare yourself to others on staff or ask why someone else received a raise when you didn't.

5. *Lifting the Veil of Secrecy*

Before coming back to work at this company, you thought veils were only worn by brides. But a veil of darkness has descended on the whole organization and extreme secrecy cloaks the machinations of others. Hidden agendas unfurl in meetings held behind doors shut tight. Every message from your boss seems to carry a certain subtext that's difficult to decode, and others on staff have picked up his flowery (read: "obtuse") way of speaking. So now you're all speaking in tongues! Clarity has gone by the wayside, and it's hard to get a straight answer from anyone. You keep your head down and your temporary door open, wondering if you are the only staffer who finds the new ambience creepy.

Transparency, a Definition
The full, accurate, and timely disclosure of information.[10]

---

103   A vocal newbie gripes that "things aren't transparent enough." You don't mean to sound jaded, but this is how the atmosphere has been for awhile. What should you do?

A. **Trust your own insights, but confirm with others.**

"Transparency" is a cliché these days with different shades of meaning depending on who's saying it. You will need to sit down with the employee to tease out exactly what he means by his accusation. Bolster or dispute his claims with your own observations and take notes. Be sure to discuss your findings with others. Your team may be more opaque than you realize.

Solicit the opinions of various colleagues at different levels to round out your perspective.

Try to create an atmosphere that fosters constructive criticism instead of finger-pointing and blame. If a report doesn't meet your expectations, nicely explain why it doesn't and offer some pointers for how it can be improved. Did an employee do a spectacular job? Praise her for it publicly.

If you're in a managerial role, try pointing the finger at yourself sometimes. Tell your people when you feel disappointed in your own performance and share how you intend to boost it. Self-deprecating gestures like this will allow workers to feel like you're being honest with yourself and others.

Some Straight Talk About Transparency

Transparency thrives in an atmosphere where doors stay open, corporate secrets don't fester, and morale is high. Financial transparency keeps companies honest and dissuades employees from putting their hands in the proverbial cookie jar.

If workers feel like they can tell the truth, it also contributes to a more open atmosphere. If, conversely, employees are yelled at for every little mishap, then they have more of a reason to keep mistakes bottled up. People hate being screamed at.

---

104 **A reporter catches wind of something at your company and asks for your opinion. Should you talk to him?**

A. Definitely not.

Don't be the Deep Throat who gives a newspaper all of its hottest tips. Instead, figure out the person at your company whose job it is to handle reporters with kid gloves, and be sure to pass the request on to that individual ASAP. If you are at a loss, consult with your friendly HR person.

105   Everyone's tittering about the upcoming merger. Meanwhile your boss told you all of the details, under strict orders to keep it hush-hush. When others ask you about the rumor, is it okay to fib and pretend you know nothing?

A.   That is the right course of action.

In the words of Sergeant Schultz from the old *Hogan's Heroes* sitcom, "I see nothing . . . I was not here . . . I did not even get up this morning."[11]

Keeping a stiff upper lip is especially important during times of change. You don't want to set off a panic. Better to plead ignorance.

That's a Wrap

1. If someone conveys that a matter is top secret, you have no choice but to respect his wishes.
2. If your former company asks you to freelance or consult for them, it's practically an admission that they shouldn't have let you go. Try to capitalize on the fact in your interviews elsewhere, or turn it into a full-fledged, bona fide offer from your ex-company.
3. An open door policy is not the same thing as keeping your door open. If your company has an open door policy, don't use it as an excuse to go over your supervisor's head.
4. Four-day work weeks, telecommuting from home, and alternative "flextime" schedules may hold your career back if you work at a company that's not open to them. One person alone cannot a corporate culture change!
5. "Transparency" is not a synonym for talking to reporters.

CHAPTER 8

The New Dress for Success

The runways of most companies have little in common with catwalks. In these hallways, timelessness is more valued than trendiness unless you work in an industry that gears very young or ultra hip. The best role models for your sartorial cues are the executives working at your company.

Women shouldn't dress like ornaments and men shouldn't dress like dandies. Women need to keep their party dresses at home—even for office parties. Men should limit the number of patterns competing for the eye's attention, lest these gents convey an image wholly out of character with the dominant culture of the corporate class.

Strive to fit in before you ever worry about standing out. It's a great piece of wisdom to follow, not just for your wardrobe requirements but also for your business conduct in general.

Start with some classic pieces and master the basic rules of dressing first. Be slow to deviate from these rules, unless the rising stars at your company all do. Accessorize sparingly: Keep jewelry, charms and ornamental trimmings, and perfumes and colognes on the light side.

Finally, treat your clothing like an investment. As the Roman poet Juvenal once wrote, "Seldom do people discern eloquence under a threadbare cloak."

1. Don't Flash Your Hardware Unless You Work in a Hardware Store

They finally kicked you upstairs to the executive suite where the view is better. The people on this floor dress two tax brackets richer than they do down in the Cube Farm. In this rarified echelon, no one wears plaid; everyone sports pants with actual pleats; and you've even spotted several guys modeling those long skinny nooses known as ties. Every day is like the Easter Parade. Wow! A woman just walked by toting a designer handbag that didn't come straight off of a truck! For the first time since returning to the company, you find yourself curious about what the official dress code is (and concerned about what fate might befall those in violation). The locked room near the Men's room isn't housing a secret fashion prison, is it?

106 You've heard it's okay to flash a little personality in your vestments. How little is too little and how much is too flashy?

A. If you have to ask, it's too flashy.

Unless you work for someone named Midas, keep the gold in your outfits to a minimum. Don't wear gargantuan belt buckles with chunky gold logos, gold shirts, or horsey gold bangles. A gold tie doesn't convey "Golden boy" as much as it does "fashion impoverished." Gold nail polish, metallic pants, and gold sunglasses are not the gold standard of office fashion that you may think. Even silver has its limitations. Tempted to festoon yourself with scads of skinny bracelets, multiple earrings, or (God forbid) a nose ring? Don't be a metal head.

———————————— THE STRAIGHT SCOOP ————————————
Metallica is a heavy metal band, not a clothing style.

107 This year, bronze is the new black. Can you wear it to work?

A. Heavy metal is for rock stars, not corporate superstars.

Why follow what the supermodels are wearing when you have so many real role models to emulate?

Look up everyone in your company who's a VP or above, and follow them for your sartorial inspiration. Whatever they happen to be wearing coordinates perfectly with the managerial vision for the company dress code.

Do you have a passion for fashion? Rein it in. Unless you work in the fashion industry or in a "glamour" area, such as advertising, temper your fashion flair with a fastidious attention to what others at the company are wearing. You needn't worry about being a fashion plate, just a model of a successful businessperson.

The Office Runway

The fashion industry should be commended for unveiling new colors each season that tempt us to dip into our wallets and buy ever more clothing. And, as more colors infiltrate the mass market, our collective eyes adjust to the glare and fashion mores loosen at the workplace.

But, thumb through any copy of *Vogue, Harper's Bazaar* magazine, or *GQ* and it should be apparent that most of the clothing displayed in those lustrous pages is *not* appropriate office attire. It's targeted to fashion-forward women and men while most companies are distinctly *fashion-middle.*

Who Knew?

Psychophysicists, those friendly folks who study human responses to color, have demonstrated that human beings can see thousands of levels of light-dark, hundreds of levels of red-green, and hundreds of levels of yellow-blue in a lab. That means that the total number of colors we can observe is roughly 10 million (1000x100x100).[12] Hence, there are plenty of fashionable colors to choose amongst—without resorting to wearing an acid green suit.

108 **If the logo shouts "hideously expensive," can't that be considered a sign of good taste?**

A. Conspicuous consumption is not a message you want to broadcast.
Somewhere on this planet there is a humongous logo adorning a woman's handbag or man's tie clip that will prove to be the glorious exception to this rule, but in general, corporate fashion is discreet rather than distracting, subtle rather than screaming, and elegant rather than brash. Most logos, frills, and other ornamentations are too ostentatious for business attire.

Instead, invest your hard-earned money in lustrous fabric drapes, invisible seams that are the telltale sign of superior craftsmanship, and flattering cuts. Pay extra for exquisite tailoring, and have a tailor eyeball every item you ever wear to the office *before* you purchase it.

Trust that eagle-eyed superiors will be able to sense when you've spent a fortune on an outfit—with or without the supersized logos.

Ostentatious Ornamentation Sends Clients the Wrong Signal
Because flashy clothes and jewels draw so much attention to themselves, they may also draw the ire of your clients who may secretly question why your clothes are so much more costly than their own. Wearing flashy outfits is particularly dicey during a recession or during a down business cycle when company layoffs abound. During the Great Recession of '09, many luxury goods companies suffered conspicuous sales declines as executives and others with seven-figure salaries cut back on buying showy clothing in deference to the millions of people who lost their jobs.

---

2. *Clothes Make the Man; Shoes Make the Woman*

After several weeks of fastidious observation, you have concluded that there are three official office dress codes: "Golden Boy," "Rising Star," and "Grunt." As an ex-Grunt, you are massively unprepared to now outfit yourself like a Rising Star. You'd love to plead ignorance of the corporate dress dictates but have a hunch that the office fashion police won't take kindly to it. (Ignorance of *this* law is no excuse.) At any minute you expect the fashion police to come pounding on your brand new door. Meanwhile, you recall reading in a glossy magazine that before any sort of major wardrobe upgrade, one is supposed to conduct an "audit" of all current clothing. Well, at least that part is easy: seventeen plaid shirts; three pairs of shoes. In spite of all odds, you embrace the challenge of turning your meager threads into a killer, dress-for-success wardrobe!

109 If the suit is dark, are there any rules that govern the color of the shirt underneath?

A. Decide whether you're trying to achieve a high-contrast look or one that is more monochromatic.

Your skin, eye, and hair color are part of the equation.

If your hair and skin are both light, wearing light colors near your face can be more flattering.

If your hair and skin are both dark, dark shirts can look polished when expertly paired with dark suits. (Feel compelled to wear a white shirt to work anyway? Try balancing it with dark accessories, such as a belt, tie, or shoes in dark colors.)

A shirt in a light color against the backdrop of an exquisitely cut dark suit tends to be the more conservative choice for the runways of the Fortune 500.

110 Must belt and shoe color always match?

A. It's the safe choice.

"Safe" may not be the message that you want to advertise about yourself, and you should trust your judgment on this matter. Simply recognize that people will make snap judgments about you based on the clothes you wear. *Everyone* is a fashionista—when it comes to *other people's* fashion selections.

That said, black shoes have no business ever being paired with brown belts, or vice versa. You don't want your accessories to appear disorganized, disheveled, or discombobulated. They should not compete with each other or cry out for attention.

Five Rules of Wearing Pantyhose You Should Adhere to Like a Girdle

Unless your name is Florence Nightingale, forgo wearing white hose to the workplace. They will make you look like a white elephant, causing people to wonder if your cost is out of proportion to your usefulness.

Navy pantyhose work beautifully—but only if your shoes are navy.

Neutral hosiery is always in fashion, even if it can be a bit ho-hum or hum-ho.

Black opaque hose are appropriate office attire during the winter, but sheer black hose are really meant for eveningwear. (Hint: Just because you're working until all hours of the night doesn't mean that you should dress as if you're on a date.)

Courtney Love can get away with torn pantyhose, but alas, you can't.

---

111   **Are there any clothes that women should avoid wearing to work, even in a casual office?**

A. There is a whole closet's worth of "don'ts."

If the shoe doesn't fit your corporate culture, don't wear it. This effectively eliminates Birkenstocks, clogs, hiking boots, sneakers, sandals, flip flops, stilettos, spike heels, granny shoes, or any boots that make you look like a sex kitten. (Meow!)

Moving up your leg, beware of pantyhose that clash, color-wise, with the rest of your attire. Blue pantyhose look atrocious with black skirts, making you wish you had a black eye so you couldn't see 'em. Also, pantyhose must be lighter than your shoe color, not darker.

Still traveling from bottom to top, skip shorts, skorts, skirts that cling too tightly to the butt, skirts that ride up your butt, and skirts that are so short all anyone can see is your butt. (You don't want to be the butt of jokes and office pranksters even if you have a glorious butt.)

But wait, there's more. Shy away from belts that support too much hardware or anything sparkly, unless you're a rhinestone cowgirl.

Put tank tops on your official "don't even think about it list." (Seriously, put this book down and write yourself a note.) Shun anything sleeveless, backless, shapeless, or (ironically) anything that's too clingy and lends too much shape. Is your shirt tugging, pulling, or exposing cleavage? Pull it off and replace with a Brooks Brothers button-down. (Just don't peel it off in the corner office.)

Most sweaters are innocuous, but steer clear of anything cutesy or that your mother might have worn to the office. These days, that's *How (Not) to Succeed in Business Without Really Trying.* Retro clothing has a campy feel wholly at odds with modern business values.

Jewelry: Keep it small and discreet. Don't ornament your arms, fingers, or ears with riches, or no one will understand why you have to work for a living.

Jackets: Have a tailor inspect any that you intend to buy. Your entire ensemble can devolve over a poorly fitting jacket (and you don't want to look like a jacket-ass). Obtain a professional opinion about sleeve length and the fit along your shoulders and back. A jacket shouldn't feel too snug or hang too loose.

3. Formal Yachting Attire to Cocktails at 7 in the Billiards Room

The good news is that your former client missed you while you were in "Siberia"—your code name for the brief interlude that you spent pounding the pavement. The bad news is that he wants nothing more than to celebrate your return to "civilization"—at his country club. You have never set foot in a posh country club before, unless you count the seventeen times you watched the movie *Caddyshack.* Will the two of you hit the tennis courts, and if so, must your shorts and polo shirt really conform to the "80 percent white" rule? And what instruments do they use to measure the percentage? Or will you both simply exercise your right to swig mint juleps poolside all afternoon? What *is* the country club lifestyle, and exactly how is your client planning to entertain you?

112   Your client wants to host you at his country club for the afternoon. Any helpful dressing hints?

A. Find out the club dress code in advance.

With all due respect to tennis superstar Roger Federer, he sets a poor example. He can wear any color under the sun at the U.S. Open, and hence, cannot be considered a proper sartorial role model. The Williams sisters are no better. And Agassi, well . . .

Country clubs are considerably stricter than any tennis league about what is and isn't appropriate court attire. Here is the last bastion of "white on white" clothing rules for tennis courts and strict rules for golf attire. You never want to be kicked out of a club for what you're wearing, or worse, be sent to the pro shop to correct your 80-proof goof! Pro shops can be excessively costly, plus there is the embarrassment factor. (High.) Ask your host in advance about the clothing requirements. If you're still unsure, call the club to double-check their guidelines.

Don't trust Google when it comes to scouting out the club dress code! Call the club directly and ask to speak to someone in the manager's office. If there's any possibility that your day at the club may extend into night, don't forget to investigate the dining room dress rules. Ask if it's jacket and tie (if you're a man) and what attire is specifically not permitted (if you're a woman).

Watercooler Wisdom

Emily Post's take on what constitutes good manners in clubs is as accurate today as it was back in 1922 when she first penned this sage advice: "A club is for the pleasure and convenience of many; it is never intended as a stage-setting for a 'star' or 'clown' or 'monologist.'"[13] It sounds clever, but "What on Earth is a 'monologist?'" you ask. A monologist is someone who performs monologues or an entertainer who performs alone.[14]

How Not to Get Kicked Out of a University Club

Inside this secret enclave, wooden panels cushion against ambient sounds and club etiquette forbids any loud discussion of business while dining.

How will *They* know, you wonder?

At most university clubs today, dining demeanor is based on a strictly enforced set of rules. In the dining room, one is not allowed to:

- take notes
- take calls
- answer pages
- text
- read or mark up papers.

Violate these codes once, and a waiter will cheerfully remind you of the House Rules. Transgress a second time, and you may be asked to leave the dining room! Inside these paneled parlors, gentle discourse on pressing social engagements is encouraged.

One *is* allowed to:

- speak in dulcet tones about tennis, golf, or one's last vacation
- hobnob with other alumni and make appointments to play tennis or golf or take a vacation with them, preferably to an island starting with the word "Saint," as in St. John or St. Bart's.

As the Columbia University Club of New York bluntly states on their website:

Business Meetings, which require obvious use and display of papers, are disruptive to other members and are not permitted. A quiet business conversation among two or three people is permissible. Club employees have been instructed to call attention to violations and to request that the member conform to the rules. Members who refuse to remedy a violation may be escorted from the Clubhouse.[15]

---

113 **Your client's father just passed away and you need to attend the funeral. You never met his father. Must you wear black?**

A. No, but your clothes must be subdued.

Black is the new black. Then again, so is eggplant, maroon, and elephant's breath. Midnight blue discreetly fades into the background, as do navy and charcoal gray. Appropriate funereal colors don't draw attention to themselves. They are somber and quiet, an acknowledgment that death is serious business and, for everyone but Shirley MacLaine, inevitable.

Speaking of business, you must leave it behind. Mobile paging devices are one accessory that's always unappreciated at a funeral. Don't bring your Blackberry, iPhone, smartphone, pager, or cell.

Do you feel separation anxiety when you must be apart from your mobile paging device? Then have it on your person, but keep the device turned off. Don't use it to call your office, text your buddy about meeting for a post-funeral drink, or check the scores at halftime. (There is no halftime at funerals. By the time one's funeral rolls around, the game, as it were, is over.)

THE STRAIGHT SCOOP

If you are a close personal friend of the key mourner and you intend to sit with his or her family, then it *is* appropriate to wear black.

---

114 You're looking forward to your first out-of-town convention. How does the clothing differ from what you would ordinarily wear at the office?

A. Wear your everyday business uniform, but take it down a notch.

You can't spell "conventional" without the word "convention." Don't let the sun, saltwater, and boondoggle ambience boggle your mind to the point that you forget you're with business associates. You can be less formal, but don't let it all hang out. Resolve to leave much to the imagination.

Don't expose real cleavage, toe cleavage, bare shoulders, or hairy legs. You work with these people, remember? What if *they* expose their cleavage, toe cleavage, bare shoulders, or hairy legs? Then can you? No. But you might want to don blinders.

Do you ordinarily wear a suit to the office? At a convention, you can downgrade the outfit to a jacket and slacks.

If a jacket and slacks is your everyday getup, then roll back the level of formality one notch—and show up in slacks and a nice sweater instead.

If you usually wear slacks and a nice sweater to work, you may be able to get away with slacks and a nice shirt at the convention. This level of dress is sometimes referred to as "smart casual." But be smart, and don't get too casual.

THE STRAIGHT SCOOP

Stay away from shorts, bathing suits (except at the pool), flip flops, Birkenstocks, and blue jeans.

Don't Tell Your Dry Cleaner I Told You, But . . .

Dry-cleaning chemicals prematurely age clothing by damaging the internal structure. Dry cleaned too often, jackets, skirts, and blouses will wrinkle, fade, tear, and shed buttons. It's actually a poor investment in your clothes' preservation! Unless your clothes are soiled or smell musty, don't dry clean them more than four times a year. If your outfits are merely wrinkled, you can always bring them to a professional dry cleaner and have them ironed.

---

4. Interpreting "Festive Attire" and Other Meaningless Phrases

It's that magical time of year again when the office is abuzz with the tinkling sounds of a party. It's not an office party. It's the annual July 4th shindig at Satan's sprawling suburban palace. However, the fireworks started early this year over two new words on the invitation: "festive attire." One of the interns claimed that "festive was meaningless"—he intended to wear the football jersey of his favorite player. Then your assistant Ashley chimed in saying that she was pretty sure that's not what Mrs. Satan had meant by the word "festive." The intern rebutted, saying that, clearly, Ashley didn't understand the meaning of the word "festive," as she had never experienced the unadulterated joy of watching his favorite player score a 60-yard touchdown! While the B-team bickered, you tried to look up "festive attire" in a couple of etiquette books, but couldn't find the popular phrase cited in any of them.

115 Is it better to show up an office party underdressed or overdressed?

A. Underdressed, but conservatively clad, if you're a woman.

Ideally, you will arrive perfectly dressed. But it's better to arrive in a casual jacket and pants rather than in a dress that reveals too much leg, arm, back, or cleavage. Don't show your bust unless you want it to air on the office *Boob Tube*.

No matter how buff you are, you never want to expose yourself to your colleagues' ridicule.

Stay away from anything too girly-girly. Avoid ribbons, ties, frou-frou ornamentation, beads, studs, shimmers, or anything that says, "I am Girl, hear me giggle."

A. Overdressed, if you're a man.

Always aim to arrive in the correct attire. But, given a choice, it's smarter to show up in a suit and tie rather than revealing yourself to be a "boy toy." Don't use the boss's party as an excuse to model Hawaiian shirts, shorts, baggy jeans or sweats, hoodies, T-shirts with clever sayings, cute belt buckles, or any gear that makes you look like a cowboy (unless you herd cattle for a living). Jeans, sneakers, Birkenstocks, and hiking boots are best parked in your closet at home.

Trust that your coworkers already appreciate that you're the life of the party and don't use your clothes to shout the message, or it will certainly be overkill.

116 One of your colleagues is getting married, and the invitation says "black tie." Any advice for reinterpreting the dress code since there will be people at the office in attendance?

A. Discretion is the better part of business (if you're a woman).

You can wear exactly what you would normally wear to a black tie gala, as long as it doesn't scream, whisper, or flirtatiously imply sex. At a business function, you want the guys in the room to think noble, business-like thoughts and keep the gents staring at your perky face, instead of at the twin peaks due south.

A. Traditional black tie attire will work just fine (if you're a guy).

A black tuxedo, white soft shirt, and bow tie will see you through the most formal of occasions. While tuxedos do come in a rich palate of exotic colors, please remember that you are not a peacock displaying your plumage. Stick to basic black. If you have a creative streak, it's best expressed through jazzy studs or a handsome cummerbund in a socially preapproved contrasting color such as crimson.

Five Fabulous Fashion Finds

"The well-dressed man is he whose clothes you never notice."
—William Somerset Maugham
"Only great minds can afford a simple style."
—Stendhal
"Fashion is what you adopt when you don't know who you are."
—Quentin Crisp
"The fashion wears out more apparel than the man."
—William Shakespeare
"I base most of my fashion sense on what doesn't itch."
—Gilda Radner

---

117 Out with it. What does "festive attire" actually mean?

A. "Slightly dressy."

Always keep your own dress code focused on the boardroom rather than the bedroom even if you happen to find yourself in the living room of your boss's wife. For women: "Festive attire" can be articulated through fabric selection and a change of texture. Instead of either wool or cotton, you might consider wearing something crafted of velvet in the winter or lace in the summer. (If it's made of lace, make sure the lace has a backing and zero peek-a-boo factor.) If you ordinarily wear a suit to work, you might relinquish the boxy "two piece" ensemble and opt for a dress instead. Because you're at a party with colleagues, take care to keep the cut conservative of any dress you sport. It may also be wise to wear long sleeves.

For guys, "festive attire" translates as "wear a suit, and if you want to get slightly creative, wear a tie in a spiffy color."

Bing! Confusion solved.

5. Whatever Happened to "Casual Fridays?"

In the Cube Farm, the dress code couldn't have been more relaxed. Truth to tell, it wouldn't have shocked you if it had turned out that half of the Cube residents didn't always remember to shower. But now that you've moved into the high-rent district, it seems like you are working in a radically different, structured, formal company where dress mores are taken seriously. One Friday morning, you tumble into work wearing a plaid shirt, pleated pants, and a sweater. The HR-Assistant-Who-Only-Wears-Black stops you in the hallway. "Oh, haven't you heard?" she asks, sniffing down her surgically perfect ski jump nose, "We've gotten rid of Casual Fridays." You feel like you're about to receive your first clothing ticket—a misdemeanor for wearing plaid. "Better not let anyone see you today," she says with a conspiratorial wink. "Today?" you feel like screaming, "Honey, this is the nicest outfit I own!"

118 **A few years ago, everyone sported casual garb to work on Fridays. Now the proverbial pendulum appears to have swung back again and Fridays resemble Mondays in terms of what everyone's wearing. What's going on?**

A. A dot-com bubble burst here, a real estate bubble burst there.
During the dot-com heyday, college grads ran dot-com empires from their parents' garages and a more casual look infiltrated even buttoned-up companies who would allow their employees to dress down on most Fridays.

But Casual Fridays were one of the casualties of the dot-com bubble burst. And with the more recent Great Recession of '09, numerous companies have returned to stricter dress codes.

THE STRAIGHT SCOOP

When shopping for a new suit, always wear the same shirt and tie that you intend to wear with it later. Doing so will help you see the suit pattern more clearly against its ultimate canvas. The same rule applies to women on the hunt for a new skirt or dress. Wear the same shoes that you plan to accessorize with the outfit, as then your heels will be the correct height should the garb require the attention of the in-store tailor.

---

119   **Is there a rule for mixing and matching the different elements of a wardrobe?**

A. Stick with just two patterns in colors that complement each other, unless you have a professional wardrobe specialist.

You've heard of male pattern baldness. This is male pattern blindness. Dots and checks and stripes can quickly morph into a three-ring circus that interferes with getting real work done. Oooh, the glare is getting bright in here.

Simple is both chicer and easier to pull off.

Most suits have a pattern or grain to the fabric. It may be subtle, but the eye still takes it in.

Plain worsted, herringbone, fine stripes, and tweed are all patterns. Windowpane, hounds tooth, and Prince of Wales are larger, more obvious patterns. But whether your suit pattern is barely visible or really obvious, for business you're safest mixing it with a patterned tie and a *plain* shirt.

Very subtle chalk striped suits can easily take on an additional striped pattern in the shirt, even with a striped tie. And some suits with a "barely there" pattern—such as the type found in linen suits—can also look dashing with the addition of a checked shirt.

(Be sure to keep the pattern fairly simple and brandish a *plain* tie.)

Look in the mirror. If you think you resemble a dandy, remove at least one patterned item from your ensemble and replace it with a plainer version.

If the Suit Fits . . .

No man should buy a suit off the rack, slip it on, and automatically assume that it looks divine. Don't be afraid to seek professional help, not to mention tailoring. When buttoned, there should be no bunching or wrinkling across the back of the jacket. If your shape is slightly rounded, there should be enough "give" in the jacket so that, when buttoned, it lies flat across the front of the chest or stomach. When open, the jacket should hang straight down at the back and the front. With arms at your sides, your knuckles should be even with the bottom of your jacket. Between a quarter and a half inch of the shirt cuff should be visible.

If the trousers have cuffs, they should fall with one break across the shoe.

120 Who helps whom off with their coat these days?

A. Business today is gender neutral, but socially, the old rules still apply.

The business world is light years ahead of the social world. Today a man should help a woman off with her coat in business, and it's equally gracious for a woman to help a man off with his coat. It may seem a bit other-worldly at first, but this simple gesture of respect needs to be extended, regardless of gender.

The person being helped with his coat then offers to reciprocate the gesture. It's a brave, new, well-dressed world.

That's a Wrap

1. Flashy hardware doesn't reflect well on your professionalism.
2. At the office, coloring yourself beautiful is less important than looking polished and smart.
3. Country clubs have their own codified rules covering dress. Endeavor to fit in by finding out what the rules are in advance.
4. At an office party, it's better to show up underdressed if you're a woman and overdressed if you're a man.
5. Casual Fridays have been replaced by formal Mondays, Tuesdays, Wednesdays, Thursdays, and Fridays.

II

Virtual Meetings

As we migrate to a business world increasingly dominated by email communication, emails are replacing in-person meetings. Are your e-voice and e-personality *advancing* your career or holding you back? Part II spells out the new communication rules for the 21st century and teaches you how to integrate Facebook, LinkedIn, and Twitter into a personal communication strategy that can help you accomplish your professional aspirations. Learn how to win Facebook friends to extend your influence; how to catch clients even in a down market; and why LinkedIn is like the headhunter you never had.

CHAPTER 9

Social Networking for the Hard-Wired

Back in the olden days, that is, before the dawn of Facebook, one's contacts used to be zealously guarded secrets. We were all private gatekeepers of our own networks and we rarely gave away the key.

Exceptions were to be made, of course. If someone we knew was desperately seeking a job and we felt fondly towards him, we might give our hapless friend the names of five people in his field who might be able to help. For that highly privileged information, naturally our friend would feel eternally grateful and, if the contact we provided worked out, perhaps forever beholden to us.

With the dizzying speed of a stealth bomber, Facebook has turned the "private gatekeeper" dynamic on its head. The gatecrashers have arrived; the walls of privacy have crumbled; and now that one's friends of friends can easily pick through every contact on our Facebook list, there's no such thing as a closely guarded secret anymore.

Today, the average person knows 300 people by name and the average person on Facebook has 130 Facebook friends. By inference, this means that you needn't "friend" every person who ever asks. But who should you friend, who should you ignore, and where do you draw the line?

This chapter examines what friendship means in the new, closely intertwined, online social networking world of Facebook, LinkedIn, and Twitter.

1. The Average Person Knows 300 People by Name, and Other *Believe-It-Or-Not Friendship Factoids*

When Satan first informs you of the change you don't believe him. "You want me to play with *Facebook*—at the office?" you stammer. You always figured there were rules *against* having fun at the workplace, and you have certainly lived up to them. "Don't be daft!" Satan screams. "I want you to friend a million strangers. Then let them know about our corporate initiatives in a way that doesn't sound like *marketing speak* but really is. Get it?" "But that's not my job," you stammer, and then wish you could retract the words. "We are *all* in media now," Satan snorts, his nose flaring like a dragon's. He flicks a talon in your direction with a dismissive back wave. "By the way, how many Facebook friends do you have?" he asks, a competitive glint in his marbleized eyes. "None," you say. "I'm not *on* Facebook." "Tempus fugit," Satan says, turning on his tasseled loafers to go torment someone else.

121   **How many Facebook friends does the average person have?**

A. 130.
Friends don't let friends stay off Facebook.

Today, the average person knows 300 people by name and has 130 Facebook friends.

By inference, that means you don't have to "friend" every last person who ever asks. But if you are using Facebook as a networking tool, then you may need to cast your Facebook net pretty wide.

Who Knew?

Robin Ian MacDonald Dunbar, a British anthropologist and evolutionary biologist specializing in primate behavior, is best known for formulating something called "Dunbar's number," which is roughly 150—the number of individuals with whom any one person can maintain stable relations.

122 **There's a hipster who you've hated since high school. If you become "Facebook friends" with him, is your relationship with him likely to improve?**

A. Not much.
Facebook may be the great democratizing force of the 21st century. But even Facebook can't radically alter the lines that were drawn in your high school classroom, crystallized in your high school cafeteria, and solidified during your school dances.

Those lines will never be crossed!

Sometimes the Truth Really Is Stranger Than Fiction
There are tons of fictional profiles on Facebook, that is, seemingly real profiles of people who don't exist. Sometimes, the fictional profile is created as a campy inside joke that's cute and fun and makes people laugh, and sometimes the fictional profile is a creepy inside joke that doesn't hit everyone's funny bone the same way. I know of one friend who was harassed by a fictional person. Alas, discretion prevents me from revealing more.

---

123 **If you ignore a Facebook request, will the person find out?**

A. Yes, because you won't show up on his friend list.
There is no mechanism for saying, "No." You can simply ignore a request. The person will never receive any sort of notification that you turned him down. However, you can assume that he will know and may even bristle if *he* considers *you* a good friend. To soften the irritation factor, you can devise a canny way to explain *why* you turned down his request if and when you get together with him in person.

There are two ways to ignore a request—the passive route, by which you do absolutely nothing, and the active route where you actually hit the electronic button marked "Ignore." Both will have the identical impact on your rebuffed friend (i.e., he probably won't hold it against you forever unless he really overthinks it). But if you hit the electronic button, his photograph will disappear instantly—a genuine benefit if you truly can't stand the person!

2. Become Facebook Friends with the Rich and Famous

Nothing that you studied in college or grad school adequately prepared you for the etiquette conundrums that happen on Facebook with the regularity of an RSS feed. Your boss wants to friend you (but you don't even like him). You mother wants to friend you (ditto). Your coworkers and colleagues are all eager to friend you. And, once you let one of them in, it's as if the floodgates have opened! You have no choice. You'd better let them all in. Yet, mysteriously, one of your barhop buddies adamantly *refuses* to become your Facebook friend. (What's up with that?) What *is* the protocol? How do you befriend the people you like but keep out those you don't? And are all of the people on your Facebook friend list *really* your friends?

124 A total stranger asks to friend you. Good idea or bad?

A. Probably bad—if you're more than two degrees of separation removed from him.

You can tell almost everything you need to know about someone by his friends.

If you and the stranger share more than five mutual friends, then he's already in your greater network, so chances are better that he's not a scam artist or someone who's fishing for your personal information. Still, with stories of identity theft headlining the news, you can't be too careful. It's smart to check out strangers' credentials with any mutual friends who you happen to share. How well do *they* know him?

If you have zero friends in common, and he doesn't belong to any of your networks, don't friend the person.

Watercooler Wisdom

"Like virginity in the '60s, privacy has become something to be gotten rid of—as soon as possible." —Jay McInerney[16]

125 What are the pitfalls of becoming Facebook friends with a stranger?

A. It's like hitchhiking with someone you've never met. You just never know.

Every time you let in a stranger, you expose all of the people on your friend list to someone with whom you have no personal acquaintance. Where did he grow up? What school did he go to? What are his values? You haven't the slightest idea.

If the person happens to be respectful of people's boundaries, then probably there is no harm done.

But what if the person is a social predator, an email junkie, a psychopathic poster, or worse, an identity thief?

An unscrupulous individual can amass reams of personal information about even "friends of friends" on this social networking site. Facebook is a stalker's paradise. Guard you and your real friends from inadvertently sharing information with a stranger in your midst.

126 How can you build your company's network without letting total strangers into your inner circle?

A. Join the blogosphere.

Empower a few plucky employees to speak on behalf of your company. Then start a company blog and have the chosen ones contribute to it. Give them the freedom to blog about anything that's not earmarked as a corporate secret—engineering plans on the drawing board, product improvements, product suggestions, upcoming contests, and promotions.

Ideally, you want to choose your corporate flag bearers to be "true believers." They shouldn't have large gripes with the company since they may have to fend off customer complaints about it!

Think twice before handing the task over, by rote, to the corporate communications group who may be besieged these days with requests to bombard the Facebook, LinkedIn, and Twitter space with glowing messages about your company's initiatives.

Instead, cherry pick people from various departments who will view blogging as the career opportunity of a lifetime and who are receptive to feedback from the public. Because, be forewarned: Once you open the doors to a two-way communication between your company and its customers, you *will* receive a lot of feedback!

Not Everyone Is a Born Writer

Fortunately, everyone on the marketing team is a born editor. It's their job to communicate objectives, editorial considerations, company voice, plus nettlesome items, such as which topics to steer clear of. Bloggers are acting as ambassadors for the company. Give each designated employee-blogger a statement that outlines his responsibilities, and make him sign it.

What if the Customers Complain?

If you have a faulty product or service, your customers *will* let you hear about it, sometimes vociferously. But often, they just want to be listened to. Show them that you are listening by placing human beings instead of robots at the helm of blog command control. Train all bloggers not to respond with *corporate speak*. It's a huge turnoff that is likely to enrage your company's base of core supporters.

---

3. Electronic Posters in Search of a Strategy

You wish there could be a whole separate department of your company to handle the social media behemoth in the conference room. "There is," your boss says curtly. "It's you." You stare at your nemesis as if one of your eyes is going to pop out of your head and roll like a marble on the conference room table. How are you supposed to predict what the next "new new thing" will be? What do you look like, Warren Buffet? Between blogging, Facebook groups, LinkedIn, and Twitter, there is a dizzying array of electronic choices. You're convinced that the first step should be to develop a strategy but you are unclear about the mission. "Just do it," your boss orders, pointing a well-manicured talon in your direction and staring at you as if you are a truculent child having a tantrum. "That's why he makes the big bucks," you think, nodding sadly.

127 A few weeks into your company's social media foray, some of your people have already begun to experience burnout. How can you keep them engaged with the new media long enough to develop an effective strategy?

A. Align their interests with your company's interests.

Only the Bee Players are drones. A-players tend to be out for themselves. So always put yourself in their Cole Haans and ask yourself, "What's in it for them?"

Build in rewards—more money, better title, exposure to top management, possible keynote at the company mission retreat, the chance to be on the ground floor of a thrilling pilot project—to keep them merrily blogging away.

For Extra Credit

Add a gaming aspect to kick-start your project. Why not incentivize the blog squad with a contest and promise that whoever logs the most blogs will win an all-expenses paid weekend in the Bahamas? Tout the benefits of being able to communicate to the market directly.

---

128 Where does most social networking fail?

A. Before it ever gets off the ground.

The lack of a content plan and poor strategy can sabotage your company's social media efforts. Sit down with your key players and force them to write an outline of blog topics covering the next six months. *Do not expect them to take kindly to this.* They may feel that writing an outline is remedial. Ignore their whining; make them do it anyway!

Most blogs have a readership base of one person. You want your company blog to have a readership of a million and one.

The content plan is like a book's table of contents. It's an extensive list, but each topic can be encapsulated in one sentence.

Next, have your people consider which cool content feeds they can post. Brainstorm with them on contests they can initiate and on questions they can pose that will engage your company's core public.

For example, let's imagine that you work at a company that manufactures handbags. You could feature a contest where blog readers take photographs of the contents *inside* their bags. The most interesting photo, or the one that tells the best story, wins. All winners receive handbags! Runners-up receive 10 percent discounts!

The content plan should include an exhaustive outline of topics, contests, and other interactive material from website launch through the first six months. It needs to feature a calendar of events and a reposting strategy. Sticking with the handbag example, let's suppose that Fashion Week is around the corner. Are there any events that your company can host that could be the toast of your blogging community?

Train your people to think and post visually. If one picture is worth a thousand words, one video is worth ten thousand.

How to Start a Blog in the Next Five Minutes

Sign up on www.Blogger.com or www.WordPress.com or any of the other free blogging services and write about any topic that strikes your fancy. (Of course, that would be a boo-boo the size of Mount Everest since you need to start with a content plan first!) Starting a blog is really simple. It's maintaining it that's the hard part. Sort of like diets and New Year's resolutions.

———————————————— THE STRAIGHT SCOOP ————————————————

There are many brushes to play with in your social media paint kit, and it pays to experiment before committing time and a lot of staff to the effort. Blogs, podcasts, social networks, and virtual worlds (i.e., Second Life) are some of the tools of engagement, and each one involves a steep learning curve.

---

129 **There has been excessive turnover at your company recently. Won't a blog expose that your organization is really just a front with a revolving door?**

A. Focus the blog on topics, not people.

Change is a harsh reality for all companies. Time does not stand still.

There are reassignments, layoffs, and firings. Good people leave. Better people are reassigned, switch departments, and get transferred to the foreign office.

There are mergers, acquisitions, moves, relocations, new bosses, and new employees. There are also some early and ardent blogging enthusiasts who just become too overwhelmed with their core jobs to continue blogging.

Focusing your company's blog on topics rather than on people is your best insurance against the ordinary changes in the life of a company that you may not want to disseminate to your blog's readership base.

Change happens. The blog lives on!

4.   *LinkedIn: Like the Headhunter, Agent, or Matchmaker You Never Had*

You don't even like the HR-Assistant-Who-Only-Wears-Black. But now, due to the grand social media experiment, you're "friends" with her on Facebook and MySpace, connected to her on LinkedIn, following her on Twitter, and listed in her Plaxo address book. You have her home, work, and "emergency" emails. Clearly, a glutton for *your own* punishment, she even provided you with a link to her personal blog about Viennese pastry. That's *nine* ways to connect with someone who you wouldn't even deign to invite to a New Year's Eve party! Then one day, just for laughs, you ask her for a "colleague recommendation" on LinkedIn and she writes pure poetry in praise of your many stellar attributes. Now, what can you say, you love her!

130   **What site can best help you build your platform as an expert?**

A.   **LinkedIn—right now.**

The technology can sometimes feel a bit creaky, but LinkedIn has a few superb applications that can help you build your "personal brand," whether you are doing it because your company has crowned you spokesperson or because it's a clever job-hunting ploy.

LinkedIn reveals your professional affiliations and helps you decode other people's. It also has a "Recommended By" feature that allows colleagues and business partners to sing your praises publicly (and that's one song future prospects will find hard to ignore). Members can also make introductions to others in the greater network and these online introductions can be very powerful! LinkedIn even has a feature that awards members points for giving helpful answers to other members. Every time you answer another member's question, it helps you position yourself as an authority in your field.

131 **Someone from a competitive organization found you through a mutual connection on LinkedIn and asks you to write a guest blog. Is that ethical?**

A. Check with your boss.

Everyone's a writer these days, and preventing you from expressing yourself freely practically interferes with your First Amendment rights. Your boss probably won't have a huge problem with your guest blog, as long as you don't use it as a soapbox to spill company secrets or badmouth anyone at the company. (Especially him.) Still, do yourself a favor and ask him before agreeing to it.

Today, everyone really is only one degree of separation removed from everyone else (except for Kevin Bacon . . . We are all still six degrees removed from Kevin!). And it is one small, intertwined, interconnected world.

Have fun. In the words of Google's great tag line, "Don't be evil." And don't write anything blasphemous or that would embarrass your grandmother.

132 **Should you friend your boss on Facebook, and connect with him on LinkedIn, and follow him on Twitter, and . . .**

A. Yes. (Sigh . . .)

It may not be today. It may not be tomorrow. It may not be a week from next Tuesday. But sooner or later, your boss will be on Facebook. It may take him longer to get there than it should. But chances are, he's not quite as clueless as you think.

And then one day, very shortly thereafter, you will open your own Facebook account, and there it will be. A request from Satan asking you to be his Facebook friend!

When that magical minute happens, the only politic thing to do is to accept his request. (If you don't, you will have to explain *why* you didn't, and that will be one incredibly awkward discourse. What will you tell him? That being his Facebook friend cramps your posting style? That you don't want to friend him in case you ever need to vent about him in a public forum?)

Once you allow the man whom you secretly despise to become your "friend" on Facebook, there really is no persuasive reason *not* to connect with him on all of the other social media. (Just try to remember that he *is* one of your "friends" and don't post about what a miserable day you're having at the office!)

5. The Big Three

There is a superficial way to deal with Facebook, LinkedIn, and Twitter and a deeper level of understanding that, to date, has eluded you. The "aha! moment" is out there, you're sure of it, and you're looking forward to it dawning on you any day now. On Facebook, it seems like there are so many posts that you just don't have time to focus on any of them. LinkedIn diligently lets you know who in your greater circle of contacts is now connected to whom, but in the most mundane manner conceivable. And Twitter tweets, ever constant, are not all that appealing unless you thrill to the constant chirp of the self-promoter. (Personally, you don't.) Moderating a social networking group on behalf of your company seems time-consuming beyond compare. How are you supposed to monitor posts, upload videos, ban inappropriate content, and still get the rest of your work off your computer desktop?

Facebook and Its Harvard Pedigree

Facebook was founded by Mark Zuckerberg with his fellow Harvard classmates Dustin Moskovitz, Chris Hughes, and Eduardo Saverin in February 2004. Within one month of going live, it had signed up half of its undergraduate population. Originally, Facebook was "just a Harvard thing." Then, with the help of his roommate Moskovitz, Zukerberg introduced Facebook to Stanford, Dartmouth, Columbia, Cornell, and Yale and then to other universities with contacts to Harvard. Initially, the site was restricted to university students. Today, Facebook still has dominance with four-year universities—as well as with everyone else on the planet.

---

133 **It seems like social networking gears very young. Should you simply assign this task to your most junior people, call it a day, and leave early?**

A. Social networks are older than you think.
Today there are well over 400 million people on Facebook. Here's a newsflash: They are not all twenty-somethings.

Journalists bemoan the fact that Facebook is no longer hip, that it's turned middle-aged. Social scientists declare that Facebook is so immense it challenges *homophily*—the tendency of individuals to associate and bond with others who are like them in terms of age, gender, class, and organizational roles.

Young staffers may be more adept at using the tools, but you should include some older staffers on the project as well. Think of Facebook as a pair of blue jeans. No matter how old you are, a pair of jeans can fit your lifestyle.

Watercooler Wisdom
As Malcolm Gladwell wrote in his book *The Tipping Point* with astute prescience: "Acquaintances, in short, represent a source of social power, and the more acquaintances you have, the more powerful you are."[17]

134 **What is the difference between friends, followers, and connections?**

A. Semantics, mainly.
As the song lyrics tell us, "People who need people are the luckiest people in the world." Or the biggest influencers, anyway.

Join Facebook, and the friend connection will need to be made by mutual consent. LinkedIn connections work in exactly the same manner.

With Twitter, a member can elect to follow another, unless he is blocked by that member.

Influence is judged by the number of one's connections. But, by necessity, the more connections one has, the less privacy.

The Psychology of Friending

Some people want to make a lot of Facebook friends just to become more influential within the beehive. *What's the buzz? Tell them what's a-happening.*

Others friend folks to reconnect with those whom they haven't seen in awhile, such as high school buddies.

Others are looking for love on Facebook, masochists mainly. It's the wrong medium for love, although it's helpful if you're tracking down one person, such as the paramour you dumped during your freshman year of college.

Still others view their Facebook network as a sprawling, and somewhat random, group of acquaintances—not so much a *Who's Who* of their friends as a *Yellow Pages* of everyone whom they ever met once. (Hey, we're all friends.)

Some super bloggers have *thousands* of Facebook friends. Other people confine their Facebook friends to people who are already part of their greater network, through an alumni association or club to which they belong.

Regardless of motive, "friendship"—however one defines it—is the glue that holds the vast sprawling social networks together.

Who Knew?

People care about other people. They don't much care about brands (unless somehow the brand can prove that it truly "gets" them—the way Volkswagen did in the 1960s, McDonald's did in the 1970s, and Facebook did in the 2000s). This is why it's crucial to blog as if there is a human being behind the corporate mask. If you don't, your efforts will backfire.

135 How much information is too much?

A. Once it's out there, it's out there.

One day your boss stops you in the hallway and says, joshing, "Hey, I didn't know you rode mechanical bulls. That picture of you falling on your butt was hysterical." You're confused. You feel like you just fell off the bull all over again and are sitting on the floor, dizzily rubbing your head. You deliberately put your boss on your list of Facebook friends who *couldn't* see your posts.

There's only one way to guarantee that the photo you *think* you're posting to a select group of friends doesn't leak out into the blogosphere, and that's not to post it in the first place.

You can place a check mark by all of Facebook's privacy settings. But one of your Facebook friends may fail to realize that the picture you posted was only intended to be seen by a small, intimate audience. Thinking nothing of it, she reposts your photo and—vavoom!—you feel outed and betrayed.

But in truth, it was all your fault.

Just the Stats

1. Many employers now check out postings on Facebook and MySpace before offering a candidate a position.
2. Some colleges have revoked admissions for students because of inappropriate postings on Facebook and MySpace. (Cruel and inhumane, but true.)
3. Your boss can learn of something that you post online even if you don't friend him. (A mutual friend could tell him about it or send it to him.)
4. Law enforcement officials can obtain court orders to view your online profile information.
5. President Obama has stated that we all post too much information. Take it under advisement.

Who Are These People, and Why Did I Ever Become Facebook Friends with Them?

You never want to ask yourself that. You want to know in advance who your Facebook friends are and *why* you friended them.

Proper etiquette is based on sound principles. Apply these principles to your online experience and it will be more enjoyable for you and less potentially humiliating. Start with a strategy. Decide whether you will:

1. friend every person who ever asks
2. friend only those whom you know and like
3. friend only people from certain organizations or affiliations to which you belong
4. friend only people from your former schools and businesses.

The great news is that all friendship requests stay in a pending folder for months so you will have plenty of time to change your mind about a particular request while you're figuring out your overall Facebook strategy.

Always remember that "it's your life," and you shouldn't feel compelled to squander your precious time on people whom you neither care about nor respect. Never be afraid to set your own rules for engagement and stick to them.

Of course, depending on your aspirations, pursuing a "friend all" strategy might have certain benefits. If you are a politician or have political aspirations within a certain club or organization, you can take advantage of the posting option and post messages to numerous constituents. President Barak Obama's Facebook strategy was widely credited with helping him attract millions of voters. (And Facebook cofounder Chris Hughes was kinged "The Kid Who Made Obama President" in an April 2009 *Fast Company* cover story.)

Conversely, if you are just starting out in the workforce, you may want to *avoid* friending your boss or coworkers (until they ask you, of course).

No matter which Facebook strategy you pursue, it's a bad idea to have ribald photos of yourself "out there" in the public domain. Never use foul language in any public posting on Facebook. (If the language used is severe enough, you could even be kicked off the site, and that would be a most painful form of ostracization!)

The great bard William Shakespeare once wrote, "To thine own self be true." Only you can determine where you draw the line between friend and acquaintance, and beyond that, what Facebook friendship means to you.

That's a Wrap

1. If you ignore a Facebook request, the person won't receive any sort of notification.
2. Guard against unscrupulous strangers by refusing to friend anyone who isn't already in your greater networking base.
3. Many corporate social media drives die at childbirth due to lack of coherent content planning in advance.
4. LinkedIn and Facebook can both aid in a job search—LinkedIn by helping you position yourself as an expert; Facebook by introducing you to groups of professionals in your field.
5. While Facebook, LinkedIn, and Twitter have all gone mainstream, many companies do not yet fully grasp their potential.

CHAPTER 10

The Lost Art of Good Phone Manners

By wired, Skype, and text standards, picking up a landline to call someone seems rather Alexander Graham Bell. One might have to wait several rings before contact. If the person called picks up, one may have to engage in a few moments of mindless small talk before getting to the point. While it's the most spontaneous of the old media, the phone requires a deft touch.

Clients and customers tend to be busy and appreciate callers who are aware of it. Still, most calls will go more smoothly if you take a brief time out to discuss something personal.

"Did you have a nice vacation?", "How was Christmas day in Ann Arbor with your parents?", and "Was the new Italian bistro as phenomenal as the reviews said?" are all ice-breakers.

One pattern to follow is to quickly introduce the purpose of the call, backtrack to a brief personal remark or question, and then plunge forward with the stated reason for the call. The segue to the personal is the pause that refreshes.

"I know we are covering scheduling today. Speaking of scheduling, did your flight to Rome go off without a hitch?" This allows your client to either say, "Yes, thanks for asking," or to relay a quick anecdote about how he was stranded in the airport for six hours. After the ice has been broken, you may officially conduct business—like civilians!

1.   *Will He Call? Will He Call? Leaving a Voicemail Message That Drives Action*

Staring at the phone, you long for it to ring. You have left him message after message to no avail. Now your heart pounds with a thousand possibilities. He dropped dead of a sudden heart attack on the 6:04. He's cheating on you—the bastard! He's found a prettier model—that business model you sent him *was* pretty lame. He fell into a black vortex with no phone or email access. That last one must be it. Waiting for your boss to return your call makes you want to tear each hair out of your head, one by one. Snap! You really wish your boss would take your urgent messages more seriously. He could at least have the decency to return your call before Friday afternoon and not drag out the suspense through the weekend.

136 **You leave messages for your boss but he doesn't return them. What can you do to make him?**

A. Ask for a specific action.
Make certain your boss knows that you want him to return your call. Give him clearly delineated instructions: "I need you to approve this four-page insert. Please return the call by tomorrow at 10 AM and let me know that you buy in. Thank you."

137 **You've left your boss a polite message asking for a response. That was over twenty-four hours ago. Now what?**

A. Step up the urgency.
Give your boss an explicit reason why you need his approval. Keep the irritation out of your voice. Sweeten your voice with a loving spoonful of honey as you say, "Apologies for the second message, but we need your approval by tomorrow at 10 AM or we will miss the first press deadline. Please call me ASAP and give me your final blessing. Thank you."

Why This Technique Works

Politely and steadfastly you are asking for your boss to weigh in and *act* like a boss. That is not too much to ask! He is there to approve ideas, offer feedback, and provide direction. You are persistent, but he is unlikely to mind as long as you keep your messages brief, direct, and cordial.

138 **Your boss didn't respond to your last urgent call. Now you are beginning to panic. What should you do?**

A. Leave him a final voicemail message that is a really a "negative option clause." Be sure to duplicate the message in email.

Your boss is acting childish and irresponsible. He abdicated responsibility on a time-sensitive project and left no instructions on how to handle his curious disappearance. But that's okay. You can work around this bizarre eccentricity.

Commit your phone message to an email message that duplicates it verbatim—in case you need to cover yourself later.

Allude to your last two messages:

"I'm leaving you a message on this urgent matter and committing it to email in case you haven't received my previous two voice messages. We need your approval ASAP or we will incur cost overages on this project that we will not be able to pass on to our client. If I don't hear back from you by 10 AM tomorrow, I'm afraid I will have to sign off on the project in your absence and we can debrief about why I did when you return. Hope everything is alright with you. Take care."

For Extra Credit
Close your message with your office number, including your extension, and cell phone number.

2. *You Can't Make Heads or Tails of His Message. Now What?*

You may as well flip a coin. If it's heads up, your boss meant to say X in his voicemail message. If it's tails, he meant to say Z. Do you want to call it? "Heads!" "Tails!"

"No . . . Let's do two out of three." Your boss speaks like Yoda if he were 20,000 leagues under the sea. Help! If you can't all collectively get inside your boss's head, he will take it out on all of our hides. But it's getting really crowded inside the boss's head, and the whole team is stressed out from the strain of trying to figure out what his bewildering voicemail messages mean. Yet to him, you must report! You ask your boss's secretary to let you know if the Jedi Master calls in and resolve to spend the weekend catching up on escapist, science fiction movies.

139 Your boss finally calls and leaves you the all-important voicemail. But his message is an alphabet soup of confusion. You can't make out a word. How should you proceed?

A. **Guess what he said and commit your supposition to voicemail and email.**

The only way to sort through confusion is with dead-calm clarity.

Refuse to feel guilty.

You are just doing your job (and you do it well, thank you very much).

"I got your message," you can say, "but it was abruptly cut off. I am intuiting that you approve of the work. If this is correct, then there is no need to call me back. If this is wrong, please call me back ASAP. I am also committing this message to email."

Then send him an email that references your voicemail message. If you can copy others on this important communiqué without appearing to get your boss into scalding coffee with his superiors, by all means, do so.

You need to respect his exalted position. But you also need to cover thy lowly butt.

140 Your boss leaves a rambling message. You can hear every word but *still* have no clue about what it means. How do you translate it?

A. Ask for an interpreter's help.

Find someone on staff who knows your boss considerably better than you do and play back the message to her.

Perhaps it will be his trusted assistant or one of your boss's former protégés. Have the person translate what your boss is saying in clear English so that you can understand it.

When you follow up with your boss on what she infers he *must* have meant, explain that you *both* listened to his message together and arrived at the same interpretation.

> ### Why This Technique Works

When you rely on one of his former protégés to help crack your boss's garbled code, you gain credibility. Your boss will realize that his message was confusing and will most likely trust that you tried your best to take it seriously.

141 Your boss leaves one message for you and a message for your colleague that directly conflicts with it. Which message is the right one?

A. Call an old-fashioned powwow.

At trying moments like this, there is a power in staying detached.

Call a meeting and arrive at a group consensus. Then leave your boss a message explaining that the group received both of his messages and came to the conclusion that what he really meant was the message he left at 11:06 AM, rather than the one he left at 11:04 AM.

Ask him to check back with you if he feels the group misunderstood.

Make sure your voice sounds super-friendly rather than obnoxious and miffed.

Sugarcoating Your Voice and Other Closely Guarded Secrets of the Professional Voiceover Club

Pour some sugar on it. On what? On your voice, of course! Do you have a difficult phone call to make? Sugar your voice sweet—in the name of amicable relations.

To achieve this sound, pitch your voice a half register higher than you would ordinarily.

Your voice should feel as if it's emerging from just inside your mouth rather than from either your nose or deep inside your chest.

Take a deep breath. Sip some water. Then throw your voice up into your mouth.

Another way to brighten your voice is by putting a "smile" in it. Think of something delightful such as an explosion of saffron and purple snow crocuses bursting from the ground heralding spring's arrival. See the picture in your mind's eye, smile, and pick up the phone.

If given an opportunity to replay your message, always listen to it once or twice before hanging up the phone. Verify that the sentiment is crystal clear, cordial, and above all, concise.

3. How to Puzzle Out Someone's True Communication M.O.

When you first met your client, he warned you that he was "a big emailer." You understood that to mean he would send frequent emails to *one* of your email accounts, not bombard all of your accounts including Facebook and LinkedIn. Your client was quite the email maniac! But after you lightly chided him about his persistence, his communication style suddenly morphed, becoming erratic and difficult to pin down. He calls, emails, texts, Skypes, and even sent you a word document in an electronic drop box once just to prove he was more technologically savvy than you. Does he have an electronic multiple personality disorder? Or is there a rhyme and reason to his communication style that you are simply failing to parse out?

142   You leave your client a voicemail message. He replies with an email. You email him back. He responds with a text message. You text him back. He sends you an IM. The two of you have had six communications yet *still* can't find the time to meet in person. What's going on?

A. Your relationship is strong, but your closure skills are wobbly.
Your client is telling you (without spelling it out) that he doesn't have time for a sit-down meeting. Try to use each electronic touch point to move your project forward in the absence of a face-to-face appointment.

Can you deconstruct the project into small, manageable chunks and conquer it bit by bit electronically?

Of course you can!

— THE STRAIGHT SCOOP —

Some people have a preferred communication style: It's their default "go to" style. Others vary their style according to their mood, perhaps gravitating to the phone when they're in a good mood and using email when they're feeling rushed and anxious. Since email allows recipients to access it when they are psychologically ready, always use it to reach those who are excessively moody.

---

143   You write four emails to your client asking for a response, which go unheeded. Out of frustration, you finally shoot an email to his boss. Then your client responds with wrath. Hell hath no fury like a client scorned! Quick, what's the solution?

A. Ask how your client would like the two of you to communicate.
No doubt about it, your client is passive-aggressive.

The first four times you reached out to him, he passively ignored you. Then he aggressively lashed out at you for going over his head.

However, whether or not you recognize it, your behavior was atrocious! If there are seven deadly sins, the one you committed was certainly the eighth. It showed no respect for your client, so his anger was actually justified.

Instead of feeling forlorn about his righteous display of temper, you should feel relieved that at least he's honest enough to share his feelings with you.

First, profusely apologize for your error. Then use the opportunity to map out a plan for reaching out to him that will work better for him next time.

To Take Foot out of Mouth, Pick up Phone and Press "Send."

We make mistakes. We are human, after all.

But if we have offended, there is only one way to correct the gaffe, and that's via the phone. A calm tone helps pacify irate clients but so does sincere regret on your part as well as a promise not to renew the behavior. There is no one-size-fits-all script for erasing an offense. But here is a generic version of one, anyway:

1. "I'm sorry I offended you." (Then listen to your client's reaction.)
2. "I did not mean it the way that it may have sounded."
3. "Here is what I meant to say." (Then explain.)
4. "I really hope you can see it in yourself to forgive me."
5. "And I promise I will never do it again."

---

144   Your client delivers messages to you indirectly via your underling. You're disturbed by this behavior and suspect your client is deliberately circumventing you. Do you air your frustration or keep it concealed?

A. Air it, but recognize that you have little power.

Before you discuss it with your client, meditate. Try to gain some emotional composure. Then, peer deep inside yourself, and ask, "Am I doing anything to prompt this behavior?"

Your client could be avoiding you because he doesn't like your personality. Conversely, his behavior might have nothing to do with you. He might simply find that your underling is considerably easier to manipulate! It's also possible that there is some verbal tic that you have which your client finds irksome. Maybe every time he calls you about one topic, you breezily say, "Oh that reminds me . . . " plunging you both into a discourse that lasts far longer than the time he allotted for the call.

Your job is to service your client and make it comfortable for him to communicate his needs to your company. So you will have to do some detective work on why your client would rather break protocol than communicate with you directly.

A conversation like this is best reserved for an in-person meeting. At some point when you are getting together in person anyway, you might try soliciting his feedback. Make sure that you're alone with him when you pose this question. "I was wondering if you could share with me your impression of how things are going with our company." If he claims that he's generally pleased, then gently probe him on specifics. Is he happy with the way that you have been servicing his business?

Don't use the conversation to point out the error of his ways! Instead, gingerly suggest that it's your job to field any questions or issues he may have. Convey that you hope he knows that he can call you at any time.

Why This Technique Works

In psychological parlance, this is referred to as an "embedded command." You are not ordering the client to call you, just nimbly reminding him of protocol.

THE STRAIGHT SCOOP

You can never coerce a client to obey decorum. Rules are often bent for those who pay the bills. Money may not buy happiness, but it sure buys a heaping helping of tolerance!

4. In a 24/7 World, 24 Hours Is a Lifetime

You receive fifty emails before lunch and two hundred by closing time. You are strung out, burned out, and beyond exhausted. Somewhere during your career, Time collapsed into a black hole and now you find yourself at the mercy of slave drivers who can reach you anytime, anywhere (and frequently do). Once, when you were in Boston for pleasure, your client's smartphone somehow managed to geolocate yours and he insisted on meeting you for a drink! With privacy fading faster than a meteor, is there any way to carve out some time out of Time, or are you forever at the mercy of others who don't believe in any time off?

145 **Your boss leaves messages on both your home phone and cell at 9 PM Friday night on a non-urgent matter. By when do you have to answer this intrusion?**

A. Saturday morning.

Go wild. Take the night off. Rebel, but get it out of your system—fast. Because by the very next morning, you'll need to be accessible. Now that we can all reach each other 24/7, it feels strangely off-putting during those few instances when we can't.

While you never want to encourage your boss to assert himself into your weekends and precious time off, the occasional phone interruption probably won't ruin your whole weekend.

Answering a random call that isn't strictly necessary helps build strong boss-employee relations in numerous ways.

146 **Hallelujah! You are finally traveling to Paris for a much-deserved vacation. How should you field calls in your absence?**

A. Put a vacation message on your voicemail.

Leave a cheery outgoing voicemail message. Don't be afraid to interject a little personality into it.

"I'm in Europe *en vacances*," you can say with a French accent that con-jures up visions of brie, baguettes, and chardonnay savored on the banks of the River Seine. "While I am away, please direct all inquiries to my assistant Ashley at (000) 123-4567, extension 215. *Au revoir*, and I look forward to catching up with you on my return on August 13th."

> ### Why This Technique Works

You have no intention of ruining your vacation to take phone calls. Your lighthearted message lets frequent callers know this is a playful way.

147 **You are leaving on an extended business trip abroad. Is there a benefit to saying that you won't be reachable by phone and your email access will be remote?**

A. Yes.

Claiming you will have only remote email access is one of those under-promises that work beautifully. Upon reading your message, no one will wait on tenterhooks for your reply. (No one knows what "tenterhooks" actu-ally are, so they are difficult to wait on in the best of circumstances.) But if and when you do answer your emails, the recipients of your "away message" will be most pleasantly surprised!

You may discover that you have *a lot more downtime* on your business trip than you suspected, so alerting people about your remote access also gives you the freedom to circle back and answer emails when jet lag deals you an incurable case of insomnia. (You can also write back at any hour of the morning. Everyone knows there is a substantial time difference and no one will hold it against you if your emails are sent at some ungodly hour in the morning.)

On your outgoing *voicemail* message, direct callers to one or two people at your firm who can help them while you're away. Mention your "remote access to email" status on your *automatic email reply* and direct everyone to the same two people to contact in your absence.

When Your Boss Calls You at Home Too Often

It's bad form to say, "Hey, you're calling me too much," even if it's true. It's more etiquette-savvy to either dissuade the calls by setting boundaries on each call's length via slight fibs designed not to hurt your boss's feelings. "Woops! I think I hear my uncle in the driveway," "My cousins are descending on me in precisely five minutes," and "I'm afraid I may burn the chicken if I stay on too long" are polite ways of conveying that the conversation must be kept short.

A somewhat more aggressive stance is to screen the call, and then "return it" via a different media, such as email.

—————————— THE STRAIGHT SCOOP ——————————

Always try to return phone calls with phone calls, texts with texts, and emails with emails.

---

5. *Be Spontaneous, but Write Down Your Important Voicemail Messages in Advance*

Your client calls you so often that it borders on stalking. You feel like his prey and deliberately try to avoid him. Recently, you screened your calls and noticed his number pop up four times. You wish he'd trust you more and stop abusing you with these constant check-ins! Yet you need to keep all channels of communication open for those times when you really have to reach *him*. Recently, you've started this crazy habit of writing down all of the voicemail messages you're planning to leave for anyone on paper so that you can practice them in advance. Will you ever be polished enough to pick up the phone and call someone directly without rehearsing what you are going to say a million times? Or is being super-cautious the sign of a consummate professional?

148 You wish to leave your client a voicemail message but don't have the time to talk to him if he picks up the phone. Is it okay to leave a message for someone if you know for a fact that he won't be there?

A. Yes, but you'll get more credit if you leave the message during office hours.

Tag! You're not It. Leaving voice messages for people at six in the morning or very late at night is the coward's way out.

Instead of actively listening to your message, your client will be sitting there meditating on why you deliberately tried to avoid him.

Avoidance behavior can also have strange repercussions when you call and accidentally reach the person by mistake! Sleuth out your client's hours. If you want to avoid talking to him, aim to leave your message just fifteen minutes before he walks in the door or fifteen minutes after he leaves at night.

Always endeavor to look like you tried to reach him in person, even if you didn't. Chances are there won't be a polygraph test so you won't get caught. But if you leave him messages at strange hours when no one works, it's almost like turning yourself in.

149 You reached your client by phone. But he sounded flustered and not altogether pleased to hear from you. How can you correct this gaffe going forward?

A. Set up the parameters of the call.

"Surprise!" everyone screams at your boss's office birthday party. Satan cracks a grin. Someone takes photos of the event on their cell phone. It's a moment.

But in general, everyone hates to be surprised in business. People like to sound smart. And that takes plenty of advance preparation.

With all clients, customers, and vendors, schedule calls in advance if possible. Set an agenda. And try to keep your calls on the short side (twenty minutes, tops).

If you can't set a call in advance, at least introduce yourself and the call's purpose when your client picks up the line.

"Hello, Wyatt. I hope I didn't catch you on your way out the door. But there has been a significant delay of the product launch. The supplier has told me that there was a small defect in one of their parts which will delay the launch for six weeks. We need to discuss how that impacts the marketing, shipments, and distribution. Do you have a few minutes to chat with me right now? I expect it will take approximately fifteen minutes."

150 Are there any topics that shouldn't be handled by phone?

A. Subjects that need to be discussed for more than forty-five minutes.

Don't turn all techie on your clients unless forced to because they've turned all techie on you.

Nothing is as effective as an in-person meeting for ironing out differences, hammering out next steps, brainstorming on tactics, and fostering good relations. Naturally, it's easier to meet in person when you live in the same geographical area as your client. If you don't, your next best option is a video conference call although some find the technology a bit intrusive.

That's a Wrap

1. If you want your boss to call you back, give him an ironclad reason and a deadline.
2. Crystal clarity in your own voicemail messages can help cut through other people's confusion. Script yourself first.
3. Going around your client is the eighth deadly sin.
4. Opportunity rings once. Don't wait for over twenty-four hours to respond to a call.
5. The phone is the medium of choice for short, transaction-oriented conversations.

CHAPTER 11

Alternative Media

There are so many new ways to communicate, ranging from texting to Twitter to location-based social gaming platforms. But it's fair to ask: Are they bringing us any closer, or are they pushing us farther away from each other? Are we all building circles of acquaintances, rather than friends, and if so, what are the ramifications? Or have the lines between business and personal, friend and passing acquaintance, completely vanished?

Beyond that, what are the new rules of engagement in this brave, new, media-centric world? Is texting a proper business tool? Or should it be used purely to communicate with friends and family?

Is Twitter a fad that we'll one day look back on as a blip on the social media scene? And what are we to make of the location-based social networks sprouting up everywhere? Are they just fun and sport for singletons looking to hook up with people in cities, or is there an underlying gaming model that we would be wise to apply to our own businesses?

Some of the alternative media require a large time commitment on our part. We are expected to build our networks, import our contacts from other networks, and in general, pretend that we know what we are doing, when really, we are all just muddling through. This chapter will spell out the rules for these new media and suggest some ideas for how they might integrate into an overall life networking strategy.

1. Two Thumbs Up, Two Thumbs Down. The Pros and Cons of Texting

When you first started working at the company, you were surprised that everyone texted each other so often. It added a spirit of gamesmanship and camaraderie to the most banal of work scenarios that made you feel like you were part of the team. Your officemates would try to outclass each other on the latest and greatest text lexicon, sometimes tripping each other with acronyms that meant two things and challenging each other to become fluent in this initial-centric language. But now you feel as if the texting craze has taken on a life of its own that is OTT (Over The Top). OLN (Online Netiquette) has you scurrying to RYFM (Read Your Friendly Manual) so often that you're afraid others may think you're an ACORN (A Completely Obsessive Really Nutty Person).

151   **Your colleague's spouse died. Is it proper to text your condolences?**

A. Not unless you want to be considered an insensitive dolt.

If texting were a dress code, it would be "shorts and Birkenstocks." It's casual because the technology is cumbersome, which in turn forces an informal language on the medium—one devoid of punctuation, proper spelling, and sentence structure.

Each number on your cell corresponds to three letters from the alphabet. Hitting the number two, for example, will bring up the letters "a," "b," or "c" as text. Due to the fact that it takes three strokes of the thumb just to arrive at the letter "c," texting has evolved its own shorthand.

"Dinr @ 8?" is perfectly acceptable textspeak among friends. "Sorry 2 hear about M" is not the proper way to express your condolences to anyone!

Send your officemate flowers and a handwritten condolence card instead.

152 **What's the protocol of texting while eating dinner with a client?**

A. Inexcusable, unless you can claim a family emergency.

Every client wants to feel as if he's the most important one on your roster. Help your client *maintain* this delusion by keeping your mobile device off during dinner!

On rare occasions, you may be able to plead a special case. For example, you might ask if you can keep your mobile on "because you're expecting your mother to text you from the hospital about the birth of your older sister's fourth child." But that's the only type of texting scenario that won't offend most clients.

Never claim that you're waiting for a family text when you are simply awaiting a text from a buddy with whom you maintain intimate relations. When you type "See u l8r," your client will sniff the scent of sex.

The Net Net on Net Lingo, or How to Say It Shorter

Here's a quick dictionary of some of today's texting terminology.

02 – Your (Or My) Two Cents Worth
121 – One To One
2G2BT – Too Good To Be True
511 – Too Much Information
AATK – Always At The Keyboard
ACORN – A Completely Obsessive Really Nutty Person
ADAD – Another Day Another Dollar
AFPOE – A Fresh Pair Of Eyes
AISI – As I See It
AYK – As You Know
B4N – Bye For Now
BCOZ – Because

BRB – Be Right Back
BTD – Bored To Death
BTDT – Been There Done That
C/S – Change Of Subject
CTO – Check This Out
CWOT – Complete Waste Of Time
DBEYR – Don't Believe Everything You Read
DNC – Does Not Compute
DQMOT – Don't Quote Me On This
E123 – Easy As One, Two, Three
EML – Email Me Later
FOMCL – Falling Off My Chair Laughing
FUD – Fear, Uncertainty, and Disinformation
G2G – Got To Go
GFI – Go For It
IDK – I Don't Know
JK – Just Kidding
JM2C – Just My 2 Cents
K – Okay
KWIM – Know What I Mean?
L8R – Later
NTW – Not To Worry
OLN – Online Netiquette
OTT – Over The Top
RMETTH – Rolling My Eyes To The Heavens
RNN – Reply Not Necessary
RYFM – Read Your Friendly Manual[18]

153 **Woops! You sent your boss a liquor-induced lust sex text intended for your new squeeze. How do you explain that?**

A. **Mea culpa.**

Call your boss and apologize. Tell him that you inadvertently sent him a text message intended for someone else who's right next to him on your mobile contact list.

P.S. Going forward, don't send texts while under the influence and never send sex texts, period.

Text's Curious Subtext: Some Rules to Live By

1. Follow the KISS rule, otherwise known as "Keep It Simple, Stupid." Is your text over 160 characters? That's an email.
2. Don't text and drive!
3. Some texts are instant and some aren't. If your text is time-sensitive, ask the recipient to write back to confirm receipt.
4. Spare your elders. Young eyes can read texts easily. But anyone over the age of forty will need to reach for his reading glasses to read your texts.
5. Communicating via text is supposed to be fun. Don't deliver bad news via text.

---

2.   *TigerText—For Cheaters Only?*

Good morning. Your mission, should you choose to accept it, involves pitching a top secret client, worth millions of dollars, who has been known to text information of the most confidential nature to all prospects. You may select any two team members to help you fulfill the assignment, but it is essential that they share no information about this project—code-named "White-Blue"—with each other or with anyone else on staff. This message will disappear in sixty seconds. It sounds like an episode of the old TV show *Mission Impossible*. But as the rapidly disappearing TigerText on your phone just revealed, this, in fact, is your life.

154 What is Tiger Text?

A. A phone application that enables text to disappear after a specified amount of time.

You can set message deletion from one minute to five days. Or you can set it for immediate deletion after the message is read. TigerText messages are stored on a TigerText server instead of on the recipient's phone.

When you see the tiger claws appear, it means that the message has been permanently deleted.

TigerText covers both text messages and phone call histories.

155 How does TigerText destroy the evidence?

A. It stores all messages on its own server and eliminates them at your command.

Most text messages leave your phone are routed through a server, and then arrive on the recipient's phone. The message you send lives on in your phone under "SENT" and also resides in the receiver's phone "INBOX" until he manually deletes it. The text message also continues to exist on the cell phone company's server for an unspecified amount of time.

TigerText looks exactly like a normal text message. But the content of your message is never sent to the recipient's phone. You control when the message is deleted. The message is displayed on both the sender's and the sendee's phones until it is zapped from the TigerText server. Once the message is deleted, the telltale TigerText paws appear.

Who Knew?

TigerText was not named after Tiger Woods.

---

156 Can you erase the record of the conversation?

A. Yes.

"Delete on read" allows the message to be deleted one minute after the recipient opens the message. A countdown clock begins at 59 seconds. When the timer reaches zero, the message will permanently vanish from the TigerText server and won't appear on the receiver's phone any longer.

There is also a "delete history" in settings that will permanently destroy the record of your conversation on your device once you exit the application. When you next log on, there will be no record of your ever having had a conversation on your mobile phone.[19]

THE STRAIGHT SCOOP

As of this writing, TigerText messages can only be sent to other iPhones or iPods (although Blackberry and Android are not far behind). Also, you can still snap a photograph of the texts with your iPhone before they are deleted—a small bug that has not escaped commentary in the blogosphere.

---

3. Foursquare and Seven Goofs Ago

As part of your company's new focus on social media, you have been asked to check out foursquare. (The name of the company starts with a lower case letter—how very e.e. cummings.) Your assignment is to figure out if there could be a business benefit to this game that rewards people for checking out restaurants and bars, and if so, how to ensure that your clients and customers will reap the perks. As you mentally groan in anguish at the prospect of spending yet another second of your off time on servicing your business, you notice that foursquare has now crowned you "Mayor" of your office for checking into this location every day. Oh, how cool! However, seconds after receiving the mayoral crown, your boss shuttles into your office, eyes afire. "You may be Mayor," your boss says with a dismissive grunt, "but I'll always be boss."

157 What is foursquare?

A. It's a cross between a geolocator, a friend finder, a walking Zagat's guide, and a game.

Foursquare is a mobile application that rewards you for checking out new places and for checking in each time you do. Here are the bold mobile brush strokes.

Each time you check in to foursquare, a GPS device displays a list of places near your location. If the *exact* bar or restaurant isn't cited, simply type it in and add it to the foursquare listings. You will earn points the very first time you check in to a new locale and for adding venues to the foursquare list. (You rack up fewer points for return visits.) Once you've checked in to a venue more often than anyone else in the foursquare network, you will be crowned "Mayor" of that hotspot. But if someone else then tops you, he will supplant you as Mayor. Many bars and cafés offer Mayor specials—free drinks or hors d'oeuvres for Mayors (who also tend to be really good customers). You can win other badges for being adventurous and testing out new places. You could be deemed a "Local" if you've visited the same place multiple times in one week or an "Adventurer" if you've checked out many different venues.

Each foursquare user has the ability to create tips for his friends and a To-Do list for himself, which almost functions like a "note to self." When you check in to a place, you'll receive a pop-up tip from one of your foursquare friends. There are also ways to check in "off the grid," enabling you to accumulate points without alerting all of your foursquare friends as to your whereabouts.[20]

What They're Called

Do you want to sound like you're on the cutting edge of geek chic? Of course you do! There's no reason for Geek to sound like Greek anymore.

Here's some vocabulary to master while you're tooling around town with foursquare, Loopt, and Gowalla. All three are called "location-based social gaming platforms." They are phone applications but not all are available yet for all phones. Many users link these social gaming platforms to their Facebook and Twitter accounts.

All Thumbs? Some Special Thumb Exercises to Make Yours More Proficient

Learning how to type with your thumbs can feel weird. Take away your index fingers. Subtract your two middle fingers, ring fingers, and pinkies. And you're left with your two fattest fingers poised over those miniscule keys.

But, never fear! Your thumbs can learn how to type without developing tendonitis! Thumbs are very clever, you know.

First, cup your mobile device as if it's a tiny book. Then, stretch your thumbs towards the keyboard. This will allow your thumbs access to all keys, and then you will simply need to practice your technique.

But, note well: Once you get the hang of thumb typing, seek ways to type less often! Make your emails as short as possible. Attach a line at the bottom that alerts recipients that your message was sent from your mobile so they'll understand if your response sounds a bit curt.

Whenever possible, master the shortcuts. Blackberry users have online forums where they share the short strokes on how to save thumb strokes. One thumb-sparing device is the autocorrect feature. iPhone actually corrects spelling mistakes as you type, which can save numerous keystrokes!

Your thumbs will be the first to let you know when they need a coffee break. Thumbs are awesome communicators. Listen to your thumbs. Massage them. And, sometimes, consider picking up the phone to reply instead.

158 Is it dangerous to let the foursquare network know your exact whereabouts?

A. It all depends on who you let into your circle.

Don't like the person? Don't friend him.

When someone signs up for foursquare, he can pull in all of his Facebook friends and Twitter followers. If you receive a foursquare invitation from someone who you know *only* through those networks (and have never met in person), don't add him to your foursquare network.

Foursquare and the other location-based networks let your friends in the network know where you are when you check in. That's information that shouldn't be readily available to total strangers!

———————————————— THE STRAIGHT SCOOP ————————————————

Be smart. Why tell everyone on your Facebook and Twitter accounts where you happen to be 24/7? Remember that if you're exploring a great street fair in Paris, it means that you aren't home. This information could be quite interesting to thieves, burglars, and possibly even to some so-called "friends" of yours on Facebook and Twitter.

---

159   Is there an etiquette to how many cross-posts are acceptable?

A. When your friends beg you to stop, you're over the limit.
Cross-posting annoys the paparazzi. What? You don't feel like you're famous enough to *have* paparazzi? All the more reason not to let people know of your every move! If you have friended your boss and coworkers on Facebook and you cross-post about every restaurant that you ever visit, your colleagues will reprimand you for telling them too much information, and rightly so.

Take care not to let your social networking universe know about any indiscretions on your part. Your real friends may think it's adorable that you're the Mayor of Kooky Karaoke and that the last six times you visited it were at two in the morning, but that's not proper information for your boss to have.

On Cheating on Foursquare

Some diehards "cheat" by checking in to every bar or restaurant they can find on the foursquare listings without setting foot inside the venues. Thus, these system hustlers wrack up badges and Mayoral accolades that they don't deserve. This hurts businesses that are trying to offer promotions to legitimate repeat customers.

If a cheater becomes Mayor and gets financially remunerated for scamming the system, it also robs others who legitimately visit the venues.
Politics and cheating. Who would ever imagine they'd go hand in hand?

4. *Skype Me Up, Scottie*

For a "mature" medium, video conferencing certainly brings out an immature streak among your cohorts. Your assistant Ashley has been running around all morning asking everyone to weigh in on her yellow silk scarf. In your humble estimation, it's too horsey for her horse-shaped face, but you are the *only person* whose opinion she didn't solicit. The interns have been tinkering with the equipment for hours; and yet, par for the course, the techie is nowhere to be found. You haven't seen an agenda for the meeting, a list of participants, or even an estimated length. God knows what the video conference goals are, but you don't. As for personal goals, yours is simply to survive this meeting, unscathed!

—————————————————————— THE STRAIGHT SCOOP ——————————————————————
As of this writing, Skype does not offer multi-person video conferencing.
But there are ways to integrate browser-based video conferencing services to achieve an ad hoc video conference among multiple parties.

160 It's the moment of truth. Everyone from all four offices has gathered around their respective conference room tables when suddenly the technology goes on the fritz. By the time the techies fix it, nerves are frayed and patience has run thin. What's the best way to prevent mishaps like this?

A. Test the equipment in advance.
When it comes to technology, you can count on one thing: If anything *can* go wrong, it will. Make sure that the day of an important video conference, a techie is in the room to help with setup and to fix any glitches. If he claims that he'll "be nearby," don't believe him. You don't want to have ten

workers twiddling their thumbs (or even exercising them on their mobile devices) while someone concludes that the techie must have dashed outside to Starbucks!

Give all participants a practice session to familiarize them with the equipment and setup. Sometimes people are unpleasantly surprised when they first see themselves on the screen. It can distort their faces and give the eerie resemblance of peeking into a funhouse mirror. A rehearsal allows them to overcome the shock. Conduct test sessions of the video link.

Design an agenda in advance, just as you would with any important meeting. Set clear objectives and keep expectations realistic.

161 You hate the way you look on the videoconference! Any tips for looking semi-decent?

A. Avoid the moiré effect.

Moiré is a type of textile with a rippled or watered appearance. In a video conference, moiré can rear its ugly watermark when there are too many images and patterns competing for the "eye" of the lens.

Dress simply but elegantly and in solid colors. Aim to make your outfit a "no fuss" zone. Stay away from patterns: plaids, windowpanes, houndstooths, checks, and stripes. Women may want to wear clothes that gear a bit brighter than normal—without going electric. For example, if you ordinarily wear navy, try robin's egg blue instead. If you gravitate to dark brown, try lightening your look with beige. Scarves, jewels, and fussy hardware sometimes distort on screen. Keep these and other gewgaws far away from your face.

Sit up straight and avoid gesticulating if possible.

Colors to Avoid on Screen

1. **Red**—bleeds into other colors and can "pop" the pink or red undertones in skin
2. **Bright Pink**—adds ruddiness if there are pink undertones in the skin

3. **Black**—absorbs all color from a person's face, lending it a "grim reaper" complexion
4. **Muddy Brown**—adds creases and other sure signs of fatigue
5. **White**—washes out skin and makes it fade against the background

---

Who Knew?

Conference room lighting can cast weird shadows that make faces look shinier, redder, or sometimes deathly pale. If there is a practice session, view it as an opportunity to inspect how you look on camera and make any tweaks accordingly.

Lights . . . Camera . . . Do I Look Fat?

Almost everyone who has ever sat in front of a camera has heard it at least once. "Don't be shocked when you see yourself on screen . . . it automatically adds ten pounds." But is it true?

Most people agree that video cameras *do* add poundage. But it's not due to the pixels per se. Usually, it's a result of horrific lighting.

Light projected straight onto the subject will help the camera flatten someone's image. In addition, most video conferences shoot people sitting down. You may not be used to seeing yourself filmed in bad light, at an unflattering angle, and just from the top.[21]

162 Are there any special etiquette considerations for video conference meetings?

A. Maintain a polite distance from the camera and mic.

After the initial shock of seeing yourself (as well as others on screen), the video conference may seem like an ordinary meeting. But it isn't.

It's a smart idea to set up giant cardboard nametag tents in front of all participants so that no one will have to struggle to remember anyone else's name. When you speak, make a special point of enunciating. Microphones can sometimes distort words, and everyone needs to be able to hear clearly.

That said, take care not to bogart the mic. Never interrupt other participants by stepping on their lines or speaking over them. Establish eye contact with the camera without leaning in too close to it. And don't forget to make eye contact with the other participants at your table!

Avoid loud noises. Rustling papers and tapping on the table may disturb other people's ability to hear. When your side isn't speaking, have someone set the audio to "mute."

5. What's the Buzz about Twitter?

When you first checked out Twitter, it seemed like it was the Jet Blue of social media. It had so few frills as to appear almost deceptively simple. However, you quickly learned that being forced to confine all posts to 140 characters or less stretched your editing muscle beyond capacity; plus, you were never sure if those following your Twitter account were competitors, customers, or professional spammers! Yet, somehow, the Twitter effort took on a life of its own. Your company *did* manage to attract a lot of followers. And one morning, Satan jetted into your office to ask if you would mind posting your photograph on the company's Twitter account. And just like that, you became the face of the company. Directly afterwards, three newbies pounced on you to inquire if they could tweet on behalf of the company. *Achoo*! Boy, this Twitter craze is catching!

163 "What's happening?" Who cares?

A. There's an audience for your product and Twitter can help you find it.

Twitter. In 140 characters or less, it lets you send a message that answers the burning question on everyone's lips: "What's happening?" It's a form of microblogging that, when combined with other social media tools, can help you tap new customers, network, and build deeper relationships with your partners, clients, and other constituents.

But there's a way a right way to talk to them and a wrong way. Now that anyone can launch a website, write posts, upload articles, and create videos and comment on them, the conversation is always two-way.

Customers want to feel as if they are talking to a person and not an entity!

Who Knew?

Social media offers content that is created by its audience. The audience participates by joining the conversation. And the conversation helps create communities and build loyalty.

---

164 **What is the most effective way to gain followers on Twitter?**

A. Start following them.

Begin by asking to follow people on Twitter. They will receive a message stating that you are. And then sometimes, they'll even return the favor by checking out your home page and deciding if they want to follow you.

Don't worry if you happen to be following more people than are following you. That's perfectly normal, especially when you are first starting to build your online presence.

Twitter's Personality Profile

If Facebook is a relatively young, Ivy-educated man or woman, Twitter is older, wealthier, male, and independent. Fewer than 25 percent of its users are stable career types. As sites like Twitter and Facebook become more popular, characterizations such as these are likely to go by the wayside and it will be harder to put a face on each of the social networking sites.

165 What personality should your company portray if it wishes to have a presence on Twitter?

A. Friendly, laid-back, and above all, human.

Your tweets shouldn't sound like they were crafted in a corporate communications office. They should not double as PR announcements because then followers will just tune you out. Your messages need to feel as if they are coming from a real, live human being and can cover topics such as company news. If you can add a personal comment about the news, that's even better. Sprinkle in special offers, but don't overdo it. You don't want to sound like the electronic version of a Sunday circular. Instead, use Twitter to "soft sell" your company. A pushy marketer is like a pushmi-pullyu, Dr. Seuss's legendary two-headed animal with both ends pulling in opposite directions. The more that the marketer tries to push his wares, the more his followers will pull away.

That's a Wrap

1. Don't text anyone bad news or use text to evade an unpleasant in-person discussion.
2. TigerText is not about cheating on a loved one. It's about maintaining the human right to privacy.
3. Don't ever let anyone but your *real* friends know where you are going to be.
4. If technology can go awry during a video conference, it will. Prepare for the unexpected by rehearsing in advance. Have a back-up plan.
5. To be effective on Twitter, companies need to show a human face.

CHAPTER 12

e-Etiquette Truisms We Hold to Be Self-Evident

We are all telecommuting, even those of us who sit in offices and have in-person meetings. The distance an email travels could be halfway around the globe or halfway towards the office kitchenette. Either way, the email will arrive in seconds. And, unlike a phone call that may not go smoothly, a bad email is irreversible.

As our email inboxes crowd with more and more communications, our tendency will be to want to "stop the noise" and race through our mail as quickly as possible. While this is a bold move, it's a big mistake. Rashness is fatal.

Train yourself to go against your instinct as it pertains to email. The more irate your reaction to a particular email, the less quickly you should answer it. And some flames will need to be doused in novel ways.

Always decode who the intended recipient is for an email. If an email is particularly venomous, never feel compelled to reply if you are not the real target for the message.

People will judge you by the emails you send. Yours need to remain placid and professional even under adversity. This chapter discloses ways to stay in control even when there is a four-alarm e-fire burning down the hallway.

1. Balancing the Need to Be Ethical with What Clients Want to Hear

Your boss has a feverish charisma that holds clients in awe. They believe he can work miracles for pittances. Even clients to whom he has fibbed in the past are all too willing to buy into his special brand of over-enthusiasm—in his presence. But the nanosecond that he is out of earshot, they force you to commit his ramblings to email, which, in all good conscience, you can't do because his promises are unattainable! You feel like a translator—an underpaid one. Your job is to rework your boss's pipe dreams into solid action plans with real numbers and timelines. You are the new, modern version of a miracle worker and yet *he* is the one who's treated like a saint.

166 **Your boss will say anything to close a deal. He has the ethics of a con man and makes outlandish promises that can't be kept. Meanwhile, you are the person who has to commit it all to email. How do you backpedal?**

A. As gracefully as possible.

Your boss's promises are worth the paper they're written on. But email is a legal document. Never overpromise in email or you *will* be held accountable.

Consult with others about realistic fees for your company's services. Map out an achievable timeline for delivering work. Try to soften the news that the product may be costlier or take more time to deliver than your boss originally promised with a light joke. Perhaps you can position your boss as the rosy-eyed optimist and you as the hard-nosed realist, but make it clear to your clients that your word is sacrosanct and that you intend to live up to it.

167 **Someone pointed a gun to your head, and so, regrettably, you agreed to a deadline that's as tight as a vice. How can you let your client know that your company can't follow through?**

A. Tell your client early, and give him a realistic date this time.

Nothing infuriates clients and customers more than knowing a deadline won't be met as it's hurtling towards them. That leaves them with few options.

Leak the news as soon as you realize it, so that, together, you and your client can arrive at Plan B. If it's crucial to meet a particular deadline, your company may have to farm out some of the work to outside vendors or hire freelancers to help brave the time crunch.

Explain the problem to the client as succinctly as possible via telephone. Then commit the problem to a politely-worded email and propose solutions. If missing the deadline isn't as grave an issue as going back on your word seems to be, you might make the situation more palatable to your client by throwing in a small "make good." For example, you could offer him a discount rate (either on this project or future ones), waive a service charge, or charge him less than your normal commission. Make sure that any new deadline you promise is realistic and commit it to email.

168 To you, they resemble "hockey stick projections"—venture capital-speak for projected revenue growth that remains flat for a period of time and then rises sharply. How do you politely ask for more realistic numbers?

A. Set your mumbo jumbo detector to "high."

Beep! Beep! Beep! When your mumbo jumbo detector starts ringing off the hook, it's a sure sign that you need to gather documentation. Ask for a profit and loss statement, a balance sheet, and a cash flow statement. It's completely within your rights to figure out (if and) when the company plans to reach breakeven. Request a copy of the presentation deck and review the math yourself to make certain it all adds up. Challenge yourself to think conservatively. Here is the one time when you may want to take off the rose-colored glasses and view the projections through more cynical lenses. Ask yourself what would happen if you cut the revenue projections in half and doubled the projected expenses. Doesn't look so pretty, does it?

2. An Email Doubles as a Legal Document

You've always considered the profusion of email to be a sign of corporate laziness. It's so much easier to dash off a quick email than to rouse yourself out of the ergonomically-designed chair housed near your computer and mosey three feet down the hallway. So you're a bit flummoxed one day when your boss, who practically personifies sloth, turns all lawyerly on you. "Don't put anything in your emails that you wouldn't want your grand-mother to read," he says, his cowlick standing at attention. "If you receive anything discussing money from our client, show it to me immediately," he commands. "Our company servers do not delete emails," he continues. "So if you have anything sensitive to say, best to relay it in person." "By golly!" you think, staring at the intelligent creature temporarily inhabiting your boss's 5' 11" frame. "What have you done with my boss?"

169 You receive a scathing email from a client complaining about overages. Should you pick up the phone to resolve it or draft an email?

A. Both, but write a draft of the email first and follow your boss's lead.

Your client is posturing through email. He may be using it as a negotiating ploy to have your company cut his rate or offer him a "make good."

Don't panic. Draft a courteous, but carefully-worded communiqué defending your company's position and save it in your *drafts* folder. Then cover yourself by showing the email to your direct supervisor and possibly to his boss before you ever hit "Send." Follow their instructions: Chances are excellent that they have been through this rigmarole once or twice before with other clients. You may need to show your letter to your in-house counsel as well.

When you finally send the email to your client, copy every person to whom you've shown the communication unless counseled otherwise. In the body of the note, suggest times when you'll be available to discuss your client's concerns over the phone. If necessary, invite some of the "Big Guns" to sit in on the call. Stand firm, but also be cordial. A strong relationship conquers most.

170 **Your boss asked you to talk to one of your underperforming underlings about his dismal record. You did—and what an excruciatingly unpleasant experience it was! Now your boss claims that you need to commit the exact same sentiments that you said in person to a strongly worded email. Must you obey?**

A. Absolutely. Think of it as covering corporate butt.

Your boss wishes to establish a "warning date" in the event that the employee needs to be sacrificed or put on probation. It's smart. Your boss is also proactively trying to avoid a "He Said–She Said" situation, which can happen when serious issues are handled solely via conversation.

To prevent the employee from feeling completely betrayed, you might warn him about the email before sending it. "Hey, Buddy, Satan asked me to write up our talk yesterday in an email and copy the folks in HR. Please don't shoot the messenger," should do it.

171 **A colleague shoots you a caustic email claiming that you stole credit for one of her ideas. Should you dignify the preposterous accusation with a response?**

A. Yes, indeed!

Never a credit-snatcher be.

If the idea was hers, write an email publicly, if belatedly, thanking her. Was the idea originally hers but then shaped and molded by others? Use your email to bestow credit where it's due.

"Thank you, Shelley, for first suggesting that we reward seniors. As a marketing gambit, your input was very solid. I would also like to thank Danny for all of the energy he devoted to coming up with a title. And even though 'Early Bird Special' migrated to 'Senior Sunday' and later to 'Yellowbird' (thanks to Petra), everyone on the team deserves a lot of credit for their hard work and diligence. I consider myself truly privileged to be working with such a plucky and dedicated team. Thanks again, Shelley, Danny, and Petra!"

Be sure to copy your boss on this email. Remember that publicly crediting team members can only make you look better due to Trickle Up Theory™. (But next time, stave off criticism by giving credit *before* a teammate whines for it.)

Who Knew?

According to the Rand Corporation, one aspect of email that separates it from other forms of communication is its ability to stir emotion in the recipient.[22] Another item that can fuel someone's anger is the lack of a reply. If you are the intended recipient, you generally *do* need to respond. But you don't necessarily need to do so via email.

Top Five Email Mistakes Smart People Make

Emails are the most efficient form of communication to date. But while they are fast, they often lack context—especially if the author is careless. Following, are the top five e-boo-boos that even highly intelligent business people make.

1. **They don't change the subject line.** Why bother, you ask? After all, you and your client both know the subject intimately. The problem with this approach is that months from now when you are trying to find the *one* email where the client agreed to the price hike, you won't be able to. Every new email deserves a new subject line—particularly emails to clients, customers, and vendors.

2. **They hit "Reply All" when the only person who needs a reply is the sender.** This is a display of egregiously bad manners. Why squander ten people's valuable time when you don't have to?

3. **They call people out in email.** Let's suppose that your boss's secretary sends a meeting agenda but neglects to mention what time the meeting will start. Inevitably, some wise acre on the cc list will write in to say that *she* didn't receive the time for the meeting. She hits "Reply all." Then another person on the thread will comment that *she* also didn't receive the meeting time. Suddenly everyone on the chain is privy to fifteen emails about this trivial oversight. It's so much more considerate to both the sender and the entire copy list to email only the sender about the oversight and let her take care of it. Plus she won't think you grew up in *Jerkdom*, the capital of *Asserica*.

4. **They don't set up their emails to carry forward the previous communication.** Thus, all responses are automatically read out of context. This is really goofy, not to mention darned inconvenient. Don't do it.

5. **They abuse the Blind Copy function.** Don't be like the proverbial blind leading the blind or watch yourself get blindsided by the same heinous tactics. There is almost never a good reason to use the blind copy feature.

3. This Flaming Email Was Made for Dousing

The e-atmosphere around the office is lethal. Emotions bristle near the surface ready to combust. There is also serious language dysfunction. Between the spelling mistakes, lack of punctuation, and rampant sarcasm, you find yourself having to re-read even mundane emails two or three times to figure out the sender's *intended* meaning. Yet the barrage of email never stops long enough for you to do so. The e-volleys are relentless. The closer that two people sit, the more emails they seem to send each other. (You've been considering replacing two particularly pernickety cube mates with their much nicer avatars!) Every time you try to talk to anyone in the HR department about training people on correct email usage, you're greeted with a derisive snicker that's the equivalent of a sarcastic email. And the beat marches on.

172   **You receive a torrid email from someone four levels your senior about your team's pitiful performance in a pitch review. You feel your skin blotching up as if it's a tomato and hives bubbling up on your chest. Well, at least you know you're alive! In a matter of seconds, you compose the kind of scathing email that will make you a hero on your floor. Why not send it?**

A. Because you can never take it back.

No doubt about it, email evokes strong emotions.

Unlike a phone call, email sits around forever, and, mishandled, a nasty one can be like a ticking time bomb. First, the insult comes hurtling across the transom with ten important executives copied on it. "Sorry," you think, "but this is war."

Naturally, your tendency will be to defend yourself and up the ante with a few pointed barbs of your own. Add a sarcastic comment about how the author of the email had a chance to air his opinions long before the failed pitch and didn't, but you are certainly *delighted* to hear them now, and you might be today's hero of the 14th floor but at the expense of your long-term job security.

Your impulsive email response may languish in mailboxes or be printed, circulated, and discussed. It may acquire a level of importance that you never foresaw. Instead, write the email response that you deem appropriate but save it in draft form. Let it marinate for twenty-four hours or as long as it takes for you to calm down. Then review your message. Are there any astute points that you made? Excellent! Now rewrite the email to say *exactly* the same thing in dispassionate language. If you can't keep your tone professional, it may be more productive to take a walk down the hall and air your feelings in person.

Why the Smartest Email Is the One You Never Send

You are seething. Red-faced with anger at an employee's nasty email, you are one step away from either demanding his resignation or turning in your own. You believe that you are too young to have your first heart attack; but the shake, rattle, and roll of your hands suggests otherwise.

It's at moments like these that you need to bow out gracefully. Leave the office and walk around the block if necessary. Do not allow yourself to even write a draft of the response that will tear the underling a new space in his posterior. You are too provoked to think coherently! And rage can act like a depressant on par with alcohol.

Think about how road rage works: One moment the driver is sane and singing aloud to "Because the night belongs to lovers" on the radio. The next, some car cuts him off nearly knocking out his headlights. Quite suddenly, he wants nothing more than to pummel the other driver into oblivion!

If you are too incensed at a coworker to see straight, then you are too irate to write back to him.

173 **An underling accuses you of slipshod management in a public email designed to humiliate you. What are your next steps?**

A. Do not send an email!

Take the opportunity to set up a time to sit down and chat with the venting employee. Tell him that the step you have just taken—sitting down with him—is the *only* acceptable way to air any future grievances he may have with you. Then hear him out.

If he makes some shrewd points, humbly apologize for his perceived mistreatment. But reemphasize that he should take great pains not to publicly flog you. Along with working out his grievance of the moment, you need to suggest ways that he can air any issues he may have with you going forward *without* involving others.

After declaring a truce, it's a good idea to circle around to your boss and disclose the contents of your conversation. (Even if your direct report didn't copy the boss, it's likely that news of the email reached the boss's ears.) Briefly explain the problem and the solution that you set up with the employee to address his issues. Summarize and be businesslike.

After these two crucial steps have been addressed, send an email to the whole team announcing that you and the distressed employee have cleared the air.

174 Someone on the team flames another teammate, copying you as their boss. What actions, if any, should you take?

A. Use this as an opportunity to demonstrate your leadership.

Sit down with the flame-thrower and tell him that pyrotechnics are not appreciated at the office. Encourage him to air his issues directly with the person that he flamed. Do your utmost to stay as far away from the problem as you can muster. You want to encourage your people to thrash through their own issues without sending nasty emails that demoralize the whole team.

Resist the urge to take sides in the dispute. You are certain to have an opinion, but keep it to yourself.

Avoid Being an HR Target: Keep Offensive Language out of Your Emails

Did your boss use a cuss word? It's boorish behavior, but he's the boss.

Did your underling curse in email? Write it off. He was probably raised by wolves and doesn't know any better.

Did your coworker and exact equal use a four-letter word in her email and get away with it? She was probably just having a brutal day.

Do not use curse words or foul language in your emails. Everyone else may do it with abandon. But consider it an axiom of Murphy's Law: If you do it, you will get spanked.

4.   *The Careful Pruning of Your Cc List*

There is an executive who you met once in the office elevator for five seconds. For some unknown reason, you're copied on all of his emails. Meanwhile, there are six new employees and one of them added you to his email loop even though he shouldn't have. Then again, one of your direct reports never copies you on any of his communications even though you are most curious as to how his projects are progressing! But you never ask him about any of them because, in truth, you're deluged. If you could ever wrest back the time you spend reading the countless emails that you really don't need to see, you are certain you'd be a most productive employee!

175   **There are twenty people on the team. How many of them need to be copied on an email?**

A.   Only those who touch the project.

Each person that you add to a cc list multiplies the number of responses you might receive exponentially. So pare down the copy list to the *fewest* number you need to handle the project. The only exception to this is if you happen to report to a *Big-Sister-Is-Watching-You*-type boss who is anxious to know what's happening under her 24/7. In that case, add her to the cc list to keep her up to speed on what you're doing. And hope that she will quickly become deluged by the number of emails and beg you to cease and desist!

176   **You have trouble exerting your authority in email. After multiple email requests that dance around the issue, you can't manage to corral all of the key players together in one room. Some people who report to you don't bother showing up to internal meetings. Suggestions?**

A.   Have them RSVP to your boss's assistant.

Discuss it with your boss first, of course. But there are strong arguments in favor of using his assistant as meeting watchdog cum laude.

First, including her name on the cc chain is a polite, non-threatening way of informing rebellious team members that status meetings are mandatory.

It makes the cavalier, inconsiderate people on the team recognize that the boss supports the meetings, even if he never bothers to show up to them.

For Extra Credit

Assign someone to take notes in the meeting. If the absences persist, have the designated note-taker mark those who were present and those who were absent on the conference report. Be sure to copy your boss on the document. That ought to improve attendance.

—————————————— THE STRAIGHT SCOOP ——————————————

When staffers miss meetings, morale takes a nosedive. Those in the room wonder why they are wasting their time and secretly envy those who somehow finagled out of being there. For those with a tendency to skip meetings, you need to create a motivation to come. One incentive is the fear factor if the boss will learn of their delinquency. Another ploy is to hold more productive meetings that will jazz up recalcitrant staffers.

---

177 Should cc lists be organized by seniority or alphabetically, and if alphabetically, by last name or first?

A. It depends on how hierarchical your organization is and what you're trying to accomplish with the email.

Whatever system you employ, realize that everyone on the team will always scan the cc list frantically in an attempt to read messages into the order in which people are listed.

If the email is an "invitation" (you use the term loosely) to attend a status meeting, there is no reason to use a hierarchical ranking. An alphabetical listing is in keeping with the "all hands" cattle call. But if the email is detailing a problem—either internal or external—it often makes sense to write the note to the actual people doing the work and copy their supervisors.

For example, if Danny and Petra are equals and they are both directly responsible for the project, you might list them alphabetically on the "To" line and then copy their supervisors listed by hierarchical rank, top to bottom.

When employing the alphabetical system to organize cc lists, choose whether you will alphabetize by first or last name, and then stick with that system. If your corporate culture is formal, last name alphabetization makes sense. But in a less structured environment, people often alphabetize by first names.

5. *You, Only Better: How to Give Your Email a Personality Lobotomy*

Over a holiday, you took a quiz on an online business website and discovered that your e-personality was only a C+. That hurt your feelings as you never got a C on anything in your life before, not even a Semiotics class at your alma mater. As a result, your strong "A personality" tendencies kicked in and you challenged yourself to improve your e-personality to at least an A-. While you have hundreds of emails piling up that need to be answered, at least you've stopped automatically responding to every last message. You would love to take the online test again, but sadly, suspect it's time to get back to work. Meanwhile you'll take it on faith that your e-personality GPA has at least improved to a B+.

178 When is it okay to send an Internet joke to colleagues?

A. **Only if you have never done it before.**
It's a paradox. If you never send Internet jokes around and suddenly succumb because you read one that is absolutely hilarious, everyone on your cc list will forgive you.

You don't have a record. You're not a spammer.

But each time you blast an Internet joke to sixty-five of your closest cohorts, it adds a little tarnish to your reputation. Bosses will assume that you're underemployed. Colleagues will correctly conclude that you're bored. The Watercooler Wag will intuit that you're available for a quick dish—at someone else's expense.

Forwarding Internet jokes erodes your professionalism bit by bit, as surely as citrus juice erodes tooth enamel.

Death to Extraneous Emails!

People should feel less prickly about an email chain ending and be more sensitive about wasting people's time.

Instead of writing, "I'll get back to you on that when I know the answer," just wait until you *do* know the answer and correspond at that time.

Never send anyone the equivalent of an email chain letter. Break the chain, and hit "delete."

---

179   **Is it true that the most important person in an email exchange should write a note slightly shorter than the one he received?**

A. It's not about the length of the email, it's about the courtesy factor. When it comes to email, "curt" is a four-letter word.

Tone has a short shelf life in this electronic media: it fades fast! Compensate by adding some courtesy filler words around your message whenever you write to someone who is important to you, be it a boss, esteemed colleague, or friend.

Use phrases such as, "I'm looking forward to seeing you," "I can't wait to get together with you in person," "please," "kindly," and especially, "thank you." Forgo excessively casual words such as, "Hey," or, "Hey there." Substitute, "Hi," or even an old-worldly "Good morning."

For closing an email, "Best," is an all-purpose polite sign off. Slightly more cordial is the ever-popular, "All the best." Words such as, "Cordially," and, "Sincerely," work nicely in more formal email communications.

Email's Noblest Purpose

Email is particularly well-suited for short, transaction-oriented communiqués that used to be handled via telephone (but also used to involve several laborious rounds of telephone tag). If your emails tend to be one-liners, always double check them for tone. Strive for friendly, upbeat, and informative.

"Are you free to meet me at 3 PM on Monday to debrief on the international initiative?"

"Can't wait! Your place or mine?"

"I think our office would be ideal if that works for you. We have teleconferencing, so if necessary, we can loop in our affiliates."

"Sounds great. Thanks so much for taking the lead on this."

"I'll blast an email and let the troops know. Happy weekend."

In the words of an old song, "Let the sunshine in."

A Couple of Phrases to Avoid in Email

1. "That's the dumbest idea I've ever heard."
2. "What bozo (yahoo, idiot, moron, substitute appropriate insult) thought of this?"
3. "Maybe it's the lawyer in me speaking, but . . ."
4. "Thank you for that incredibly astute insight."
5. All acronyms. (They're fine for texting.)

180 Does the most important person generally end the email chain first?

A. That's a myth.

In the earliest days of email, the most important person in an email exchange between two people may have made it a special point to nip the e-chain first, but that is no longer the case. Today, once the email topic has been discussed and dissected, with next steps detailed, there is usually no reason to write any more. So either party is free to drop the communication.

If you end the email chain first and you happen to be subordinate to the other correspondent, just be especially courteous.

That's a Wrap

1. Email is an iron-clad commitment so keep any overpromises out of it.
2. Email is often an essential ingredient for solving a monetary dispute with a client, customer, or vendor.
3. Email is dangerous when it's used to fan the flames of a personality clash.
4. To avoid e-bloat, keep cc lists trimmed to the minimum. Only the key players on a project need to receive every last email associated with it.
5. All emails must stay courteous. Don't write them unless they can be cordial.

CHAPTER 13

e-Gaffes, Egads!

So many new ways to communicate with each other, so little time! But each new communication vehicle carries with it a slew of novel ways to offend, insult, and hurt each other's feelings. And sometimes it may seem as if the ever-present misfirings are reason enough to return to snail mail and courier pigeon!

Is a party invitation sent via Evite somehow less deserving of an RSVP than one sent by snail mail? Should the "blind carbon copy" line on email ever be brandished as a weapon of stealth? How different should one's e-personality be from one's real, bona fide personality? And is there a reason to create a completely different persona in the form of an avatar? Is an e-firing so much worse than the in-person variety—especially when staffers have been warned in advance of an impending layoff?

These are just a few of the potential pitfalls caused by the new media. Another major hurdle is how to handle the disappearance of privacy. Is it acceptable to have companies peek into your private emails if you're writing them after hours on the company server? Does your company have the right to insist that your avatar dress a certain way, and what if your avatar wants to let loose after hours?

In these pages, find the brand-new rules to negotiate the ever-changing media landscape.

1. Evites

Everyone loves an office party, or so you thought, before you sent a bowling Evite to the team at your boss's command. That was three days, four hours, and six minutes ago. But while you included the spiffiest picture imaginable of a great big bowling ball, and even a shapely bowling pin, no one has bothered to RSVP. The party that was supposed to boost morale looks like it may be one big morale bowling bust. Every time your boss trolls by, a scowl etched into his gruff, wizened face, he glances in your direction as if to say, "Heard anything yet?" You have been trying to ignore him, but it's getting progressively more difficult. He snorts rather loudly.

181 **How do people feel about Evites?**

A. There is an e-generation gap.

The great divide isn't so much about the Evites. The philosophical schism is about whether there is such a thing as a free lunch. Most people over fifty years old have learned that there isn't. Thus, anything that works beautifully and happens to be free is automatically suspect. Evites are one of those items. They are often startlingly attractive to use and eminently practical.

People under the age of fifty grew up with a different worldview. Facebook, LinkedIn, and Hotmail are free. Everything is free, lunch included.

So it all depends on whom you're inviting. Is your party targeting a younger crowd? Send an Evite. If your audience gears older, better to send an old-fashioned party invitation via snail mail.

182 **You were invited to a colleague's coed shower via Evite and mention it to someone at the office. It turns out that he wasn't invited and feels upset. Is there any way to repair the damage?**

A. Tell the hostess what happened, and hopefully she'll extend him an Evite, too.

The e-delivery vehicle may seem casual, but don't relax your guard. No one appreciates hearing that he was overlooked for an invitation.

Evites reveal every invitee by publicly displaying the names of those who replied "Yes," "Maybe," and "No." It even shows a list of "Not Yet Replied." To prevent foot-in-the-mouth disease, check all four lists before discussing events like this with anyone.

183 **How old should one's kids be before they are too old to include on a holiday greeting card?**

A. Fifteen, or once they start looking like adults.
You can thank Facebook and cell phone cameras for the profusion of photo postings. And there's no age limit to any photos that you choose to post online.

But the new photo-centricity has spilled over into holiday greeting cards delivered via snail mail with strangely off-putting results!

You tear open a card and immediately wonder who the adorable couple is in the photo. "I have *no idea* who these people are," you think. "This was a mistake." You snatch up the envelope just to be absolutely certain that your assumption was correct and then peer for a moment at the return address. Something about it looks familiar. Wait a second . . . you *do* know these people. This was no mistake! Perplexed, you stare at the photo on the holiday card again. At last, you have an epiphany. *This man and woman standing close together with their arms wrapped around each other are not some young couple in love. These are your friends' children!*

Even in today's blended families (where the kids share one parent but not the other), matriarchs and patriarchs should resist the urge to send friends, family, and colleagues photographs of kids once they look like adults. At the point that they do, it's time to invest in holiday greeting cards from a Hallmark store.

2. e-war

Your company used to be more civilized until they fired all of the people over thirty and hired some brash young things to replace them. Every day, the Millennials arrive en masse armed with their Blackberries and smartphones, which they use to text each other ferociously when projects are going well. Meanwhile email, which used to be the primary method of communication, has been promoted to the number one stealth weapon whenever two staffers disagree with each other about tactics. And lately, the intrapersonal volleys have been particularly vitriolic. You try hard to be well liked by your massively difficult compadres. And how do they repay you? By sending you *scores* of email marked "bcc" or "blind carbon copy" over their inane turf battles. You believe that the whole team is gearing up for a bloody e-war and you are unsure which side to take. It would be nice if everyone would continue to regard you as decidedly neutral, a.k.a. the "Switzerland" of the 14th floor.

184 One of your coworkers constantly interrupts you during staff meetings. You want her to stop this outlandish behavior and feel strongly that she should be reprimanded. What's the protocol of using the bcc function on your email and blind copying her supervisors?

A. Dangerous and obnoxious.

Write a seemingly constructive email while blind copying someone's bosses and you are engaging in e-war. You may be able to get away with it once. You may be able to get away with it twice. But eventually, you will develop a reputation as one who plays "dirty email." At that point, you should anticipate swift and massive retaliation!

If you have a problem with someone, raise it with her directly. Take the time out of your busy schedule to sit down with her. Explain why it's bothersome to have her step on all of your best lines. Add some humor to the situation by asking her if she's "an only child" or by saying how much you hated being one (if true). Then ask her to please stop stepping in to complete your sentences!

> **You Heard It Here First**
> An e-personality can be a considerable improvement upon your own.
> After all, in email no one ever has to see you sulk. Did your boss send
> you a scathing email? Painstakingly draft a pleasant, upbeat reply.
> You might try thanking him for his critique. Then suggest some steps
> that you will take to answer his concerns. If you retain your dignity in
> email, it's more difficult for those around you to lose theirs.

185 **An underling emails you, copying your boss on all of her communications. How can you persuade her to stop including him on the most mundane items?**

A. Don't hit "Reply All."

The cc function is overused and abused. If you are certain that your boss
shouldn't be on the chain, simply write your rejoinder email and hit "reply."
That should convey the message clearly. If the behavior doesn't stop, sometime you might ask your boss how he feels about receiving emails from
your direct report. Should your boss concur with your assessment that it's
a total waste of his time, you might share that with her at some point down
the line—but in person and in a casual, off-handed way that won't make
her squirm.

186 **Your boss asks you to fire an employee for inappropriate web surfing. This strikes you as an invasion of privacy. Who's right?**

A. Your company is.

It may be uncouth. It may be untenable. It may be tacky in the extreme. But
it is not illegal. The law is a snoop enabler.

A survey by the American Management Association found that three-
quarters of employers monitor their employees' website visits. Some lob-
bying groups are fighting the trend. But in the interim, several workplace
privacy cases have been decided in favor of the employer.

An email lasts forever. Email systems retain messages in memory long after they have been deleted. Over half of employers review electronic mail messages.[23]

If you have a computer terminal at your desk, it could be your boss's window into your work habits. Employers can use computer software to peek at what is on your screen or stored on your computer terminal. They can monitor your Internet usage including both email and web surfing activities.

What Privacy?

1. **Your work habits are an open book.** Are you in a word-processing or data-entry job? Your company's system may allow your employer to observe how many keystrokes per hour you perform.

2. **You can't screen your screen.** Since your employer owns the computer network, he can use it to monitor what's on your terminal while you're working.

3. **You won't know if you're being watched.** Most surveillance equipment lets employers spy without the employee's knowledge. But over 80 percent of employers disclose their monitoring practices to their workers.

4. **Your emails are being read.** If an email system is used at the company, the employer owns it and may elect to read its contents. This policy also applies to messages sent from your terminal to another company or from another company to you. This includes web-based email accounts, such as Yahoo and Hotmail.

5. **Messages marked "private" are often not.** Many email systems have this option, but it doesn't guarantee that your messages will stay private. (If your employer's official email policy states that messages marked "Private" *will* be kept confidential, then you do have some protection. However, even in this situation, there may be exceptions.)

Encrypted Messages Are Not Necessarily Safe!
Encryption scrambles an email at the sender's terminal and then unscrambles it at the receiver's terminal. This technique guarantees that the message can be read only by the sender and the intended recipient. It may stop coworkers and industrial spies from reading your email, but your employer may *still* have access to the unscrambled emails.

---

3.   e-sex

If everyone fantasizes about sex every seven minutes, you see no harm in writing about it once a day from your terminal. Your flight of fancy feels like a coffee break: providing just enough mental stimulation to help you plough through the deadly research reports, pages of interminable financial accounting, and reams of social marketing minutia that are now apparently part of your job description. The "mystery person" to whom you're writing is single, completely available, and works on neither your floor nor in your department. (You would reveal the enigma but fear that someone may be reading your computer screen even as you write this.) You never use risqué language in any of your top-secret communiqués. Doesn't everyone deserve a little bit of R-rated fun?

187 **Isn't e-sex at the office fairly harmless? It's not like you're using the desks or the copy room or the supply room. It's just email.**

A. You could get caught.

Do you really want some techie with a goatee to get his ya-yas off reading your steamy emails? Granted, he wears blue jeans to work, which don't show stains readily. So he may wait a bit longer to turn you in. But one day, after the pure release of getting off those aforementioned ya-yas, imagine him turning all corporate on you—by reporting your e-orgasmic literary masterpiece to some guy in senior management who then reports it to your HR person. They all have a chuckle (if not quite a bit more) at your expense, and then write it up in your dossier as if you have committed the sin of the century. Naturally, you will be informed of your breach only when it's time to deny you a raise.

Don't have sex on other people's property. The email server is your company's property.

188 **Only one person knows about the e-sex relationship you're having with gr57@hotmail.com. So what's the harm?**

A. Employee morale could plummet.
If others on staff find out about your e-dalliance, they will only laugh, you think.

Pity it's not true. Some will be offended; some will feel grossed out; and all will gossip about the affair mercilessly. You and your paramour's emails will be the subject of other people's emails and blogs. And tongues will wag.

Studies show that gossip lowers employee morale. Do you really want employee performance to plunge while speculating about your performance? "Don't dip your quill in company ink" or write all about it on the company server. Remember these immortal words: "Eeee-www."

189 **Your e-liaison is no one else's business. True?**

A. False. It's company business.
Are you and a subordinate having e-sex? You could be exposing your firm to a law suit. Email doubles as a legal document. And watch out if the subordinate later turns around and claims it was sexual harassment!

Are you having e-sex with your boss? Everyone will automatically assume that's the reason you're receiving all of the plum assignments while they choke on the prunes.

Are you having e-sex with someone at your own level? "Unfair!" will shout the wags to the exposed rafters in the industrial ceiling. You and X now have a secret alliance that you will both use to further each other's careers while banding together to keep others from succeeding.

No one on staff really cares all that much about whether the two of you are *actually* having sex. It's all about politics.

Watercooler Wisdom

According to www.urbandictionary.com, e-sex is "the online version of sexual contact. Where there is no real contact, all interactions occur via the Internet." [24] That's one definition. Plenty of times when people are engaged in e-sex they are also having real sex. E-sex leads to real sex and real sex sometimes leads to e-sex. And e-sex leads to skipped raises on a seemingly trivial, but massively stupid, indiscretion.

4. e-firings

Your boss fired a staffer by email and copied ten people on his brusque communiqué. The irate staffer sent the entire company a scathing rebuttal via email, the contents of which are unprintable. Now everyone is in an uproar. Half of the staff is holed up behind closed doors bad-mouthing your boss for acting like a rube, while the other half is behind closed doors proactively calling their headhunters. You are the only person working with your door open today! Gee, it's nice and quiet around here. You can actually hear yourself think for a change. Suddenly the phone jangles, its discordant bleating belying the sounds of silence. "Can I see you in my office, now please?" your boss says. Your heart skips a beat, uneasy. But this time around, you are dead certain that you're not on the firing line. "He's not going to fire me," you think with a flash of ESP. "After all, it's the first time Satan has ever used the word, 'please.'"

190
Your boss informs you that you have to let go of one of your employees. You ask if your boss might "script you." Snarling, he says, "Ah, just do it via email. That's the latest trend." What are the ramifications?

A. Your employee will resent you forever.

If firing is a real slap to the self-esteem, firing via email is like a punch in the face. Not only are you cutting off that person's livelihood and pushing her into the big, heartless world out there, you're also revealing that it's not even worth your time to discuss it with her in person. She has every right to think of you as the slipperiest kind of weasel!

You may believe that you are dodging the "shoot the messenger" syndrome, but in fact, long after she's left the company she *will* want to shoot you.

191
Your company announces it needs to fire fifty people and that the victims will be notified via email. Is this really any different than calling a series of meetings with the unfortunates, and if so, how?

A. It's radically unfair to the victims.

Firing someone in person is a horrific experience. On a scale of 1 being "fun" and 10 being "going to the dentist for a root canal," firing someone clocks in at around 15. Have you always despised working with her? She will automatically assume that you masterminded her downfall whether or not it's true. Did you passively support her? She will deduce that you knew of her fate long in advance and didn't try hard enough to save her. She may curse at you, scream, rant, or dissolve into tears. She may accuse you of being soulless or selling out to the establishment. She may claim that she is far more talented than you and rave about how life is unfair.

But if you try to avoid the painful conversation by decapitating her via email, it doesn't allow her to air any of these feelings. And she has no opportunity to experience closure. You've robbed the worker of this important rite of passage. She also has *no idea* where her performance fell flat or how the company may spin it when people call for references about her. This puts her at a severe disadvantage when she has to trample the tarmac and look for a new job.

By avoiding a face-to-face proper firing, the company is treating her like an hourly migrant worker instead of like a white collar professional. And then you wonder why no one feels any loyalty to the companies where they work!

192 Can a generous severance package ever take the sting out of an email firing?

A. No. It just proves that the company has a double standard.
No company would ever hire by email. They would insist on an in-person meeting, if not several.

The same standard should be upheld for cutting employees from staff. In fact, if possible, it's a smart idea to bring in *the same players who hired the person*—the boss, an HR manager, and possibly a direct supervisor. Let the employee ask any questions that she needs to in order to understand how she failed to live up to expectations. If your company has an outplacement firm, urge the worker to take advantage of it. Can your company afford to let her use office resources, such as the secretarial staff, the Xerox machine, and mailroom center? Allowing her these simple courtesies will go a long way toward helping her recuperate from the dreadful experience of being fired and move on.

Show her compassion. Refuse to treat her as if she's the Invisible Woman. Recognize that one day you may be in her identical situation, and treat her the way you would want to be treated.

5. Avatars, Cartoon Versions of Yourself, and Other Aliases—Enough Already!

You would like to thank James Cameron for creating the movie *Avatar*. Were it not for that phenomenal film, you sincerely doubt that avatars would have had a "second life" at your workplace. But suddenly, avatars are omnipresent! Now, all of the geeky guys from the MIS department drop by constantly to talk to your team about the benefits of going virtual. "It will save you money on travel costs!" they shout in unison. (Nothing wrong with that, you think, recalling your ill-fated business trip to Costa Rica.) Some guy bedecked in blue jeans and a mildewed flannel shirt even has the chutzpah to discuss avatar dress codes! You think it's hilarious when he recommends that *your* avatar wear a suit to a virtual meeting. It wasn't so long ago that the only thing you'd ever sport to a meeting was a plaid shirt. If it's all virtual anyway, why are protocols important? And what are those rules?

193 What is an avatar? You thought it was an awesome movie, but...

A. An animated version of yourself that's possibly taller and even better looking.

Avatars are two or three-dimensional incarnations that are often animated and resemble human beings. In a business setting, they are usually used as a visual representation of workers. Just as with social networking sites and individual webpages, an avatar's appearance and behavior are a reflection of an individual and the company for whom he works.

If your company has a code of conduct for other Web activities, such as blogging, it should be able to extend those principles into virtual environments, such as Second Life.

194 What are avatars being used for in business?

A. Training and virtual meetings are the two top uses.

If your company is expanding or merging—necessitating a shift in employee roles—virtual meetings can be hugely helpful. There are also other uses that work nicely, such as virtual tours of a facility. As corporate travel budgets tighten, avatars can also help bridge the gap between overseas offices.

Companies on the Virtual Edge

According to the *Harvard Business Review* blog, firms such as Accenture, Cisco, IBM, Intel, State Farm, Wells Fargo, and others use virtual worlds, populated with avatars, to train, sell, and brainstorm. Controlling the avatar is not always intuitive or easy, but the price is right.[25] Other uses may include employee recruitment, managing programs, and collaborating with company groups around the world.[26]

---

195 Is there anything to be particularly sensitive about with an avatar?

A. People take pride in their avatars.

Avatars make life at the workplace more lively. But behind the fun is a level of primitive engagement, and people care deeply about their avatars. They want their avatars to be treated properly!

As in the real, non-virtual world, standing too close to other avatars may violate cultural standards. Research shows that tall, attractive avatars are more persuasive. Virtual touching is a real "no-no" in business.

Game Theory

Virtual worlds feel like a game, and that can have a positive impact on your company's business. Games require teamwork, data analysis, strategy, and decision-making ability. They can also help prevent employees from feeling bored.

That's a Wrap

1. People over fifty years old sometimes have trouble accepting that Evites can be beautiful, well-designed, eminently practical, and yet *free*. Mail these late adapters an engraved invitation instead.

2. The blind carbon copy is a lethal weapon of e-war. Don't use it, or be prepared to face retribution.

3. Resist the urge to have e-sex on someone else's server. Things could get e-messy.

4. Firing someone via email doesn't give her a chance to achieve closure the way that firing her in person does.

5. Some of the same etiquette rules from the real world carry over into the virtual world. Don't stand too close to another person's avatar, and think twice before touching another person's avatar.

III

EATING

Part III is a crash course in all the things you need to know about restaurant dining but feel too humiliated to ask—such as how to handle late arrivals and sudden departures, how to pass sauces, butter, and the salt and pepper, which dinner partner to engage in conversation first, and when to switch partners. When wining and dining a client, you can't afford to reach for the wrong wine glass or nosh from the incorrect bread plate! But master a few easy rules and you will have the confidence to eat any culinary creation that a restaurant chef can concoct.

CHAPTER 14

Tabletop Rules and Regulations for the 21st Century

Knives and spoons have been around since the dawn of the Iron Age, but somehow these simple tools, along with forks (which came later), are deceptively difficult for modern Masters of the Universe to master. Put a client or other notable dignitary at the table, and the discomfort becomes palpable.

Fortunately, mastering utensils becomes easy with the acceptance of a simple truth. To every tabletop, there is a system, along with the corollary: There are precious few departures from the system.

One can read utensils at a place setting like a book. Only you can decide whether that book will have a happy outcome or an embarrassing one.

Etiquette is both a code of conduct that you can use every day, as well as the specific routines for handling more formal dinners and get-togethers with clients, CEOs, business prospects, and other superiors. At the end of the day, even if their etiquette is lacking, yours should be as polished as a place setting from Tiffany's.

The great news is that etiquette rules, relentlessly practiced, eventually become innate. You will know them without thinking twice about them.

1. How to Read a Tabletop (The Monarch Notes)

You hail from a long, celebrated line of spaghetti slurpers. You grew up using bread to wipe up spare sauce on the plate. Before you watched reruns of *Seinfeld*, you had no idea what "double-dipping" meant, or even why it was unseemly. And, before taking this job, you ate most of your meals standing six inches from your home refrigerator, so as not to waste any time in the event you required a second serving. Yet somehow, in spite of your humble roots, you've finagled yourself into a position where now you're expected to entertain clients, visitors from the foreign office, and even your boss. Luckily, you've arrived at a safe place where you can learn everything no one ever taught you about table manners (but you're expected to know anyway).

196 **In this four-star restaurant, there are a slew of utensils at your place setting, all set in military alignment. You just want to eat without drawing attention to yourself. You heard that, when in doubt, you should follow your host's lead. Is that really a good idea?**

A. No, no, Nanette (or Ned).

Don't fret about whatever your seatmates are doing, because it's likely to be dead wrong. Following their lead is like copying the homework of the dumbest person in a class. You'd never stoop that low, right?

With all due respect to those with whom you work, it's highly unlikely that most of them will be well schooled in etiquette since it's rarely taught at school (or at home, for that matter). So stop looking frantically around the table trying to decipher what others are doing. They know not.

But in a nanosecond, you will.

197 Is there some cardinal rule for knowing which fork, knife, and spoon to use?

A. Follow from the outside in.

The place setting before you is like a MapQuest of the evening's meal. Just follow the directions it gives and you'll never get lost. (If you're a guy, no worries. You never have to *ask* the place setting for directions. It just gives them to you.)

Pick up the fork on your farthest left for your first course. Use it.

Are you done with that course? Good job! Place the fork on the plate and let the waiter whisk it away.

Ready for the second course? Pick up the next fork that's now on your farthest left—and so on, all the way through until dessert.

Follow the same routine with the knives on your right-hand side. Keep working from the outside in. Voila! Now you're a pro.

198 What about the dessert fork and spoon?

A. Life is uncertain. Eat dessert *last.*

An old adage advises to eat dessert first. Ignore it.

Eating dessert first will destroy your appetite, add unnecessary calories to your waistline, and get you all muddled about which fork and knife to use.

That's because eating your courses backwards will completely screw up the order in which you pick up and utilize the utensils at your place setting. Then you'll be using the wrong utensil for every single course during the meal! It will be the decline of civilization, starting at your tabletop.

To repeat: Never eat dessert first. The outermost fork on your left is *not* a dessert fork! The outermost spoon on your right is *not* a dessertspoon!

The dessertspoon and fork can generally be found *above* your plate, lying horizontally, where they should remain untouched—until you eat dessert *last.*

Watercooler Wisdom

In Edward Lear's whimsical poem, "The Owl and the Pussycat," the two protagonists "dined on mince and slices of quince/Which they ate with a runcible spoon." It sounds adorable, but what, pray tell, is a runcible spoon? Funny you should ask. The word "runcible" was a nonsense word coined by Lear that meant absolutely nothing until half a century later when it came to mean a spoon with three short tines like a fork. Does life imitate art or what?

2. The Taming of a Fork: American vs. Continental Style

Before you had European clients, you never really considered how life was different on the other side of the Pond (that's British for "ocean"). Of course you knew that the British had that odd habit of driving on the left side of the road and that in certain countries it was beyond gauche to eat certain foods with one's hands. But your recent travels abroad opened your eyes to something far more significant. There are two entirely different ways to eat food—Continental versus American—and in general, Americans are in the *minority* in preferring "the American style" of eating! Now after a brief stint abroad, you almost need a refresher course in how to eat American-style. What are the key differences between the American and Continental styles, and is it alright to switch back and forth?

THE STRAIGHT SCOOP

Residents of the United States and Canada are the *only* ones in the world who use the American style of eating, commonly referred to as the "zigzag" for the way that it requires switching hands. (Of course, we all know that the shortest distance between two points is a straight line, right?) You can use the American style of eating for dinner and the Continental for lunch, or vice versa, or even vary them according to which country you find yourself in at mealtime. But get proficient at both, please, because switching back and forth during one seating is considered horribly rude in every country.

199 You don't mean to stare but your European client eats his food completely differently than you. Who's right?

A. You both are—assuming that you're using the American style and he's using the Continental style. Let's talk about the American style first.

The American style is a bite-by-bite operation. Cut a bite. Switch hands. Eat a bite. Cut a bite. Switch hands. Eat a bite.

Pick up the fork with your left hand and the knife with your right hand. Cut a bite-sized piece of food. Lay your knife down towards the top of the plate—cutting edge facing in—and now switch the fork to your right hand. Now, holding your fork with the tines pointing up, use it to pick up your food, either by scooping the morsel onto the tines or by piercing it with the tines.

Take a bite, chew, take a breath, and repeat the whole process.

200 What is the Continental style of eating and how does it differ from its American counterpart?

A. In the Continental style, the fork stays in your left hand while the knife stays in your right. Don't switch hands.

The American style of eating zigs and zags; the Continental style just zigs. Food makes a beeline, fork to mouth, without going off on any tangents.

Pick up the fork with your left hand and the knife with your right. Cut a morsel of food. Don't switch hands! Instead, keep the fork in your left hand, stab your food with it, and then bring it up to your mouth. In this case, the tines of the fork point *down* throughout the entire operation.

Meanwhile, the knife rests in your right hand, poised for action, and ready to be used again. If you need to nudge something onto the tines of your fork, use your knife (but gently, please).

Zippity-do-da. Now you know.

The Non-Neanderthal Rule
Cut each sliver of food, bite by bite. But never cut all of your food into tiny pieces all at the same time unless you are feeding a small child, eating with a Neanderthal, or eating with a child who is a Neanderthal.

An Airline Analogy
Imagine that American and Continental were both airlines. (Oh wait! They *are* both airlines.) The American style of eating is like flying to Miami by stopping over at Orlando first. The Continental style of eating is like flying direct.

201 **Dammit, that does it! Your server tries to whisk away your plate even though he must realize you haven't finished. There is still food on your plate. You've already glared him down twice—to no avail. Any way to convey the message without screaming, "Excuse me Waiter Boy, but I haven't finished!"**

A. Yes. Don't put your utensils in "finish" position by mistake.
Okay, you promise you won't, but what is the "finish" position, you wonder?

In the American style, the finish position is sometimes referred to as "four o'clock." What a shame that whoever coined the term didn't know how to tell time! The position should really be called "ten-of-four."

Picture your plate as a round, analog clock. In the finish position, the *tines* of your fork and the top of your knife both point to the number ten, while the *handles* of the fork and knife both point to the number four, as if it's ten of four in the afternoon. (The fork and the knife lie side by side: The tines of the fork face up while the blade of the knife faces the fork.)

Unfortunately, harried waiters, anxious to turn tables and leave their restaurants before ten of four in the morning, sometimes mistake the "just resting" position in the American style for the "finish" position.

When taking a breather in between bites, rest your fork and knife *almost* in the "ten-of-four" position, but keep your utensils well separated. This should alert your waiter that you are *not* finished (although depending on what night it is and how busy the restaurant is, this won't always work).

A little British goes a long way towards correcting the problem of the overeager waiter, even here in America.

"I'm terribly sorry," you might say putting on your smoothest Hugh Grant accent, "but I haven't finished with that plate quite yet. Thanks so much for your understanding!"

For superb results, add a little sugar to your new British persona.

For Extra Credit

The finish position is almost identical for both the Continental and American eating styles—a ten-of-four position for both fork and knife—with one notable distinction. In the Continental style, the tines of the fork point down.

However, the "I'm just resting" position in the Continental style is *markedly different* from its American counterpart. In the Continental rest position, the knife and fork form an upside down "V." The tines of the fork face down and overlap the tip of the knife.

The knife handle points to the number four on the clock (just like in the American style); but the fork *handle* points to the number eight on the clock, while the tines, face down, point to the number two.

---

3.   Utensils You Only Wish Had Never Been Invented

From the time you were a toddler, you've had to deal with utensils. So why is it that tonight of all nights, at the most important client dinner of the year, you suddenly can't remember how to use them? It's amazing that these ordinary items—forks, knives, spoons, and the occasional oyster fork—strike fear in your heart. With powerful people watching your every move, even a benign bread knife seems intimidating. Will you be cowed by a soupspoon? Will you confuse your fork with your neighbor's or reach for a knife that tumbled onto the floor by accident? Of course not! With a few quick refreshers, you'll gain the confidence you need to order *any* item on the menu, even if the company CEO is seated at the table.

202 **You order** *spaghetti mushroom alfredo* **at a client dinner, but when the steaming plate arrives, you're not sure which utensil to use. You eat spaghetti with a:**
A. Fork.
B. Fork and spoon.
C. Fork, knife, and spoon.
D. Egads! You're not exactly sure of the protocol and you're worried about splattering spaghetti everywhere.

A. Answer B (Fork and spoon.)
This takes some hand-eye coordination, but if you're good at video games, mastering the two-utensil trick is a no-brainer. First, take a deep breath. Then, pick up both utensils. Hold the fork diagonally with your right hand and the spoon in your left. Gracefully lift a small portion of spaghetti with the fork and twirl it against the cupped part of the spoon until it forms a neat, little bundle. Then pop it into your mouth. For extra points, practice this skill at home before you show it off at a business dinner. Perfect your technique until you're the Derek Jeter of spaghetti eaters—and you'll never be tempted to tuck your napkin into your shirt to protect it. One small spoon for spaghetti . . . one short step to conquering lobster and chicken with bones!

203 At the mission retreat dinner, oysters on the half shell are served with a tiny fork on the same plate. You just stab the oyster with the oyster fork and then pop the morsel into your mouth, right?

A. Wrong. Pick up the oyster shell with your hands.

When you are handed a special fork that seems like it was designed *expressly* for the purpose of eating oysters, picking up the oyster shell with your bare hands and slurping the slippery concoction can seem positively barbaric! Nevertheless, all Barbarians at the Gate who suddenly find themselves transported to fine eating establishments will eventually need to conquer the oyster—even if doing so seems like a throwback to an earlier era.

Think of the fork as a "garnish" for the lemon that often accompanies oysters (or as a vestigial item with no practical use whatsoever, much like your pinky toe).

In any case, feel free to ignore the dastardly fork.

204 At a job interview dinner, is it acceptable to blow on your soup?

A. Not unless you're willing to blow the interview.

Eating soup requires manual dexterity. But if you've ever played an air guitar, you should be a natural. Air guitar etiquette involves playing invisible chords on an invisible instrument. Soup etiquette involves using a visible instrument (your soupspoon) to describe an invisible circle.

Pick up the largest spoon at your place setting, dip it into the soup close to the edge of the bowl, and then glide the spoon *away* from you towards the bowl's center. The idea is to describe a rather large circle with your spoon—first directing the utensil away from your lips and then back again towards them. As the spoon approaches your mouth, be sure to sip the soup from the *side* of the spoon.

Circling your soup through the air, one spoonful at a time, will cool it down considerably. When finished with the soup, place the spoon on the service plate under the bowl, rather than inside the soup bowl. Be sure to leave a few drops of soup in the bowl at the end of the course. (Lifting the bowl or swabbing it with bread to sponge up the remaining soup is considered undignified, unrefined, and thoroughly unacceptable in restaurants.)

At a Restaurant, You Really Don't Want to Fork Things Up

1. Don't hold your fork like a rake (or your spoon like a shovel).
2. Don't cut your food with the side of your fork. (That's what the knife is for.)
3. Don't mix and match forks and knives with chopsticks. Pick *one* set of utensils and stick with it.
4. Don't reuse your salad fork for either the main course or dessert.
5. Don't bend over your food. (Bring the fork to your mouth, not the other way around.)

---

4. *Standing Up When Someone Leaves the Table and Other Throwbacks to Emily Post*

If only you had read the manual on "conference dinner decorum" *before* you had arrived! You can't remember what the rules are, and neither can anyone else at the table. When the most junior accountant at the firm stood up to go to the ladies' room, half of the men at the table stood up and half of them didn't. (You haven't the slightest clue which half was right.) When she returned, three-quarters of the men stood up—the new standees clearly guilted into it by the more chivalrous guys. Pretending to study your arugula salad with intense interest, you mentally review everything you know about tabletop etiquette and realize it's not all that much. You remember reading somewhere that men no longer have to open doors for women. So why do guys have to stand every time a woman moves away from the table?

205 Do men really have to rise when a woman leaves the table to go powder her nose? It seems like such a throwback.

A. Yes. But a woman doesn't have to leave the table if she's only going to powder her nose.

Stand up when a woman leaves the table for any reason. If she protests and says, "Oh, don't get up," realize that she doth protest too much and do it anyway.

If she says, "Thank you," and affects a surprised, shocked look much like a doe in headlights, do it anyway.

Even if she gives you a curt, pointed lecture on feminism, smile, and do it anyway.

Some so-called etiquette gurus incorrectly assert that gender equality at the workplace has erased this longstanding tradition at the dinner table, but most women appreciate the gesture, so why not indulge the fairer sex?

Help Me, Rhonda! There's No Room to Breathe

What if there isn't room to stand up all the way? In that case, perform a "half-rise." The half-rise is more like a genteel squat and if you've been to the gym in the last four years, you should be able to execute one easily. Stand on your feet, but keep your knees bent so that your butt lifts just slightly out of your chair. The gesture is shorthand for, "You know I'd stand up all the way for you if I could."

---

206 You're at a client dinner at a posh restaurant when one of the clients waltzes in two hours late. The rest of you are finishing your main meal. You:

A. Say "Hello, Jack, it's great to see you," and stay seated. Doing anything else would agitate your fellow diners.

B. Rise. Just because he's rude doesn't mean that you need to be.

C. Stay seated and signal the waiter so that your late client can be served promptly, and hopefully, catch up with the rest of you.

D. Stay seated and keep talking to your dinner companion, so as not to disrupt the flow.

A. Answer B (Rise. Just because he's rude doesn't mean that you need to be.)

At a client dinner, the client is the most important person. Even if he is abominably late, it's only polite to rise when he enters. Let others fuss about getting him wait service.

How to Perform Standup

Standing up is a sign of respect; staying seated, a sign of boorishness.

To not appear as an oafish, uncouth sort, stand whenever you shake someone's hand, especially if the person is older than you, someone whom you're meeting for the first time, or a high-ranking client or other important dignitary.

Sometimes standing during a meal can also be surprisingly practical. At a crowded table if you try to reach over to shake someone's hand from a seated position, you could knock over a wine glass or inadvertently brush against someone's food. True, you'd have to be mighty clumsy to do it, but only you know what you're capable of.

Why risk it when standing up is so much more genteel?

---

207 Is there room for women to groom at the table?

A. It all depends on how one defines "grooming."

Any act of grooming that takes one second or less to perform is socially acceptable.

You can apply your lipstick. But recognize that in the dim, nether light of the restaurant dining room, you may totally miss your lip line (which will have the unintended effect of making you look like Krusty the Clown).

You are also free to powder your nose. Fact: Women have been whipping out tiny compacts to powder their noses since Time Immemorial, or at least since they watched their grandmothers whip out their tiny powder compacts. However, you will need to do it at the speed of Superwoman or risk offending everyone at the table *and* their grandmothers! No one wants to watch you put on the full regalia.

Are you tempted to comb your hair? Temper the urge. Remember always, you are not a cat! Spritzing perfume is unsanitary around food. And, if you touch up your mascara in this ill-lit quarter, you're likely to hurt yourself.

All things considered, you are probably better off traipsing to the ladies' room to groom (and having all the gents at the table rise when you do).

Direct from the English-to-English Phrasebook: A Couple of Phrases You Should Plan on Bringing to Dinner

It's easy to buff up your language with the mastery of a few choice phrases. On the left side of the column are some common items you may require when eating in our native land. On the right side is the language you should use to request them.

What You Want	How You Say It
1. the pepper	1. Please pass the salt and pepper.
2. some water	2. May I trouble you for a glass of water?
3. a new napkin	3. Pardon me, but my napkin seems to have fallen on the floor. May I have a new one?
4. the waiter	4. Could you kindly ask our waiter to come to our table?
5. the check	5. When you have a moment, can you bring the check, please?

5. Passing: Don't Fake Left and Move Right

It's not worth passing out about it, but you're pretty certain that you passed the bread basket the wrong way. Of course it wasn't your fault. It was your assistant Ashley's fault. She started it all wrong by passing the dang basket to the left. Ashley is left-handed, not that it matters. Now the HR-Assistant-Who-Only-Wears-Black bends Joe Client's ear while your boss elbows her to pass the basket to Joe's most important superior, Bentley Big Shot. Bentley looks positively famished, too. If you ever survive this weekend with your colleagues, you're going to recommend that your company invest in some etiquette training for the troops. Surely your boss will approve. Deep down inside—really deep—you're sure he's not the incarnation of evil that everyone claims.

208 **What is the correct way to pass food?**

A. **Counterclockwise (or to the right).**
It doesn't matter whether you are right-handed, left-handed, or ambidextrous.

It may sound counter intuitive. But if you want your dinners to run like clockwork, then you'll need to pass all food counter clockwise.

However, keeping the food moving *in one direction* trumps the direction from which it happens to arrive. So if your assistant makes a cardinal boo-boo and passes the basket to you from the from the wrong side, *keep* passing the basket in the same direction. (Two wrongs *do* make a right.)

Vow to think nothing more of it with either the left side of your brain or the right. Right-ho then, carry on.

209 You are a pepper aficionado and spot your spice of choice on the far side of the table nestled in between your boss and the company CEO who are both engaged in a lively debate. The *last* thing you want to do is disrupt their banter. Can't you just reach over and grab the dang pepper yourself?

A. Not unless you want to demonstrate a major character flaw.

It's commonly called "the overreach." But in this case, "overreaching" is really under-reaching because you are *failing* to reach your goal for the evening. Your aim is to impress your superiors with your flawless comportment. Instead, you're showing a flaw—impatience. Ask for items to be passed rather than reaching for them unless they are directly in front of you.

As a side note, it is considered uncouth to ask for *any* seasoning before tasting the food. (If the chef could see you, he might raise one of his sharp knives in your direction. And at a business dinner, you don't want to be knifed in the front or the back.)

The Salt and Pepper Are Married

One out of two marriages in America may end in divorce, but the alliance between salt and pepper isn't one of them. These two partners have been hitched for a long time. You may prefer salt over pepper or vice versa, but always ask for them as a pair, or you risk having the person passing *only* the one you requested, which is shockingly poor etiquette.

210 Is food served from the left or the right, and does it really matter? You're starving!

A. Yes, food is generally served on the left and cleared from the right.

In a great restaurant, seating, serving, and clearing is a finely orchestrated concerto and the only reason to worry about from which side the food will arrive is to avoid upsetting the waiters' rhythm during the performance. (You wouldn't want to lean left by mistake and bang into a plate leveling straight to your head. That could cause a concussion.)

But just in case you find yourself on an etiquette reality TV show any time soon, *yes,* food is served on the left and whisked away from the right.

Beverages, however, are served from the right and cleared from the right. That's a cinch to remember because all glasses, goblets, and flutes flank the right side of any place setting. (Apparently, the reason is because most people are right-handed. Sorry, lefties!)

That's a Wrap

1. Never follow your host's lead, as chances are excellent that he's not an etiquette guru.

2. If you don't want a waiter to whisk away your plate prematurely, make sure your utensils are in the "just resting" position. Keep both fork and knife in the "ten of four" position, separated from each other. When you're finished, simply push the two utensils together.

3. Contrary to popular perception, you do *not* eat an oyster with an oyster fork.

4. Men should stand by an old ceremony and rise whenever a woman leaves the table.

5. You can reach for the brass ring, but don't reach for tabletop items that are out of reach. It's perfectly fine to ask for them.

CHAPTER 15

The Five Key Food Groups

When you are in a fine restaurant, your etiquette is under a microscope. Your manners are being analyzed, dissected, and monitored. Small flaws are magnified; tiny ignorances, revealed.

And in certain situations, such as a client dinner or job interview, the grade that you receive will have a major impact on your career. Get an A+—and you'll be expected to wine and dine today's kings and queens of commerce.

In any high-stress dining scenario, ignorance is not bliss and the lack of familiarity with certain food items can breed contempt. In this chapter, find five difficult-to-eat food groups that don't normally get covered in nearly enough detail.

When in doubt, revert to the old-fashioned, standard way of doing things pre-cell phone era. Remember that patience is a virtue and that certain technological advances were created to allow you to be pleasantly stuck at a three-hour dinner now and again without checking your "Crackberry."

While everyone hates being bullied, in a communal setting such as a client dinner, some alpha personalities may even add a peer pressure element to your meal.

Is the client ordering lobster and mandating that everyone follow his lead? Is he a dessert freak pushing you to taste the most caloric pastry since the invention of the Napoleon? Sometimes, for the sake of camaraderie, it's more important to follow his cue than to assert your independence.

1. Mastering the Humble Bread Plate

You are a real trailblazer. When you asked your boss to please pass the bread, it was as if a giant light bulb lit up and everyone on the team decided to copy your brilliant idea. First your boss snatched a piece from the wicker basket. Then the intern stole a piece. Then the first client took a piece. Then the second client took a piece. By the time the basket reached you, of course it was empty, and you had to ask the waiter for some more bread. But when he returned with the basket, he had the bad manners to put it right in front of your ravenous, bread-sucking boss again. You certainly hope these ideas of yours are getting noticed! Let the record reflect that *you* asked for the bread first!

Exemplary Bread Basket Karma: What Goes Around Comes Around
If the breadbasket is in front of you, it's your charge to pass it around the table. Pass the basket to the right and *do not help yourself* until it comes all the way back to you.

"Etiquette" Rhymes with "Baguette," but Where on Earth Does It Come From?

From the French, of course!

According to Emily Post's book, *Etiquette in Society, in Business, in Politics, and at Home,* when the Versailles gardens were first being planned, King Louis XIV's master gardener became irked because his newly seeded gardens were being continually trampled on.[27]

To keep the trespassers off the grass, he put up warning signs, called *etiquettes.* The courtiers continued to ignore directions—to his intense annoyance.

> The gardener eventually complained to the King about their rudeness in such a way that his Majesty was moved to issue an edict, commanding everyone at Court to "keep within the etiquettes."
> Now you know.

211   Oops! You think you just ate from your boss's bread plate by mistake. Anyway to correct the gaffe?

A. Own up to it, if true.

It's happened to all of us, even apparently, to the late, great Emily Post.

"Silly me! I appear to have eaten from your bread plate by mistake. Here, let me trade and give you my untouched plate," should suffice.

Or whip out Ms. Post's great line: "Isn't that just like me?" she said.

Now the *reason* that people are always noshing from each other's bread plates is because most people are right-handed. So the tendency is to reach with one's right hand for the tiny plate on the right. There's only one teeny weenie problem. The plate isn't yours: It's your neighbor's. And thou shalt not covet thy neighbor's bread plate!

Your bread plate is the little plate to your left. (It's directly across from the glasses on your right.) So if an error happens and it's your fault, look at the bright side: Now you have something in common with the divine diva of etiquette, Emily Post!

212   Is there any trick to cutting and buttering bread?

A. Trick question sighting! There is "no cutting."

When it comes to breaking bread, the only "trick" is to recall that you are *breaking* it.

You are not hacking it, cutting it, slicing it, scissoring it, or stabbing it.

(Bread is peaceful. There is no need to behave violently towards it.) Breaking bread is a ritual: time-honored, but not time-sensitive.

Did someone just pass you the breadbasket? Select the roll closest to you. (Never rifle through the basket to assess which rolls are plumper. Rolls aren't melons, you know.) Then place the roll on the bread plate to your *left*. Tear off the tiniest, bite-sized piece. Using the small bread knife that is lying horizontally on that plate, butter *only* that torn piece of bread. Pop it into your mouth. Repeat the entire process for each bite.

Watercooler Wisdom

"Bread and circuses," from the Latin, panem et circenses, is a metaphor for handouts and petty amusements that politicians use to gain popular support (instead of meriting it through sound policy).[38]

213 Eeeew. My work partner just swabbed his bread in the communal olive oil on the table. Is his etiquette correct, or is he teetering on the slippery slope?

A. He's not teetering, Darling. He slipped all the way.

Olive oil is "in" these days, as the benefits of monounsaturated fats and Mediterranean diets receive glowing press. "French women don't get fat," we're told. And just look at what they're eating! But diner beware—olive oil's rise to fame hasn't done any favors for modern manners. Most people have *no idea* how to contend with the slippery glop arriving on the tabletop via the tiniest of bowls. Waiters can also be surprisingly parsimonious with those miniscule bowls—frequently allotting just one per table without any sort of serving utensil.

So what, pray tell, are you supposed to with the oil? Do you pour it? Dunk your bread in it like a sponge and mop it around? Use a butter knife to ladle it? Slather it all over your body and get suntanned? No, no, no, and dear God, no! (The stress of worrying about it all is keeping you as skinny as a toothpick.)

Either request a real serving spoon or volunteer your own unused teaspoon as a "serving spoon" for the oil. Gingerly ladle out a dime-sized portion onto your bread plate. Then, pass the bowl and donated spoon around the table to your right. (Ask your waiter to replace your spoon at the earliest opportunity.)

2. *Lobster and Crustaceans of the Deep*

It's "Lobster Night" at The Ragged Claw. "Why don't we all order lobster?" your client suggests, an impish smile alighting his pink face. Your only experience with lobster to date was watching a live one scurry for safety in some ancient Woody Allen flick. You feel intimidated by nutcrackers (your mother is one) and aren't wild about plastic bibs as a sartorial statement. It looks like things could get messy. You consider passing, or ordering some dish where the chef has already done the work of extracting the damned lobster from its shell. You scour the menu for lobster thermidor. "No, no!" your client insists. "We're ordering lobster *by the pound* tonight. One pound or two?" he asks, winking at you until your own face turns bright red.

214 Eating lobster is time-consuming, difficult, and slovenly beyond belief. What are you missing here?

A. Lobster isn't food. It's a pastime.

Eating lobster is misnamed. It's not really "eating." It's more like a sport. The lobster, though deader than dead, must be tackled and wrestled with. The tools used are different than those designed for other foods. There's even a whole separate vocabulary for each section of the big red "bug," well known to lobster aficionados. Eating lobster requires a mega amount of work and a commitment on par with getting married. On a calorie-per-minute basis, it's ludicrous. But once you taste the sweet, succulent meat slathered in drawn butter, you'll draw a satisfied sigh of contentment, and could, quite possibly, be hooked for life.

215 What's the right way to eat a lobster?

A. With gusto. Grab a bib, a nutcracker, a tiny pick, and a shellfish fork.

Even dead, lobsters resist being eaten.

Their hard shells, spindly legs, and gooey red and green fillings make them a challenge, and you will need to develop a hunter's passion for the work involved. But some of the greatest tales you'll ever share will be told over lobster fests. And, as with any good story, there's a beginning, middle, and end to eating a lobster.

Start with the claws. Then tackle the tail. And finish with the legs.

Lobster claws are almost always cracked in the kitchen before being brought to the table, but you'll still need a nutcracker. And, if you ask really sweetly, most restaurants will be delighted to provide you with the fanciest of plastic bibs. (See "The Tackling of Lobster, One, Two, Three" for claw-to-tail-to-legs instructions.)

The Tackling of Lobster, One, Two, Three

Chapter One: It All Starts with the Claws

1. Twist and pull off the two claws from the spot where they are attached to the body.
2. Crack open each claw with a nutcracker.
3. Extract the delicious lobster meat with the metal pick or shellfish fork provided.
4. Swab in drawn butter.
5. Eat. (Mangia, mangia!)
6. Ooh and aah about how delicious the claw meat tastes. (This is mandatory.)

Chapter Two: Next Comes the Tail

1. Grasp the tail with one hand and the back of the lobster with the other.
2. Twist and separate.
3. If there is squishy, green stuff, it means that your lobster was male. It's called "tomalley," which is a delicacy so technically it's edible. (Experts may differ. Mercury and other pollutants sometimes end up here, so you may want to pass on eating it.) However, if the squishy stuff is red, your lobster was female. That's lobster roe. This is perfectly safe to eat, and many consider it one of lobster's finest yields.
4. Use the shellfish fork to extract all meat, swab in butter, and savor.
5. Discard the dark, vein-like structure that runs the length of the tail.
6. Optional: Some people break off the lobster's tail flippers and work to fish out the tiny portions of meat inside.

Chapter Three: The Last Lap—Legs

1. Gently pull each of the lobster's eight legs away from the body.
2. Bite down on each leg and suck out the meat with your teeth.

Lobster See, Lobster Do: Or Why to *Always* Order Lobster Whenever Your Client Does

Wrestling with a dead crustacean is an adventure. Here's your golden opportunity to fend against the unknown! Will the claw crack at your command? Will the butter splatter you in the eye? The communal joy of conquering these pesky crustaceans adds an element of bon vivant fun and derring-do to any client outing and therefore *must* be indulged *whenever* the opportunity presents itself. (Just don't *suggest* ordering lobster, because it tends to be *très* costly.)

216 Whenever you visit your business partners in Maryland, they insist on ordering Maryland steamed crabs. At the end of the meal, there are crab shards, shells, and carcasses strewn all over the crab-soaked table. You are a fastidious eater. Is there any way to keep things clean?

A. Not a chance. Take out your mallet and start pounding!

Think of all the money it will save you on therapy.

First, remove the claws. (Not yours, the crab's.)

Next, remove the legs. (Again, we're talking about the crab's legs.) Gently twist and pull to dislodge both. Next, place the crab on its back to reveal its underbelly. Using a knife, pull up the "apron" of the crab. Now, tear the hard shell from the top of the crab all the way off and discard. (If that doesn't help you vent your aggressions, nothing will.) Scrape out and throw away any part of the crab that doesn't look appealing. This may include the green-yellow mustard (the crab's "liver") and the lungs (sometimes called the "devil's fingers").

Break the crab's body in half and scoop out the sweet crabmeat. Use the knife to tease out the crabmeat from all of the little nooks and niches along the cartilage. Next, hum the song "If I had a hammer" for inspiration—but just inside your head.

Then, pick up your mallet and pound those claws. SPLAT! *You hate your boss.* SPLAT! *You hate messy food.* SPLAT! *You didn't get the credit you deserved on the IV Quarter report.* SPLAT! SPLAT! SPLAT!

Finally, fish out the sweet meat with your fork. Mmm, delicious. *You have never tasted anything so divine.*

How to Turn Lemons into Perfume

To clean up, wash your hands thoroughly with soap and water. If the crab scent persists, rub lemon juice over your hands and rewash with soap and water.

3. Spinach, Poppy Seeds, Sugared Walnuts, and Other Menaces to Teeth

You have no problem with exotic foods served at scalding temperatures. Your teeth are less forgiving. They rebel at the unfamiliar, which is unfortunate since your client loves to experiment with newfangled restaurant fare. Every time you pass on the steaming stews and flambé desserts, he shakes his large, pink lobster face at you sadly, absently toying with his whiskers. No doubt, he pities your conservative roots. Little does he know that it's your *tooth roots* which are the problem. For as far as your tooth roots are concerned, broiled foods and chilled desserts are at the root of all evil.

―――――――――――――――― **THE STRAIGHT SCOOP** ――――――――――――――――

Restaurants can sometimes seem like a minefield to teeth. After all, you're exposing yours to all sorts of potentially hazardous substances. If your teeth are sensitive, shun foods with temperature challenges, such as soups served sizzling hot and ice cream. (Also, experiment with Sensodyne toothpaste. And no, nobody paid me to say that.)

217 Spinach at a business dinner: dumb, dumber, or insane?

A. All of the above. (Unless your name happens to be Popeye.)

Let's take a half a step backwards and craft a "pros" and "cons" spinach list. Many smart business decisions are made this way. So let's start by evaluating the "pros" of spinach. On the plus side, it tastes good. It has a cool texture. It contains two ingredients that may even help prevent macular degeneration of the eyes.

As for the "cons"—you'd have to be blind as Oedipus Rex not to notice how horrific spinach looks when it's nestled in between teeth! But wait! It gets worse. Cooked spinach even leaves a slight film on the pearly whites that may prevent you from *feeling* the spinach huddling in between the gaps of your teeth. You mistakenly think that people are laughing at your fantastic jokes. Instead they're laughing at the spinach in your teeth.

Before you order spinach at an important dinner, just think about those huddled spinach masses yearning to breathe free! Tonight, save a leaf. If you truly care about making a good impression over dinner, please do *not* eat your spinach!

218 What is proper toothpick etiquette?

A. An oxymoron.

You can use a toothpick to pick up a cherry tomato, a tiny square of cheese, or an olive.

You *cannot* use a toothpick to pick your teeth—at least not here in America, you can't. (Not to nitpick, but in Asia, no one blinks if you use a toothpick in between courses and everyone picks away with abandon like country and western singers picking on their guitars. Still, err on the side of caution and check local customs before whipping out your golden toothpick.)

The *only* place where you can get away with using a toothpick in the U.S. of A. is behind a closed door in a restroom, preferably with the door locked. Don't let anyone pick the lock with a toothpick either.

Top Ten Tooth Menaces

Food, glorious food! Why can't you eat anything that you want? Following are the top ten tooth menaces and how they deviously work to subtract points from your etiquette mojo. Determined to eat them anyway? A visit to the dentist in time saves nine.

Top Ten Tooth Menaces	What They Do
1. Spinach	1. Nestles in between teeth.
2. Poppy seeds	2. Makes you look like a smoker . . . with dark spots on your teeth.
3. Olives	3. Forces you to gnaw around the pit like a dog with a tiny bone.
4. Beets	4. Turns teeth a garish yellow. Very Halloween.

Top Ten Tooth Menaces	What They Do
5. Coffee	5. Taints teeth dingy gray.
6. Tiny pieces of caramel in ice cream or candy	6. Lodge between teeth and the gum line until you cry for dental floss.
7. Red wine	7. Makes teeth look washed out and lifeless.
8. Beef stew	8. Stringy pieces hide between teeth. Where's the beef? You can't see it, but you can feel it.
9. Hard, sugared flowers on top of birthday cakes	9. Can crack your enamel.
10. Sticky rice	10. Sneaks under the gum line. Ouch!

219   **At a job interview dinner, are there any items that you shouldn't order?**

A. Plenty. Stay away from *anything* that you've never eaten before.
You could be allergic and have to be rushed to the hospital, mid-interview. You could despise one of the ingredients. Wincing while you bravely try to chew your way through it, you would then *fail* to impress your interviewer. You might be unsure how to handle any given item, and eat it entirely wrong.

One person's osso bucco is another person's eel sushi. But at a job interview dinner, your *unfamiliarity* with certain food items could make an interviewer think twice about hiring you.

On Acing the Dinner Portion of the Job Interview Test

At most job interview dinners, you *will* have a choice about ordering. And only you can be master of your destiny.

The choices that you make early on in that meal could well determine who you become.

If you do have a choice about ordering, why not make your life easy? Why order spaghetti and ratatouille when you could order salmon and pota- toes? Given a choice, select food that's easy to eat and designed not to spot outfits. Here are some foods to avoid if humanly possible:

1. **food with deeply colored sauces or gravies**
2. **greasy foods**
3. **hand foods, such as hamburgers, spare ribs, and French fries**
4. **food that requires chopsticks, especially if your chopstick etiquette leaves something to be desired**
5. **unfamiliar foods that challenge your digestion or allergies.**

Do you have special dietary needs? Conduct your detective work with the fastidiousness of the TV sleuth Monk. Find out which restaurant you'll be dining at in advance and look it up online. Peruse the menu before you ever get to the restaurant and decide what to order in advance. Why take chances with your food selections—especially at an all-important job inter- view dinner? You've got enough stuff to worry about.

Who Knew?

Blame the Brits for making toothpick usage totally taboo. Before the 18th century, it was actually considered a compliment to the chef to pick your teeth after dinner! The French had no issue serving tooth- picks with dessert. But the English decided toothpicks were crude, rude, and socially unacceptable, and for better or worse, their take on the lowly toothpick has withstood the test of time, at least here in America. Your heart really has to go out to the lowly toothpick. Tooth- picks don't have an army of lawyers to defend their honor.

4.   Eating Meat, Neat

They're into it. They're just not that into it. They're into it. They're just not that into it. You've heard every last detail about your employees' flirtations—with diets. Vegan. Vegetarian. Macrobiotic. Mediterranean. Fruit and vegetable. Cabbage soup. South Beach. Cambridge. 3-Day. 5-Day. 7-Day. Miracle Diets. All protein. All grapefruit. All juice. All the time. Yes, you've heard it all while trying to maintain your own diet—that would be the meat and potatoes diet—while getting your butt into the gym in between restaurant outings. Oh what? Haven't you heard about the meat and potato diet? It just so happens that you're really into it.

220 You feel self-conscious about eating hamburgers when you're out with the office gang. What if an onion shard flies out or you smear your lips with ketchup?

A.   To prevent mishaps, cut the hamburger in half.

Hamburger buns are like women's handbags. Overstuff them, and they will break. So be sure to pack light.

Add just *one* slice of tomato, *one* lettuce leaf, and *one* pickle. Spoon some ketchup on top. Clamp the bun lid firmly in place, then press down to secure it with your left hand. Then, with your right hand, take your knife and slice the sandwich in half vertically.

Resolve to be less efficient and more proficient.

It's perfectly acceptable to use *both* of your hands to lift only half of a burger at a time.

221 You're germ-phobic and really despise the idea of sharing food, even in a Chinese restaurant. How do you finagle out of it when you're with businesspeople who may not understand your reluctance?

A.   Order the moo shu pork, and skip having seconds.

The pancake protocol for moo shu pork at most Chinese restaurants will save you from ever having to share why it is that you hate to share. (You never want to tell anyone in business that *sharing* is your pet peeve. It makes you look like a Lone Ranger rather than a team player. Not good.)

Many waiters will roll up the moo shu pancakes for you. If your waiter won't, use a fork and knife to lift one of the pancakes out of the wooden basket all by yourself. Gently lay the pancake on your plate. Then, with a serving spoon, carefully place the zesty concoction of stir fried pork, scrambled eggs, and sizzling wood ear mushrooms in a skinny vertical line right down the middle of the pancake.

Do not overstuff. Less is more in terms of manageability. Now, dribble a thin ribbon of brown hoisin sauce along the top of your moo shu pork.

Then, with your fingers, roll the pancake into a tightly wound cigar. (If you have never smoked in your life, simply pretend that you have for the purpose of this exercise.) Tuck in the ends of your cigar pancake. Lift with your hands. Consume in two or three bites. Scrumptious.

Boy, You Turn Me Upside Down

It turns out that Chinese custom has a nifty solution for oversharers. Once a pair of chopsticks has touched someone's mouth, he is *never* supposed to reuse the same ends to pick up communal food. So if you've already eaten something with your chopsticks, remember to turn them upside down (so that you are using the wide ends to pick up food from a communal tray). Better yet, use a serving spoon.

The Net Net on Chopsticks

Grasp the bottom chopstick like a pencil in your right hand. Place the second chopstick right next to it, parallel to the chopstick on the bottom. Now, with your right index finger, push the tips of the two chopsticks together, so the sticks form a "V." The top chopstick does most of the moving while the bottom chopstick remains stationary in the web of your right hand.

To prevent catastrophic spills, simply hold the bowl of food under your chin. Believe it or not, this is correct etiquette in Asian cultures and in Chinese, Japanese, and Korean restaurants throughout the United States.

When you use chopsticks, is there more food on the tablecloth than either in your mouth or on your plate? Request a fork and knife.

222 How do you conquer chicken with bones?

A. Honestly, it all depends on who's watching.

At a formal dinner, imagine that the ghost of Emily Post is watching your every move, for she may well be. Do not let your fingers do the walking! Resist the temptation to pick up any piece of the chicken with your fingers. Instead, gingerly slice away as much meat as possible off the bone. Leave the rest on the plate.

However, at less formal gatherings, no one's watching you closely. Emily doesn't get out all that much. And it would be a pity to leave food on your plate when there are people starving in . . . well, for one thing, *you're* starving!

Use your utensils *first* to the fullest extent possible. Then finish up with your fingers.

When in doubt, do without. If you are unsure about whether or not an event is formal, always assume that it is (and don't pick up any chicken pieces with your hands).

Don't Be Chicken about Eating Your Chicken

In a casual setting, there is no reason *not* to gnaw everything on your plate. Here is a sensible line of attack:

1. Use the knife and fork to cut off as much chicken as you can from the bird's body. Eat.
2. Proceed to cut the leg, joint, or wing.
3. Hold the piece of bone up to your mouth. Nibble the bone clean.

Condiment Reconditioning 101

If you hail from a large clan where the kids competed for the food on the table, you may need to reset the way you view condiments to "go easy."

Items such as cranberry sauce, salad dressing, ketchup, mayonnaise, hoisin sauce, soy sauce, hot sauce, and sweet and sour sauce are best managed in small doses. Think small. Take small portions on your plate; put small portions on your food; and pop small portions of them into your mouth.

5. *Negotiating Your Way through a Flaky-Crusted Strawberry-Rhubarb Pie*

The waiter trundles out the dessert cart, and you're dismayed to see that everyone on your team wants to partake. Six courses into the meal, and your people are all still ravenous! Were they raised by wolves, you wonder, but quickly discard this cynical thought for one more empathetic. What if your employees only eat out when the company's paying? What if the rest of the time they are absolutely starving to death? Oh, the poor lambs! You overhear your client, his boss, and the HR-Assistant-Who-Only-Wears-Black strike a deal to divide and conquer their Napoleon, New York Cheesecake, and double chocolate sorbet, and decide that you'd better stay to the meal's sweet conclusion. The relationship with this client wasn't built in a day. But it could crumble in a nanosecond.

223 You love strawberry-rhubarb pie à la mode and only wish you had a clue how to eat it. Fork? Spoon? Both?

A. Your choice!

In this particular case, you have a lot of latitude (for which you should have a gratitude attitude).

For strawberry-rhubarb pie solo, you'd use just a fork. For ice cream alone, you'd use a spoon. But for strawberry-rhubarb pie à la mode, you can either use the spoon all by itself or the fork and the spoon together.

Isn't life sweet?

224 You just ordered a stewed pear and can't stop secretly stewing about how to eat it. Any hints?

A. Pretend that your spoon is a knife.

It may sound like something straight out of Lewis Carroll's *Alice's Adventures in Wonderland*. Or it may sound like it comes straight from Never Never Land.

But at a certain point in the evening, the knives retire to the kitchen. And then, the forks and spoons are allowed to take over for them. It's true. It's like a role reversal happening at your tabletop.

Hold the pear in place with your fork (tines, face down) and cut the fruit with the edge of your spoon.

For Extra Credit

Back in the old days (circa ten years ago), forks and spoons used to work together on many more dessert items than they do now. But some things never go totally out of style. It's still perfectly acceptable to use *both* utensils on a dessert item, if you so choose. So, if you want to use a dessert fork to cut your sinful chocolate cheesecake and your dessertspoon to scrape off the dollop of whipped cream on the top, at least you're not committing an etiquette sin. True, people may stare at you and feel that you're high maintenance when it comes to your utensils. But what do they know?

---

225 Your client is like a drug pusher with his drug of choice, sugar. Evilly, he insists that everyone at the table order a dessert—and that's after a gigantic meal. How do you just say, "No"?

A. You can either say, "No, thank you," or just accept the dessert and leave some or all of it.

You don't want to be a pushover, but pushing back too much can have unintended consequences. It's bad business form. It can make you look like an ingrate when your client is just trying to be jovial. He may have had a few drinks, making him even pushier than he is ordinarily.

Most resistance is made sweeter with a bit of whimsy. "I'm afraid I have to pass this time. I'm trying to maintain my girlish figure," will usually work on anyone who's not a relative.

But if it fails to, just take a slice of the calorie-laden temptation and push it around your plate. Your client will feel like you listened to him. And you will feel like you listened to your inner voice that told you the $60 million account was the real dessert.

That's a Wrap

1. When someone requests the bread, it's "first ask, first served." Wait till the basket comes back around to you before you take a slice.
2. Eating lobster is an adventure that should be pursued with the precision of a hunter.
3. It's clever to plan what you'll eat at a job interview dinner before you arrive, particularly if tooth sensitivities or allergies are an issue. Google the restaurant in advance to discover what's on the menu. (But never disclose your field research to the host.)
4. There are two entirely different ways to eat chicken with bones—depending on who happens to be sitting at the table.
5. After the main meal, knives make themselves scarce, and the edges of spoons and forks double as substitutes.

CHAPTER 16
For the Love of Grape:
A Short Primer on Wine, Dessert Liqueur, and Other Liquid Temptations

In wine mythology there are many "old saws." Some may need to be sharpened; others work just fine and should be used to cut through the newfangled jargon that seems to multiply as wine becomes more and more popular.

Saw One: Red wines complement red meat while white wine partners nicely with fowl and fish. Occasionally, there may be a reason to update this time-honored sanctum, but only when doing so helps achieve a more perfect union between the food and wine. You never want one to overpower the other.

Saw Two: White wines are served before red and dry wines before sweet. This rule was developed back in the days when it was commonplace to consume four or five different types of wine during a meal. Your company's T&E budget, not to mention new health concerns about drinking, may determine differently!

Many aspects of wine connoisseurship—from the wine selected to the glass that holds it to the way you raise the glass in your hand—still revolve around temperature.

With wine, as with all aspects of etiquette, the key thing is to refuse to feel intimidated. Remember that waiters, wine stewards, and friendly liquor store owners are all there to help you. So first, resolve to "breathe" just like the wine, and then lift a glass to your newfound knowledge.

1. A Connoisseur's Guide to Squeezing Every Drop of Knowledge out of a Wine Label

Your boss warned you that you would play host this evening. Pity he *failed* to alert you that the new business prospects would all be foodies cum laude just one step removed from oenophiles! The wine steward, a stern looking fellow with a monocle, hands you a leather-bound book and waits for your pronouncement. Thumbing through its plasticized pages, you observe that it's filled with wine labels. Should you suggest a crisp California chardonnay or a white burgundy from France? Or perhaps you should follow the new T&E guidelines and aim for a modest Chilean? You worry that asking the steward for help may be perceived as a sign of weakness and wonder if your prospects for promotion will be crushed faster than an Alsatian grape.

―――――――――――― THE STRAIGHT SCOOP ――――――――――――

French wines are described by the region where the grapes are grown and cultivated. Thus, "Burgundy" and "Champagne" are locales in France with thriving wine industries. French wine labels highlight both the country and region of origin. American wines, by contrast, are described by the grape varietal.

A Wine Orderer's Guide to the Galaxy

The vocabulary is part of the experience of enjoying wine to the fullest. Here are some delicious words to savor:

Aperitif: A wine served before a meal, such as Vermouth.

Crisp: Good acidity, pleasant balance, not sweet.

Dry: No sugar in the wine.

Decant: Pouring wine carefully from a bottle so that the loose sediment at the bottom of the bottle doesn't get mixed into people's glasses by mistake. The wine steward or sommelier decants the wine.

Dessert wines: Muscatel, Madeira, Ports, Sauternes, Sherries.

Reds: Barbaresco (Italy), Barolo (Italy), Burgundy (France), Cabernet Sauvignon (varietal*), Chianti (Italy), Claret (France), Concord (eastern United States), Dao (Portugal), Dolcetto (Italy), Merlot (varietal), Pinot Noir (varietal), Rosé (varietal), Syrah (varietal).

Whites: Cabernet Sauvignon (varietal), Champagne (France), Chardonnay (varietal), Chenin Blanc (varietal), Montrachet (France), Orvieto (Italy), Pinot Grigio (varietal), Pinot Gris (varietal), Pouilly-Fumé (France), Sancerre (France), Sauvignon Blanc (varietal), Semillon (varietal).

Varietal: Term used to indicate a wine made predominantly from a single type of grape.

Vintage: The year in which the grapes were harvested.

* Varietals are grown all over the world.

226 Are you supposed to order wine after you order your appetizer and entrée or before?

A. Order your wine with the meal, but after everyone has selected what he or she will be having.

Wine is supposed to complement food, so your guests' individual meal choices point the way to a pleasant pairing of the two. While the old rules of "red wine with red meat" and "white wine with white meat" still apply, temperature and texture also play a starring role.

Did one of your tablemates order chicken, white fish, or veal? Chilled white wines will bring out the flavors and subtle spices found in lighter fare.

Is one of your honored seatmates eyeing a heavy roast or stew? Red wines, served at room temperature, are heavier than white wines and tend to pair nicely with heavier meals.

What if a guest orders a heavy stew made with a light meat such as chicken? Feel free to ask your waiter for a suggestion, but you are probably justified in ordering *either* white wine or red.

227 You're completely ignorant about wine. Can you ask your waiter for help with your selections?

A. Of course!

There's no need to feel self-conscious about it. Most waiters enjoy helping patrons and are delighted to recommend bottles of wine in a range of different prices.

For better service, compliment the breadth of the wine list (if true), and don't be afraid to engage in a full conversation.

"Does the wine pair nicely with fish?" "Is the wine dry or sweet?" or "Do you have any rich burgundies that are modestly priced?" are all questions that most waiters are trained to answer.

At fancy restaurants, there may even be a sommelier or wine steward to assist you. (Don't forget to tip extra when you solicit help. See "For Your Convenience, A Menu Of Tips On Tipping" later in this chapter.)

228 If you are out to dinner with three other people and they all order food best accompanied with red wine but your meal needs to be paired with white, what is the correct compromise?

A. Order a bottle of red for the table and your white wine by the glass.

This is more like a sacrifice on your part than a compromise. The table has "swung red." It's time to wave the white flag and surrender your wish for a bottle of white to the collective will of the table. Order yourself a glass of white wine and a bottle of red for everyone else to savor and share.

Technically, there should be no difference between wine ordered by the glass and the bottle, but alas, there often is. Wines retain their flavor better when they haven't been uncorked. And the quality of wines that most restaurants reserve for their dinner patrons is usually higher than the swill opened for barflies and "by the glass" wine customers.

But as host, you need to be a good sport and sacrifice your own needs on the altar of your guests' pleasure. (However, if you're concerned about ordering wine by the glass, you can circumvent this by ordering a half-bottle of white for yourself when you order a bottle of red for your colleagues.)

2.   *Every Wine Deserves a Glass to Call Its Own*

Your potential clients are wine guzzlers: They drink wine like it's water. You can't keep up with them, and neither, apparently, can the waiter who dutifully poured the first bottle of white, but left the second bottle chilling nearby. Sitting there, you wonder what the ghost of Emily Post would say about delegating responsibility at this point. Is it the waiter's job to keep the wine flowing, and if so, where is he? Or is wine-pouring one of those new, glamorous tasks that you can now add to your ever-expanding job description? Or should you simply abdicate responsibility and let Mr. Bountiful take care of it? (*Mr. Bountiful* is your pet nickname for the new business prospect who seems to have only one thing on his mind tonight: drinking.)

THE STRAIGHT SCOOP

If the waiter doesn't return to pour the wine, it's the orderer's charge to do it. So that means it *is* your job. Do it like a professional: Fill the white wine glasses three-quarters of the way; fill the red wine glasses only halfway. Think of red wine as a bit more "stressed out" than its white counterpart. Red needs to breathe to become more mellow.

Who Knew?

The largest glass at the table, the water goblet, is set directly above the knives on the right-hand side of the place setting. Next to the goblet on the right is the champagne flute. To the right of this are placed a red or white wine glass and a sherry glass.

229 You're flustered when the host of the charity supper turns to you and asks you to select a wine for his guests. Some of the people at the table have ordered the rubber chicken; others will be eating the stringy steak. Is there one all-purpose wine?

A. No. Pair white wine with white food and red wine with red meat.
Your host may think he's being gallant, but he's being irresponsible. When he asks you to make the all-important wine decision, he's abdicating his responsibility as the MC of ceremonies. A monarch can abdicate his throne; a governor can leave her post earlier than planned; a mayor can extend his term limits, or not. But the host is *always* the host. Don't let your host leave you holding the bottle without your permission!

If you feel confident and wish to order wine for the table, by all means do so. But you needn't feel obligated.

"I'm flattered," you can say, "but wine really isn't my area of expertise. So I am going to turn the decision back to you. I know that whichever wine you choose for us, it will be perfect."

230 How can you tell if a wine has gone bad?

A. Sniff the cork.
Delicately bring the cork up to your nose. Does the cork smell musty or mildewed? Does it smell like moth balls have gotten to it or like anything that may be hanging in Aunt Hildegard's closet?

If the cork smells rank (or splinters into tiny shards in your hand) it's an excellent indication that the wine is past its prime. However, please note: You are only allowed to smell the cork if you are the "designated taster" for the evening.

If your host has tasted the wine and given it his blessing, you're free to either drink it or not. But you can't challenge your host or question his "wine nose" or make him feel badly by suggesting that he return the bottle.

As the expression says, "Put a cork in it."

$\mathcal{231}$ How do you hold a glass of wine, and is it different for red wine than white?

A. Hold a red wine glass by its bowl and a white wine glass by its stem. The next time you hear some old geezer shout, "Nice stems!" consider this: He may genuinely appreciate the sculpted stems of the gorgeous white wine goblets around the table.

White wine is stored at a cooler temperature than its red sibling. Lift a glass of white wine by its stem so that the warmth of your hand won't accidentally warm the wine. You also raise it from its stem so that the wine won't cool your hand by mistake. (You would never want to give any luminary arriving late a chilly reception by shaking his hand with an icy grip.) Etiquette: It can be eminently pragmatic when it isn't downright enigmatic.

Red wine is served at room temperature, so none of the white wine considerations apply. Raise a red wine glass by its bowl. The heat from your hand will help enhance the wine's flavor. Temperature rules!

The Ceremonial Wine Tasting

When the waiter or wine steward brings the bottle for your inspection, first double-check the label to make sure that it's precisely what you ordered. He will pour a tiny sample from the bottle into your glass. If it's red wine, gently swirl it in your glass. Hold your glass by the bowl, and move it clockwise once. This subtle motion allows the wine to breathe and helps unlock its full flavor potential. (If it's white wine, there is no need to swirl. Simply life the glass by its stem.)

Now, delicately sniff the wine and take a sip. Savor the wine in your mouth for a moment before swallowing. If the elixir passes muster, compliment it. "Perfect," you might say to the steward.

Does the wine taste funky or have a moldy smell? Speak now or forever hold your peace. "It tastes slightly off," you might say. If that's the case, the waiter or steward will fetch you another bottle of the same vintage if available, generally without any questions asked.

Please note that the wine not being to your liking is *not* enough of a reason to return it. With red wine in particular, allowing it to breathe may give the wine a more mellow cast. However, if the wine has turned rancid or to vinegar, then you have an obligation to your guests to return it!

3. The A–Z of Dessert Liqueurs, from Crème de Cacao to Crème de Violette

Being a modest drinker, you are secretly peeved when the waiter suggests after-dinner drinks, although you maintain a cordial demeanor suitable for the drinking of cordials. What a surprise! Your clients, all heavy drinkers, order a round of cordials with dessert. Now you're tasting Crème de Violette for the first time in your life, a purple-colored cordial that's the key ingredient in all sorts of cool drinks like "the Aviation" and "Jupiter." "That's my favorite planet," Joe Client whispers drunkenly in your ear, "you've gotta love Jupiter." You finish your drink and signal the waiter, hoping that he'll bring you the check without delay. Half an hour later, you first begin to appreciate the power of purple when the chandelier lights of the room form a purple prismatic pattern on the wall.

232 Is there any distinction between a liqueur and a cordial?

A. Yes. But it's complicated.

You can drink either of them after dinner and not feel embarrassed, so by all means experiment and have fun. Here's a quick download of the main distinctions between the two, so you'll sound like a pro.

Liqueurs are seasoned with herbs, such as sage, mint, aniseed, and caraway. The full list of herbs and proportions used are a state secret. And some liqueurs, such as chartreuse, contain over a hundred ingredients!

Some famous liqueurs include Benedictine D.O.M., Cointreau, Drambuie, Grand Marnier, Kahlua, Bailey's Irish Cream, Amaretto, and Chartreuse. Liqueurs are not usually aged for long periods of time.

Cordials are prepared with fruit pulp or juices and have names like Crème de Banana, Crème de Cassis (black currant), and Crème de Blackberry (not to be confused with an electronic instrument that helps you send email from a mobile device).

The term "crème" means "one of the best," as in "crème de la crème," and doesn't imply the use of cream.

Both liqueurs and cordials are sweet, and the sugar and liquor can pack a punch. Best to sip your after-dinner drink slowly so you won't slip on the floor when you stand to leave the restaurant.

233 Your client loves to drink champagne with the main meal but you can't stomach it. Isn't champagne just for New Year's Eve?

A. Not everyone feels effervescent about champagne, but it's become trendy.

As recently as five years ago, champagne used to be reserved primarily for dessert, although the King of Bubbles would sometimes make a surprise appearance at a particularly festive cocktail party. Today, however, champagne has received some major marketing mojo, and it seems to come out for all sorts of occasions.

If your champagne experience has been confined to a glass of Dom Pérignon once a year as you count down numbers with fifty million people while watching a ball drop, there's a quick way to sound more knowledgeable about it. Simply learn two new words and you can request your champagne "brut" (dry) or "sec" (sweet).

As a general tidbit, pair sweet champagne with sweet foods. Then, you can say, "Sweets to the sweet," and sound *très* literary, as you quote the Queen from Shakespeare's *Hamlet*.

Watercooler Wisdom

The word "toast" derives from an old English custom where a piece of toasted bread would be placed in the bottom of a glass to enhance the flavor of wine or beer. Once the toast was saturated with liquor, the person would swallow the soggy toast.

234 Your boss asked you to give a toast tonight, and you're not exactly a toastmaster. What is the secret to giving a great toast?

A. A toast is not a roast.

Speak from the heart, and everything else will be forgiven.

No one will care if you flub a line if your sentiment is genuine. Strive for a tone of sincere appreciation, and your honored guest will feel admired instead of humiliated. Where most toasts fail is when the person giving the speech aims for humor but fails to attain it.

Humor in toasts is vastly overrated! A great toast brings a tear to the eye rather than a groan to the lips.

Did a worker pitch and secure a prestigious account or extend himself for the sake of the team? Simply thank him from the bottom of your heart.

The world's greatest toasts only last for about a minute or two.

For Extra Credit

Never toast yourself. If someone at the table raises a glass to you, smile, look pleased, and express your sincere thanks. Wait until others have taken a sip in your honor before drinking from your own glass.

For Your Convenience: A Menu of Tips on Tipping

Sommelier—15 percent of the wine bill if he provides service to your table. (Your waiter still receives 20 percent of the cost of the meal, including wine.)

Restroom Attendants—$1 to $2; more if one helps you remove a clothing stain.

Cloakroom Attendants—$2 per coat.

Lunch Counters—20 percent of the cost of the meal.

Bellhops—$5 for carrying one or two bags; more for multiple bags. If he runs a special errand for you—for instance, he picks up a newspaper or suntan lotion at your request—$7 to $10, depending on how long the errand takes.

Bartenders—for drinks when you're not eating in the establishment, $2 per drink.

---

4. *What the Department of Motor Vehicles Doesn't Understand About Your Body's Reaction to Alcohol*

You remember it vividly from your trusty Department of Motor Vehicles' handbook. One glass of wine equals twelve ounces of beer equals one shot of 80-proof distilled liquor. Of course you didn't quite believe it back then, and you surely don't believe it now. While vodka and gin seem to have little impact on your ability to focus, the tiniest bit of wine goes straight to your head and has sometimes even caused an instant migraine! And yet wine is considered more socially acceptable than the "hard" liquors, and sometimes you feel pressured to indulge when dining with clients. You wonder if there's a way that you could teach yourself to hold your liquor better. Isn't there a school for that somewhere?

────────────────── THE STRAIGHT SCOOP ──────────────────

Reactions to alcohol vary widely. Here are some factors that might influence your own reaction:

1. age
2. gender
3. race or ethnicity
4. physical condition (weight, fitness level)
5. use of medications
6. speed with which the alcohol enters your system
7. genetics and/or family history of alcohol-related problems
8. mixing liquors

Keeping Your Head About You When All Are Losing Theirs

There's a lot of confusion out there about whether or not drinking is good for you. The jury is hung on this one—possibly hungover.

Some studies suggest that everyone should have two drinks per night to lower stress. Other studies state that drinking every night will cause liver damage and may cause breast cancer (a stress booster if there ever was one). Beyond pseudoscience, one's alcohol tolerance is a highly individualized thing. One person feels tipsy on one glass of wine. Another person feels sober after six mixed cocktails. Someone may contain her liquor reasonably well but descend into mean as the long night journeys into morning.

As Socrates, ancient Greek philosopher (and probably a sensible drinker), once quipped, "Know thyself."

---

235 If your guest orders an alcoholic drink before dinner, must you?

A. The meal may feel more festive if you do, but don't feel obliged.
You don't have to bend to peer pressure (or "guest" pressure).

Simply use the word "tonight" to help rescue the situation, and spare your guest any pangs of guilt. "I'm not going to order my regular vodka gimlet tonight, Joe, because I'm feeling a bit drained. But I'm delighted to see that you're ordering a drink, and next time, I intend to join you."

THE STRAIGHT SCOOP

There's one big difference between guests and hosts: Hosts rule. If you are hosting, you needn't follow a guest's lead, even if the guest happens to be your client. However, if the client is your host, then, as a matter of courtesy, you should follow his lead. Therefore, if your host does *not* order an alcoholic beverage, you can't either. If the waiter asks you first, you can always demur by turning to your host to ask what he's planning to order. "What are you thinking of having Joe? I'm still trying to decide so why don't you take the lead" will save you from making the wrong decision.

---

236 **Does champagne make you feel tipsier than wine or is that buzzing sound a symptom of your overactive imagination?**

A. Great news! You're not losing your grip on reality.

Carbonation makes you feel fizzy, er fuzzy, faster. Fuzzy Wuzzy was a bear. Fuzzy Wuzzy had no hair. Fuzzy Wuzzy wasn't really . . . Oops! There go the brain cells. Bang! Bang! Bang! It's official: You're plastered.

When mixed with alcohol, carbonated beverages will make you feel drunker faster than fruit juices mixed with the same amount of liquor. A few glasses of champagne will get you buzzed faster than the same amount of wine.

Why Can't a Woman Be More like a Man (When It Comes to Alcohol)?

Men and women may be equal, but equal amounts of alcohol do not hit women and men the same way. On average, women are built smaller than men. Therefore, the identical amount of alcohol can cause a higher blood alcohol concentration in women (due to smaller blood volume).

But hold onto your cordial glass! It gets worse. Most women have more body fat per pound than guys do. Body fat does not contain a lot of water, which would help dilute the alcohol. So here again, the same amount of alcohol causes a higher alcohol concentration in women.

Lastly, women have less ADH in their bodies than men. ADH is the enzyme that helps break down and eliminate alcohol. And that's before you factor in a woman's menstrual cycle, which can radically magnify the way she reacts to alcohol.

Dietary Guidelines for Americans defines moderate drinking as the "consumption of *one* drink per day for women and up to *two* drinks per day for men." [29]

Vicky's Vodka & OJ

I have an unusual habit, or so bartenders from New York to Miami to Los Angeles assure me. I order my screwdrivers light. I ask for orange juice with a citrus-based vodka and request that the bartender "please go light on the vodka."

This has three advantages: 1) I believe that I can order two vodka and oj's during an evening out but only get the "blood alcohol content" of one drink, 2) Bartenders love me because by going light with my vodka, their establishments save money on the margins with my two drinks, and 3) Bartenders remember me because I'm the only patron they've ever met who orders screwdrivers "light." This also helps me receive more attentive service the next time.

---

237 Whenever you drink white wine it gives you the worst hangover. You feel like your head is set to shatter into a million tiny pieces. What's the best cure?

A. The best remedy is not to drink, period. Barring that . . .

Rehydrate, reset, reboot, and reenergize.

Alcohol dehydrates, so replenish the lost liquids with water and fruit juice. Tomato juice contains fructose which helps your body metabolize the alcohol faster. Alcohol also tires you, so allow your body to sleep it off. Take a long nap if you are able, or a cat nap. (Just don't take one at your desk if you're supposed to be working.)

After your nap, kickstart your energy level with food that will give you some get-up-and-go. Is that grease? Indulge in bacon and eggs. They make queasiness vanish and provide protein, plus the "comfort" of feeling alive.

Are you more of a health nut? New studies indicate that asparagus boosts the enzymes in your body that are responsible for breaking down alcohol in your system. (However, asparagus also causes gas, so if your stomach is already feeling unsettled, you may want to lay off the asparagus.) Alleviate your hangover with a sports drink. It will replenish the lost electrolytes in your body.

Depending on your tolerance, you may also want to pop a thousand milligrams of Vitamin C. Take a brisk walk or get thee to a gym if possible. Exercise will detoxify your body and make you feel as if life is worth living again.

―――――――――――― THE STRAIGHT SCOOP ――――――――――――

Some claim that the best cure for a hangover is "the hair of the dog." Alcoholics, mostly. Contrary to wishful thinking, any "new alcohol" entering you body will not help metabolize the old alcohol any faster. So renounce the Bloody Mary for the Virgin Mary.

How to Avoid a Hangover in the First Place

Everyone's body is different, and depending on one's height, weight, and genetic tolerance one person's hangover amulet that "keeps the evil spirits away" (or at least from haunting her the next morning) may not work for someone else. Here are some items to take under advisement.

1. **Tomato juice.** Along with helping your body cycle through the alcohol post-hangover, tomato juice supposedly stops the urge for alcohol in the first place. Garnish with lemon and ice.

2. **Water, water, water.** Dilute the impact of alcohol while drinking by having one glass of water in between each glass of liquor. The idea is to rehydrate while you're dehydrating.

3. **Control your intake.** Drink one alcoholic drink per hour or less.

4. **Adjust for that time of the month.** Women who partake right before their periods often feel tipsier on far less alcohol. When estrogen levels are low, drinking any alcohol tends to pack a bigger wallop.

5. **Never drink on an empty stomach.** If there's nothing there to absorb the alcohol, it is bound to have a bigger impact. Food, water, and fruit juice dilute alcohol and help slow its absorption into the bloodstream by up to 50 percent.

6. **Don't mix liquors.** Tempted to enjoy a cocktail before dinner and wine throughout the meal? You'll feel it more on the "morning after" than if you had just stuck with one liquor.

7. **Avoid sweet drinks and sugary foods with alcohol.** Sugar can speed up alcohol's impact.

8. **Be ageist.** As people age, they are more susceptible to alcohol's influence. If you're no longer twenty-one, stop drinking as if you are.

9. **Pick your poison with care.** A teaspoon of self-knowledge can help you drink more sensibly. Some people have a higher tolerance for light liquors (gin and vodka) than dark (bourbon and rum).

10. **Remember that cheap wine has a steep price.** Inexpensive white wine is responsible for some of the world's most unbearable hangovers. If you order white wine in a restaurant and wake up with a headache that makes you question your will to live, don't order white wine at a similar price point from that establishment again. You'd don't have to be an oenologist to know which wines to stay away from. You can just keep a wine log.

5. You Know You're over Your Limit When . . .

All of a sudden, it hits you with a thud. The sun will come up tomorrow, and when it does, you will have to be at the office, bright and chipper, with at least 40 percent of your brainpower intact. As engaging as these new business prospects happen to be, they are *not* the only people who your company needs to service this week. Your boss, absent tonight, will expect a full, detailed play-by-play of the many scintillating conversations that transpired over the evening. And you will have to pretend to be alive and awake enough to fill him in. What promises were made? Did you discuss any deadlines or next steps? You have a headache the size of King Kong just thinking about tomorrow morning!

238 What's the rule about mixing your own drink at someone else's party?

A. Don't go there.

You may tell yourself that you're just trying to be helpful, but you're not. You may think that you're easing the situation for the other guests, but you're not.

Don't act like the host when you're not.

Do you still feel inclined to pour yourself a drink? Remind yourself that you are not a chimpanzee. In the chimpanzee community, the alpha chimp often changes when another chimp challenges him.

In someone else's home, the host of the party is the "alpha" person, regardless of his personality. The host should never be challenged on his ability to entertain by rude guests, overeager for their liquor fix.

Resolve to be a social drinker instead of an anti-social lush. Just wait your turn like the other guests and nurse all drinks slowly.

> **Who Knew?**
>
> When you drink alcohol, your body immediately attempts to break it down into non-harmful substances, such as water, carbon dioxide, and energy. Ten percent of the alcohol is eliminated through sweat, breath, and urine. Enzymes in your stomach and liver detoxify the rest at a rate of approximately a half ounce per hour (or half a standard drink).

239 You spent $600 on this bottle of 2005 Chateau Lafite Rothschild. But your colleagues are worth it. Is it alright to let your esteemed guests know that you hold them in such high regard?

A. Keep mum about the cost. Or be prepared to pay the price.

You may have more money than God.

You may have inherited Daddy's company or have grown up with platinum spoon in your mouth.

You may spend more on a bottle of wine than one of your employees earns in a week. But it's abominable etiquette to boast about it to your guests. You wouldn't want one of those employees to accidently conk you with that ridiculously expensive bottle, now would you?

240 You're starting to *sssssshlur* your words but don't feel like you can leave the *poddy* until you find your boss . . . or is it your coworker that's lost? How do you say your "So long, farewell" when it's been a *looooong* night?

A. Don't worry about it. Just scram.

Bid "adieu" to the host if you can do so without sliding on the area rug, crashing into a lamp, or otherwise making a spectacle of yourself. But if someone has hinted that maybe you've had too much to drink, take the cue and scramble. No one will ever remember if you slipped out the back. But everyone will recall if you slip on your butt. So if your words are beginning to skid into each other, by all means, take the opportunity to skedaddle like a paddle.

A Swizzle Stick Is Not a Straw

The next time that someone stops you at a networking party and asks you who invented the swizzle stick, boy will you sound smart!

Those skinny sticks propping up the orange, lemon, and lime slices in fancy cocktails were invented by someone named Jay Sindler in 1933.

But why? What caused Sindler to think of developing such an important thing?

As fate would have it, Sindler, an engineer, was seeking a way to extract the olive from his martini without using his fingers. Sindler was granted a patent for his invention back in 1935, and the first swizzle stick had a spear-point on one end. Today, companies often plaster the paddles of swizzle sticks with corporate logos or other designs.

Plastic swizzle sticks are made of two very thin tubes conjoined together. Although they look like "mini straws," one should take care to remember that they aren't. Even after a few drinks. Sipping liquid through a swizzle stick is considered bad form.

That's a Wrap

1. You are allowed some creativity with pairing wine and food, but ye olde "red wine with red meat" and "white wine with white meat" rules still work nicely.
2. Hold a red wine glass by its bowl and a white wine glass by its stem.
3. With rare exception, toasts should be kind and spoken from the heart.
4. Women and men have separate and wholly unequal reactions to the same amount of liquor.
5. If someone suggests that you've had too much to drink, do not pass "Go." Just leave the party quickly, without making a spectacle of yourself.

CHAPTER 17

P's & Q's:

From A to Z to Beyond Taboo

Like a diamond, there are 4C's to etiquette. They are: courtesy, consideration, camaraderie, and class. For those who did not grow up with a sense of noblesse oblige, courtesy must be extended to everyone on the office totem pole—even the Goth girl who treats you as if you're lower than a speck of dust on her keyboard. Phrases such as "please," "thank you," "kindly," "pardon me," and "might I trouble you for" should be on the tip of your (hopefully unpierced) tongue.

Everyone has two dinner partners but only one dance card in a restaurant. You'll be the Fred Astaire of dining once you know the rules: wait for the host to start first, never call the waiter "Sir," or the bartender "Honey."

Resist the urge to interrupt someone's hole-in-one golf triumph, even if you've heard the story six thousand times before. Catching a waiter's eye is no easy feat if he's deliberately ignoring you, but you must never wave at him wildly or leave the table to chase after him.

With a few, easy pointers you will learn how to network like a pro, suffer a bore, and carry yourself with ease and refinement, no matter where business or life happens to take you.

1. Everyone Has Two Dinner Partners but Only One Dance Card

You hate to seem square, but you wish the tables at these trade association dinners weren't always round. At a round table, you're always stuck with two dinner partners. Plus, there's the likelihood that someone directly across from you will lob a conversational zinger in your direction. You're a sitting target. Just once, you wouldn't mind being seated at the end of a very long, rectangular table with tons of empty chairs and only one person that you had to entertain. You really are more of a one-on-one type: a serially monogamous conversationalist. Will you be seated near a bombastic talker or a surly sourpuss who answers in monosyllabic grunts? Hmmm. You wonder what's on the menu tonight.

241 At the association trade dinner, you're wedged in between Boris the Bore and Fascinating Frank. If you have to listen to one more story about how Boris's kid trounced a chess match or received an A in Geography, you will die. It *is* possible to be bored to death! Can't you duck out of talking to Boris, due to your fragile constitution?

A. Sorry, but at a business dinner, it's imperative to give both of your partners equal time.

When you divide, you conquer.

Divide your time evenly between both of your dinner partners, even if one them is more exalted, appears to be the "real decision maker," or is just easier to talk to. On some primeval, unconscious level, business people always know whether you're treating them with respect, so it's imperative that you do.

Is one your seatmates the most tedious person on the planet? Try segueing to a topic that might hold your appeal for longer. You can start by taking his topic and "working it" by trying to make it wider, broader, or deeper.

For example, a story about his child's chess victory could lead you to inquire if the whiz kid happened to inherit the "chess gene" from his dear, old Dad. If the answer is yes, you could probe further and ask if your dinner partner plays chess electronically and how it compares to face-to-face competition. Alternatively, you could mention something about the history of chess (it originated from the two-player Indian war game known as *Chatarung*), or even segue to the fact that you believe executives should think three moves ahead in business as good players do in chess.

Amass enough general knowledge about a broad enough array of topics and conversing with bores isn't quite as deadly as it may seem at first. And that boring guy (who everyone else avoids) can't help but appreciate that he's holding your rapt interest!

―――――――――――――――――― **THE STRAIGHT SCOOP** ――――――――――――――――――

Every time you attend a business dinner of any sort, it's a test. You are being unofficially judged on your dinner decorum—your demeanor, ease, and ability to converse with the other guests. Employ charm, grace, and that magical ingredient known as "mingleability" with every person, and there is no reason why you can't ace this test.

242 After you've chatted with one of your dinner partners, how do you politely direct your attention to the other person?

A. Tell your partner exactly what you are about to do, and then pivot your body thirty degrees.

Begin the meal by conversing with the fascinating person first, so that you guarantee that at least you'll have a little fun. Twenty minutes later, if you have barely communicated with your other dinner partner, it's time to make the "switch."

Be deliberate about it. "I've loved our little chat," you can honestly say. "But I feel as if I have been totally ignoring my other dinner partner! I'm going to spend some time talking to Boris now, and I look forward to circling back to you later."

Then, press both knees together, make a quarter-pivot away from Fascinating Frank, and lavish your attention on Boris.

243 Can't you introduce Boris the Bore to Fascinating Frank and talk to both of them at the same time? Or is three a crowd?

A. You must spend quality time with both of your dinner companions, however that is accomplished.

Being someone's dinner partner is a big responsibility. You have to give him the courtesy of your active attention, and then, when he's not speaking, have enough life material to draw from so that you can add interesting fodder to the conversation. Moreover, you need to steer the interchange *away* from business to the fullest extent possible. Extract every amusing shard of trivia that you can from your partners so you can foster stronger connections between them—if necessary.

Maybe once you tell Fascinating Frank about Boris's chess progeny, Frank will disclose that he once tried to play and was checkmated so quickly he gave up on the game. He may have felt deflated at the time but if he tells the story at your conference dinner, it will make for a lively and memorable evening for everyone concerned. Conversely, if you tell Boris about Frank's tree farm upstate and there seems to be no glimmer of interest, drop it. Don't feel obligated to play "matchmaker" between two people who have absolutely nothing in common. Just be an attentive listener.

2. Let the Napkins Unfurl!

Due to technical difficulties beyond your control, this meal cannot begin. That's because technically, the meal starts when the host places his napkin on his lap, but you'd be willing to wager that *this* host has never used a napkin, period. You wonder why you're standing on ceremony when everyone else is not only sitting on their butts, but texting. Is the HR-Assistant-Who-Only-Wears-Black really scratching her inner ear with the handle of her spoon? When surrounded by colleagues who make cavemen look civilized, is there truly an advantage to playing by the etiquette rules book? And if so, can someone please tell you what it is before you need a walker to get to a dinner like this?

244 The host and one of your colleagues rhapsodize about the history of the world but haven't even reached 1 AD. Meanwhile, your New England clam chowder turns as icy as a northeasterner. Is it okay to start eating even though the host hasn't?

A. It is perfectly reasonable to start, but announce your intention.

"I recently read a fantastic business etiquette book," you can interject, "and it claimed that it was alright to begin eating before the host if one's food was getting cold. I hope you don't mind."

Keep your tone playful, and it may even nudge your host to begin his meal *and* buy this book.

Another gambit is to elect yourself group spokesperson.

"Harry, you don't mind if we all start, do you? The food looks scrumptious, and we've been so looking forward to this dinner."

245 The shirt that you're wearing cost one month's salary. Surely everyone will understand if you just tuck your napkin into your collar to protect your investment, right?

A. GONG!

If restaurants were allowed to expel customers for D-etiquette, this sartorial no-no would top the list. Never tuck your napkin into anything—a collar, waistband, or belt loop. However, in the interest of avoiding serious spillage, feel free to shun certain exasperating-to-eat food items such as drippy oysters, water-drenched clams on the half shell, squirting cherry tomatoes, spaghetti smothered with tomato sauce, onion soup, shelled lobster, game hens, small birds, lettuce, peas, fish with bones, and artichokes.

(Do you despise food restrictions with a passion? No worries. See Chapter 14, 3. *Utensils You Only Wish Had Never Been Invented* and Chapter 15.)

On Retaining Your Equanimity During a Spill

Spilled food needn't spoil the evening, especially if you can stay serene about it.

Did you drop a piece of food? Neatly pick up as much as you can with your clean spoon or your knife. Then wet a corner of your napkin in your handy water glass and dab the spot. (If a substantial amount of food spills, call the waiter because the tablecloth may need to be changed or at least covered with linen napkins.)

If you spill more than a drop or two of wine, signal the waiter immediately. Did you spill food on one of the other diners? Offer your hapless victim a sincere apology and offer to pay his dry cleaning bill. If he doesn't take you up on this immediately, follow up in a few days and politely insist.

246 You're expecting a very important call from Hong Kong and don't want the ringtone to disrupt everyone else's meal. Yet you feel obliged to take the call if and when it comes. What is the etiquette of tucking your iPhone into your napkin, so that no one will see it on your lap?

A. Poor. Keep your phone in your pocket.

Put *nothing* on top of your napkin or under it. Your napkin needs to stay unencumbered.

At a formal dinner, wait for the host or guest of honor to pick up his napkin and place it on his lap. Follow his lead. Don't whip out your napkin like a boomerang that you expect to come back and land on your lap. There is no "wrist" action whatsoever. Gently pick up your napkin and place it, *folded lengthwise*, on your lap.

The napkin rests on your lap throughout the meal unless you must excuse yourself to use the lavatory or take a call.

Do you need to use the restroom? Place the napkin on your chair with a minimum of fuss. When you leave the restaurant, fold the napkin loosely (hiding any stains you created) and place it to the left of your plate.

A Napkin Is	A Napkin Is Not
1. A cloth for protecting one's lap.	1. A bib for protecting one's shirt.
2. A signal from the host that the meal is about to start.	2. A white flag to commandeer the waiter's attention.
3. Placed on your chair, a sign that you're coming back.	3. A sponge to mop up spills.
4. Gently folded and placed on the table to the left of your plate, a sign that the bill has been paid and you're leaving the restaurant.	4. An oil blotter for makeup.
	5. A washcloth on a hot day.
	6. An eyeglass cleaner.
	7. Kleenex.
	8. A "doggy bag" for the bread.

Never Complain, Never Explain

You've probably seen the saying stitched on a pillow somewhere: "Never complain, never explain." It sounds like a cute rhyme, but at a business dinner, this homily to stiff upper lipism turns out to be excellent advice. Even if the bouillabaisse arrives stringy and the string beans are overcooked and lifeless, never complain about the food in front of those with whom you work or you'll seem like a whiner. Never "explaining" too much also makes sense at a business dinner. Unless the call you're waiting for has a direct, positive impact on your dinner companions, there's no purpose in discussing it in excruciating detail. Put your mobile phone on "vibrate" and if it goes off during dinner, just smile apologetically, quickly place your napkin on your chair, and scoot out of the dining room so that you can take the call outside without disturbing others. When you return to the table, a simple, "So sorry. This time, it couldn't be helped," should suffice. And then be sure to turn your phone off.

3. How to Catch a Waiter's Eye Without Knocking over a Wine Glass

In an ideal world, your waiter would lavish your table with the perfect amount of attention. Whenever your wine glass ran dry, he would magically reappear to replenish it—like a genie with a bottle. Should you arrive at the restaurant famished, he would intuit it and instantly place a menu in your hand while recounting the sumptuous specials. But on those evenings when you required more "alone time" with a client, your waiter would also know to hold off on all verbal interruptions until you were good and ready. Alas, most waiters are not psychic and are far more concerned with turning tables than making certain your business dinner goes off without a hitch. That's where strong communication skills can come to your aid. It often helps to understand the restaurant hierarchy and to be on superb terms with the gatekeeper.

247 Your sleepy, local hole-in-the-wall just received a glowing review in *The New York Times* and tonight the place is jampacked. The last time you stopped by, you were treated like royalty. Now they can't seem to recall your face, stranger. Any way to spur their memory into giving you the service you deserve?

A. Try the Miami Squeeze. (You don't have to be in Miami for it to work wonders.)

There's nothing quite as alluring as lucre for staving off temporary Alzheimer's. Executed smoothly, the Miami Squeeze will remind the busiest Maitre d' who you are and may help you get seated considerably faster.

Named after the protocol required in one of Miami Beach's most popular restaurants ("Joe's Stone Crab"), this tipping technique may nudge the Maitre d' to "find an open table" for you that he wasn't aware of before. Voila! What a miracle! It helps to execute this move with confidence, so you may want to practice it a couple of times in your living room before taking it out in public.

Remove a $20 bill from your wallet. Fold it in half. Then refold it, so that the amount shows on both sides. Slip the small square into the palm of your right hand and shake the Maitre d's hand. When you do, say something excruciatingly polite, such as, "I *raved* about your restaurant to my colleague who flew all the way from Paris to try your sumptuous foie gras tonight. Do you think that you might be able to seat us? He's elderly, and . . ."

248 Simmer down, please! There are seventeen people, all drunkenly singing "Row, Row, Row Your Boat" at the table next to yours. You can't even hear yourself think, much less what your client is saying. What do you do?

A. Ask your client if he wants to move to a different table. If he nods his head "yes," follow Reverse Restaurant Protocol.

If you must switch tables for any reason, tell the *first* person who approaches your table to send over the Maitre d' immediately. The first person will most likely be a lowly busser rather than a server. That's fine. Never wait for your server to arrive; it's imperative for someone to relay to the Maitre d' that you're unhappy as soon as possible so that your table switch won't bog down the traffic flow for all of the other patrons waiting for tables.

The busser may well send the server over instead. Bussers don't always speak flawless English and yours may have misunderstood your request. Don't get flustered. Just politely persist and ask for the Maitre d' again. When the Maitre d' arrives, be candid about your reasons for wanting to relocate.

"I enjoy the song 'Row, Row, Row Your Boat,' " you might say, "but not over dinner. What other tables do you have right now?"

If the Maitre d' claims that he has nothing available at the moment, negotiate to stay at your table through appetizers and then "switch" at the earliest opportunity. With any luck, those rowdy camp fire singers at the table next to yours will be rowed out by the time your new table is ready and you won't even need to move, but don't count on it. At fine restaurants that care about attracting repeat business, the Maitre d' may try to make it up to you later with a free dessert on the house or a free drink. Even if you are on a diet and counting every last calorie, be gracious. Accept the freebie as a token of his goodwill.

Why a Restaurant Is like a Hungarian Seven-Layer Cake (and Why It Isn't)

Like a Hungarian Seven-Layer Cake, there are seven layers to most restaurants. But unlike a Hungarian Seven-Layer Cake, the layers in a restaurant are all different.

Slaving away at the bottom are the bussers, who are the first to approach your table with water and a bread basket. Directly above the bussers on the food chain are the servers. In upscale eating establishments, there may also be a captain or head waiter. (If one person takes your order and another person serves, the first is the captain or head waiter and the second is the server.) The Maitre d' is the person who seats you. There may also be an Owner (who you may never encounter—a lot depends on the type of restaurant and how often you visit).

The other two layers may consist of a sommelier, or wine steward, and the chef who runs the kitchen staff. If the establishment has a liquor license there will also be a bartender, who, like the servers, reports to the Maitre d'.

249 **Is it okay to snap your fingers at the waiter if yours happens to be ignoring you?**

A. Only if you want your waiter to shun you for the rest of the night.

Silence is golden. It also happens to be the best way to get a waiter's attention.

Catch his eye and signal with your hand, with your index finger or first two fingers pointing up.

If his back is facing you, say, "Waiter," in a pleasant tone or politely ask another restaurant employee to get your server for you. Snapping your fingers is wildly insulting! Be kind to the people who wait on you or they may serve you real beer instead of virgin, caffeinated coffee instead of decaf, and yesterday's bread basket.

Kings in ancient courts had "tasters" to test their food. You don't. What's in that lentil soup anyway?

Hey There!

It's okay to call a waitress "Miss," but it's not okay to call a waiter "Sir," and never scream, "Hey there," or, "Yoo-hoo, over here!"

---

4. *Nolo Interruptus, and Other Keen Observations by Cicero*

In your estimation, there's nothing remotely entertaining about entertaining a client. "Travel and Entertainment" should be renamed "T&T" for "Travel and Torture." Your boss, rosy-eyed optimist that he is, expects you to close a deal tonight. Meanwhile, your client waxes prolific about extreme sports and his undying love for lemon meringue pie of all things. You haven't even slugged your way through the stuffed artichoke appetizer, and already you're feeling rather perturbed about tonight's outcome. The Sauvignon Blanc must be playing tricks with your head: Your client can't really be *this* boring, can he? You struggle to think of five topics to discuss, just in case your client ever deigns to let you speak as you guzzle your libation like liquid comfort food. You consider asking someone to fetch your waiter who hugs the far reaches of the cavernous room like a bat. At least doing so would break your client's monologue about—whatever it is he's meandering on about.

The Art of Conversation According to the World's First Self-Help Author

Who was the first self-help author? Dale Carnegie wrote a great book back in the 1930s. Benjamin Franklin also penned some bon mots about engaging people. But Cicero, writing back in 44 BC, wrote down a list of rules that have endured for eternity. His dictates:

1. Speak clearly.
2. Speak easily but not too much, especially when others want their turn.
3. Do not interrupt.
4. Be courteous.
5. Deal seriously with serious matters and gracefully with lighter ones.
6. Never criticize people behind their backs.
7. Stick to subjects of general interest.
8. Do not talk about yourself. (Of course, in a job interview situation, you may very well be expected to talk about yourself.)
9. Never lose your temper.
   It's hard to find a better set of rules to converse by anywhere.

---

250 Is there any polite way to interrupt a blowhard?

A.   Think of a clever segue.

Cicero, no doubt a fantastic dinner companion, said it best: "Nolo interruptus." In Latin, it means, "Don't interrupt." Cicero scribbled these legendary words back in 44 BC. Interrupting has been annoying people for over two thousand years!

However, even Cicero probably wouldn't object to a good segue. Is your client rhapsodizing about the virtues of lemon meringue pie again? Why not try a clever verbal zig zag to the topic that *you* want to discuss?

"Well, going forward, I'll certainly know that your favorite dessert is lemon meringue pie! And speaking of lemons, I thought our firm really turned lemons into lemonade for you on the GHI project. Despite all odds, Clarissa pulled out all of the stops and managed to turn a handsome profit. I hope you're as impressed as I was."

And then listen to what he has to say.

(Please note: Segueing to a business discussion is really only appropriate as your dinner heads towards dessert. But you can always segue to a general interest topic. See Chapter 18 for more details.)

251 **Your client is on a tirade about how unhappy he is with your company's performance. Pity you're in a four-star restaurant and everyone is staring your way. Should you let your client blow his gasket in public or quickly try to retire to more private quarters?**

A. Let him blow, and hopefully it will blow over.

There could be several reasons why your client is yelling at you in front of an audience, seemingly oblivious to the concerned stares from strangers.

Perhaps he grew up in an abusive home and perceives that raising his voice to unacceptable levels is completely "normal." Perhaps he's a bit hard of hearing and just wants to be positive that you hear him out (no problem there . . . everyone in the restaurant can). Or perhaps he's just a screamer—someone who deliberately squawks as an obnoxious negotiating tactic.

Regardless of his motivation, it's best to just listen to his rant. If you can stay placid, this is normally your best course of action. Try to uncover what his real problem is with your firm, and if it helps him calm down, gently rephrase once the outburst has passed.

"Tomorrow, I'll tell Stanley that you were colossally disappointed with our turnaround time on your project and ask if there's any way for the firm to make it up to you . . . Does that sound alright?" When your cantankerous client nods, gracefully attempt a subject change to a more neutral topic far removed from business. How about those Knicks?

252 You googled your client before you met with him, discovered he was really into backgammon and boomerang-throwing, and came prepared with five relevant stories. But every time you try to broach his hobbies, he refuses to discuss them and seems determined to talk about business instead. What's going on?

A. Scratch everything you learned, and start fishing.

Google makes it so easy to research anyone that, admittedly, it's tempting to use the knowledge to press forward. But when you already know everything there is to about a person, it can sometimes backfire. Your natural curiosity is diminished since you can anticipate exactly what the prospect will say. Under these circumstances, even questions about his interests can seem "canned."

If none of your conversational gambits seem to be working, try asking your client something fairly banal, such as "What did you do today?" or another open-ended question that he'll have no trouble answering.

Open-ended questions that tease out information are better for sparking conversations than questions which can be answered with a simple "yes" or "no," such as, "Did you have a nice day today?"

For Extra Credit
Where does a woman's handbag go?
A) On the table
B) Dangling off the perimeter of her chair
C) Sitting with her on the chair
D) On the floor, slightly under her chair
Answer: C or D.

5.   Please Don't Do This in a Restaurant (or if You're Going to, Let Me
*   Know in Advance so I Can Cancel My Reservation)*

If you ever take a client to another restaurant without checking it out beforehand, you will hand a gun to someone in HR and beg her to shoot you.
Your client insisted on Mexican food, and ordinarily that would have been
lovely. But this particular establishment hustled you both into the dreaded,
teeming room for out-of-towners. On your right, a family of six squeezes
into a table for four. On your left, a young, mop-haired couple French kiss,
oblivious to the disgusted stares of gawking strangers. The family presses
into your fifteen square inches of precious space, practically stuffing their
coats and backpacks onto your lap. You feel like a piñata that's about to
burst and you haven't even savored your first beef taco yet.

253   **The couple next to you on the banquette fondles one another**
breathlessly. Alas, their tablecloth isn't hiding quite as much
action as they think. Is there any way to throw some cold
water on them (metaphorically, that is)?

A. Make a joke.

If you can somehow tie their errant behavior to the purpose of the meeting
at hand (yours, not the woman's at the table next to you), you will gain
mastery over the situation. "While things are heating up on our left," you
might say to your client with a wink, "let me tell you why our company is so
passionate about your new project."

> ### Why This Technique Works

Hanky panky is a natural subject for humor. And retaining your good
humor is often the key to preserving a client's good will. He can't fail to be
impressed on three counts: 1) instead of feeling awkward about the situation, you turned it around to your company's advantage, 2) you stayed
focused when all around you were distracted, and 3) you demonstrated
sprezzatura in spades. *Sprezzatura* is an Italian word from Castiglione's *The*

Book of the Courtier, defined as "a certain nonchalance, so as to conceal all art and make whatever one does or says appear to be without effort and almost without any thought about it."[30]

(However, if you can tie the couple's behavior to a general interest topic that's *not* business-centric, you're a true etiquette black belt. See Chapter 18 for inspiration.)

254 It's date night with a twist. The blue-haired couple two tables down from you verbally spar. She accuses him of doing who-knows-what to she-knows-who. He defends his innocence, and their decibels rise. Should you and your client both try to escape from their emotional earthquake?

A. Stay where you are and count to ten.
Don't humiliate the quarreling couple further by requesting a seat change. Chances are, one of them will leave soon enough of his or her own volition. And once that happens, peace will rein once more, and you and your client can return to the business at hand. While you're waiting for order to be restored, you might try some banal banter. These days, movies that *don't* feature Meryl Streep are a pre-approved conversational topic. (See Chapter 18 for more.)

255 Your client is a check-haggler. He's whipped out his trusty calculator to re-tabulate the bill. Should you stop him?

A. To quote Shania Twain's brilliant epigram, "Don't be stupid."
You may feel like telling your client that it's impossible to dine in this town for a song. But it's better to refrain. After all, if this is his modus operandi, there's nothing you can do to change it.

He will always be the type to nitpick, find small errors, and celebrate over miniscule savings. But when you indulge his pet peeve, either outcome is a win-win from your perspective.

Should he find a mistake on the check, he will feel even more fondly about his dinner with you. He was the brilliant mathematician who spent fifteen minutes at the end of the meal to save fifteen cents!

And, should he fail to find anything amiss, then he can only believe that you brought him to a very fine establishment that would never cheat him. Just sit back, relax, and smile, no matter which outcome occurs.

Who Knew?

A pet peeve is a minor annoyance that an individual happens to find more grating than others seem to. Your client's propensity to comb through checks seeking errors should be treated like a pet peeve. Coo over his idiosyncrasy and say something charming about it, the way you would if he introduced you to a real pet, rather than a pet peeve.

That's a Wrap

1. You must give both dinner partners equal time even if doing so bores you for half of the meal.
2. You may start eating before your host, but you must announce your intention in a good-natured manner.
3. If you need to switch tables, do it as soon as possible to avoid disrupting the pleasure of other diners.
4. Let sleeping dogs lie, but let screaming clients rant. Listen well and you may be able to avoid far worse collateral damage.
5. There's nothing that you can do to change other people's appalling restaurant behavior.

CHAPTER 18

How to Have a Conversation with Almost Anyone About Practically Anything

When wining and dining a client, you can't afford to reach for the wrong wine glass or nosh from the wrong bread plate. You also don't want to choke on an item that's supposed to be effortless, but in fact requires a ton of advance preparation to make it seem so—conversation.

The ability to converse with anyone can be compared to a muscle. Let the muscle atrophy and your conversation will be flabby and shapeless. You will find yourself at the mercy of bores and challenged when it come to talking to those with whom you have little in common.

But exercise the muscle and work it out occasionally, and your conversation will attain stamina and beauty. Others will seek you out for your wise insights, your degree of engagement, and for how much life experience you bring to a project.

Underneath the innate talents we all have for our jobs is the sheer ability to get along with people. And two-way conversation is one key to doing so.

This chapter will impart some of the secrets of charisma and charm, two pillars of scintillating conversation. You will also learn the secrets of active listening and enforced optimism, which are the other two pillars.

1. 26 Pre-approved Conversational Topics in Alphabetical Order

Whenever you find yourself in a conversation with your teammates, you feel like changing the subject. Business of late is too depressing to talk about with all of the new layoffs at the company. The hiring freeze isn't thawing anytime soon; and these days, the HR-Assistant-Who-Only-Wears -Black bears an uncanny resemblance to the Grim Reaper. No one at your office has taken anything but a *staycation* in over six months. Collectively, everyone is in a rut. You know these Thursday night team dinners are supposed to boost morale, but if everyone's in a quagmire, how are you all supposed to rescue each other? Group therapy might do it, but you're pretty sure that your boss won't let you put in for it. Just a hunch.

256 You've heard that at a business dinner, you're not supposed to discuss business until dessert. What are you supposed to talk about?

A. For your dining pleasure, here's an alphabetized list.

Astronomy, Bicycling, Calligraphy, Deep-Sea Diving, English Royalty, Fly Fishing, Global Warming, Harley-Davidson motorcycle clubs, iPhone applications, Jingles, Karma, Latinate Words in Crossword Puzzles, Macrobiotic Diets, Nano Technology, Origami, Paradoxes, Quilting, Restaurants, Sculpture Gardens, Travel Taken for Pleasure, Uranus's Preeminence Since Pluto Was Downgraded from Planet Status, Vineyards, the X-men, Yoga, and *Zen and the Art of Motorcycle Maintenance.*

Yes, the letter W was skipped. Good catch. There is always the Weather Girls, Waterloo (the battle of and the song by ABBA), and Western film genres.

257 What about a client dinner? Can't you talk about business at the start of the meal?

A. No. Try not to fatigue the clients.

Surprisingly being "all business" at a business dinner is a brutally bad business strategy. Usher some pleasure into the experience.

When you introduce business into the conversation, you make the client work way too hard. Instead of bonding with you, he's sitting there thinking what a drag it is to talk to you. "Why did I ever agree to meet with this bore during my off-hours?" he wonders.

Don't bring up any business before dessert. Talk about something else.

258 You know that you're not supposed to talk about sex, politics, and religion at a meal. Are there any other taboo topics?

A. Divorces, bereavements, and these days, impending layoffs and furloughs.

Don't bring doom out to dinner or his partner gloom. They may go hand in hand, but neither is conducive to a positive business outcome. Especially at the beginning of a new venture, it's helpful to keep the conversation upbeat and convivial. You don't want to seem superficial, but you also don't want to depress your guests.

Suppose a key player at your firm was recently let go. You feel badly about it. Maybe you were even the person who pulled the trigger. You recognize that your client will be upset and so you feel justified in raising the topic at a business meal, hoping you can surface it, quickly clear the air, and dispense with it. Big mistake!

You let the proverbial puma out of the wine bottle and what happens? Your client spends the next hour kvetching about how your firm has turned into a "revolving door," while you sit there frantically ruminating about how to change the subject.

That's easy. Don't bring up the subject in the first place!

THE STRAIGHT SCOOP

Brush up on local events, but let someone else raise them. Try to keep the conversation feather-light and sparkling.

---

2. *Ten Totally Taboo Subjects under Any Circumstances*

Personally, you don't care if someone is bipolar, bisexual, or biodegradable. But others do, and lately, the gossip swill has been particularly acidic. Late hours, intense deadlines, and third quarter results that fell painfully shy of expectations have added a new bite to the chatter. The Watercooler Wag insists on full disclosure: You now know every med that your assistant Ashley consumes. (You'd never dispute the Watercooler Wag's powers of observation; when her lips are attached to that watercooler, she sees all!) You just wish there were a way to pull the team together so that instead of carping about each other, you were all urging each other onto greatness.

 Two company interns jabber nonstop about sports. Are they being rude or is it your responsibility to learn the subtle difference between basketball and baseball?

A. Both.

The average person is "long" on approximately five topics, and one of them is usually a spectator sport. Avoiding all discussion of spectator sports is like trying to avoid air. You can do it, but you'd have to live in a bubble.

So take a deep breath. With some strategic skimming, you can unearth some common conversational ground.

If you know for a fact that two people on your team are into sports, you can devote sixty seconds of your precious day to learning something about this alien topic. Surely you can spend one whole minute on this noble endeavor!

Pick up the sports section of your local paper. Yes, it may look foreign to you, but observe: It's written in English. Skim two articles and vow to spend no more than thirty seconds on each. Then, the very next time that you pass one of the sports groupies in the hallway, simply force yourself to comment on the article you read. "I hear your favorite team cleaned up yesterday. Congratulations."

If he stares at you in shock, smile. It may take him awhile to adjust to the "new you," but he'll get used to it.

Why This Technique Works

People are conditioned to pick up all sorts of vibes and signals that we don't even realize we're sending. Let's assume that your stunned officemate recognizes that you're not into sports. When you reach out to him in this way, on some primal level he'll appreciate that you made an extra special effort to bond with him. You've agreed to meet him in his conversational comfort zone instead of forcing him to meet you in yours. Further, you've congratulated him for being associated with a winning team. That makes him feel like a winner too.

How to Raise the "S" Word (Sports) When You Don't Know Sssh! About It

Don't be put off by colleagues who are interested in different hobbies than you. There are thousands of hobbies and three hundred million people in the United States. By definition, not everyone can share the same interests! That's what makes horse racing. And basket weaving. And fencing. And—well, you get the basic idea.

Instead of secretly bristling with resentment whenever the topic of sports arises among your officemates, consider if there's a way to tag onto their interests in a manner that you'll find palatable. For example, you might suggest a team outing to a sports bar after work one night. While the sports zombies gaze unblinkingly at the gigantic thirty-inch TV screen, you can quietly order a drink or watch right along with them and actually learn something! You'll get credit for having the team-building, morale-boosting idea. Plus, next time, it will be easier to discuss a topic so many leagues outside of your comfort zone.

260 Your colleague has put on forty pounds in three months. You assume that she must be pregnant. There could be no other reasonable explanation! Is it alright to confirm your suspicion?

A. No. Wait till she brings it up.

Most women will not take kindly to your asking, even if turns out that your presumption was correct.

If you're right, the woman in question may be waiting to discuss it with her supervisor before uploading it onto the office *RumorTube*. Or she may not think that she's showing—and BOOM!—your query just disabused her of that notion! Or she may not feel like she knows you well enough to discuss some of the logical follow-up questions, such as who will replace her during her leave, how long she'll be away, and while we're on the subject, who's the Dad?

If you're wrong about her "showing," it's a Jupiter-sized gaffe. You've let her know that she looks fat. And chances are, she's not going to appreciate your honesty.

261 Someone has the unmitigated gall to ask you your age. When you refuse to answer, he says, "Alright. When did you graduate from college?" What's the correct response for a nosy parker?

A. "That's privileged information. Only my mother knows for sure."

It's not PC to say it, but we live in an ageist society where plenty of people discriminate against older workers. This prejudice, while illegal, frequently prevents people from getting hired and promoted. And these days, men are just as likely to be tarred with the ageist label as women. In many cases, gray hair, real or metaphorical, will not help you get ahead. And in some industries, it will hold you back.

But you can do your part to nip this pernicious habit in the bud.

If someone asks your age, tell him as nicely as you can muster that it's none of his business. The trick is to say something that, while charming, hopefully stops the inquiry. (Please note that the answer given here is appropriate for ageist questions that arise on the job but is *not* ideal for job interview situations. On a job interview, you need to employ extra special moxie to halt the inquisition or simply answer the question and move on.)

In Memory of My Great Aunt Lynne

When my great Aunt Lynne died, she had a different age written down on all of her documents. It wasn't some mistake that happened when she first arrived in this country because she was born and raised here. Some in my family attributed Lynne's alternate ages to a deliberate act of vanity on her part. She *must* be vain, they reasoned, because she looked so damned amazing for her age—whatever age that was.

Lynne looked like a taller, realer version of Doris Day and was by far the most glamorous woman I have ever met. She had platinum hair that she wore swept into a saucy up-do, long, springy, black false eyelashes that she plastered on every single day (that would constantly fall into her eyes) and ice-blue contact lenses. She had three husbands (my great uncle was her third) and legs chiseled like a Rockette's. Her sister Trixie actually *was* a Rockette.

I once asked Lynne how old she was and was surprised when she told me that nobody knew—not even my great uncle. As a six-year old, I found this fascinating. "But doesn't he ask?" I said, incredulous at my great uncle's lack of curiosity.

"He asks," she said with a wink, "but that doesn't mean I tell him."

"Well what about at the office?" I said. "Don't they ask?"

"Honey, I work in the fashion industry," she said by way of explanation.

Whenever I teach a career seminar, inevitably someone in the audience will raise the current obsession with age.

"Do you think that ageism exists in the workplace?"

"Someone asked me how old I was during a phone interview. What *should* I have said?"

"Is it alright to Botox one's resumé?"

At that moment, I always remember how my Great Aunt Lynne resolved to keep everyone guessing.

The Taboo Topics

1. **Business**—before dessert.
2. **Sex**—your sex life; other people's sex lives; the scandalous lives of politicians and celebrities.
3. **Politics.**
4. **Religion.**
5. **Sexual orientation**—i.e., asking someone if he's straight, gay, or bisexual.
6. **Meds**—yours and other people's.
7. **Sports**—to the exclusion of all other topics. It's fine to discuss sports in teaspoon-sized doses.
8. **Pregnancy**—especially if you're not 100 percent certain that someone is pregnant. Better to wait until *after* the baby is born.
9. **Age**—how old someone is; what year she graduated from college; when she got married; how old she was when she had her kids; and other telltale markers of the passage of time.
10. **Gossip**—yours and other people's.
11. **Firings, Furloughs, Layoffs**—both past and impending.
12. **Death**—with some exceptions. If someone at the office dies, it is appropriate to collectively mourn his passing. Parental deaths are acceptable conversational fodder, particularly if a parent's passing means that you will need to take time away from the office.

3. Why Sex Is Overrated (as a Topic)

Your boss reminds you of a schoolboy with an overactive libido. When he's not regaling the table with stories about his ex-wives, he's opining on more current conquests. You would love to give him a trophy for "Most Boring Boss Alive," but know that he wouldn't even mind provided the trophy was phallic enough. Sometimes a trophy in the shape of a cigar is only a trophy in the shape of a cigar. Carefully tearing off a piece of bread and buttering it, you settle in for another recounting of how he stole his second wife from her third husband, only to eventually divorce the poor woman for his third wife, Mrs. Satan. You've heard of "kiss and tell." This is "kiss and retell and retell and retell."

262 **Can other people's sex lives ever be titillating fodder for conversation? What if a governor gets involved in a scandal and it's splashed across all of the newspapers?**

A. There's a small window of opportunity to air it, but after that the window is closed.

Sex: It's such a yawn!

Underlying all sex scandals, there is a lurid sameness.

Should you choose to focus on some sizzling item from the tabloid pages, force yourself to maintain a healthy distance from whatever the underlying issue is. Remember that you're talking about the politician's personal life and not your own.

Jonathan Swift on the Art of Conversation

He was a poet, a satirist, and probably a great conversationalist. Swift compared conversation to carving a roast in a gentleman's house with this captivating stanza:

> *Give no more to every guest*
> *Than he's able to digest.*
> *Give him always of the prime,*
> *And but little at a time.*
> *And that you may have your due,*
> *Let your neighbor carve for you.*

263 You've heard that gossip is a no-no, but if Penelope and Sam really don't want others to jabber about them, perhaps they should stop getting it on in the office supply closet?

A. Don't drink from the office swill or it may come back to bite you.

In a way, things were easier back when people could select their office vice of choice: smoking, drinking, picking up someone at the office to date (or marry), or gossiping about others.

Now it's illegal to smoke anywhere inside an office and liquid lunches are a thing of the past. Laws on sexual harassment have made it challenging to ask an officemate for a date. That leaves one big vice—gossiping—and everyone's doing it with abandon.

Gossiping about others makes you seem small, petty, mean-spirited, and bored. To an eagle-eyed supervisor, it makes you look as if you have way too much time on your hands. If you don't have anything better to talk about than Penelope and Sam's love fest, please put this book down, leave the office immediately, and go get a life!

264 You and your paramour have been keeping your intra-office love affair bottled up for months and the stress is nearly killing you. There's no policy at your company against intra-office dating. Can you both pursue a full disclosure policy like they do on certain TV shows?

A. Not unless you want to make others ill.

This may come as a shock, but most colleagues won't view your affair kindly regardless of company policy. You're worried that they're ogling you or imagining how you both look naked while getting it on. But instead, they're wondering how your affair may influence your salary and title. Are you receiving juicer assignments as a result of your assignation? Are you being treated more favorably by the powers-that-be? Even if you're dating a coworker from a different department, those in the know are likely to view the alliance with derision. After all, you and your love interest *have* an alliance while the rest of the folks just have to prove themselves on merit.

4.   *How to Extract a Conversation from a Local News Story*

"What did you think about that article in *Time* magazine?" your father used to ask at the dinner table, staring down at you with his professorial eye. Ever since, you haven't been into pop quizzes and despise putting others on the spot. Yet, to your father's point, you *do* wish the people on your team would crack open a magazine once in awhile. Their ideas seem so yesteryear; and that can't be beneficial for business. Your company is supposed to be on the cutting edge. Instead, it's teetering on the edge of a very blunt ice skate. And, clearly, Facebook is wholly responsible. You honestly believe that no one reads anything except their Facebook posts, speaking of which—it's been two whole hours since you last checked yours!

265 **Your boss behaves like he's one of the talking heads on Fox News. Whatever the topic—gridlock, local taxes, schools, national security—he has the solution and is keen to tell the client all about it. Should you let your boss wax poetic, or try to interrupt him?**

A. **Try to redirect—especially if you believe that his opinions are contrary to your client's.**

When your team is holed up together in the office or on a road trip, your boss is the most important person. Does he love to climb on the soapbox? There's nothing wrong with being an enthusiastic member of his audience.

You can listen, laugh, and even cheer him on if you happen to agree with his worldview. You can be his Greek chorus.

But when a client is with your group, suddenly the *client* is the most important person in the room while your boss is temporarily "demoted." Is your boss getting swept away by the fumes of his own voice? Be sure to glance at the client every so often to gauge his reaction.

If the client seems to be enjoying your boss's performance, hold off on all interruptions, because as Cicero noted, interrupting is rude. But if your client seems miffed with your boss's viewpoint, it is a good idea to gently steer the conversation to a more neutral topic. Seek a convenient segue.

"Your views on gridlock are really interesting, Stanley. On a completely unrelated note, I was wondering if you might help me get unstuck? I can't decide whether to order the halibut or the squid. Do you have any thoughts for me?

Why This Technique Works

Some people are better talkers and some are better listeners. When your boss is on a talking jag, it's especially important to listen with your eyes—to what your client *isn't* saying. Never pierce anyone's eyes, but do try to keep casual tabs on your client's facial expressions especially during someone else's monologue.

Watercooler Wisdom

Margaret Shepherd, author of *The Art of Civilized Conversation*, says: "Never speak uninterrupted for more than four minutes at a time." If you are the only person who still has a full plate of food, stop talking!

266 Your underlings sit around reading tabloid headlines aloud to each other. Is there any way to focus their attention back on the task that they're being paid to do?

A. Try to capitalize on their energy instead of depressing it.

Decipher why poring through the tabloids seems to be so much more mesmerizing than real work. Is reading the tabloids fun? Try to bring an element of play into the job if possible.

Are your people enjoying the communal aspect of reading aloud? Perhaps it's a cue they should spend more time with each other brainstorming. Are they laughing over those headlines? Maybe you need to invent a way to make meetings more lighthearted. Are your underlings helping each other solve today's crossword puzzle? Maybe you can add a slight gaming aspect to your own meetings by asking workers to compete on a project.

Don't automatically assume that staffers are reading the tabloids purely to idle away time. They may be trying to tell you something without being able to verbalize it.

267 If you can't discuss the scandals in the newspapers, any bad financial news, or politics, what are you supposed to glean from perusing the paper?

A. Everything else. You're just keeping your finger on the pulse.

Be a trend scout. Think of yourself as a modern day trendmeister whose job it is to predict what will happen tomorrow. Try to pick up little clues as to what shape tomorrow will take from every single item that you ever read, be it a Facebook post, an electronic newspaper, or a book on Kindle.

Collectively, will we launch into a brave new future or will we long for a cherished past? What will the new technology resemble? Which businesses will rise? Which will fall? And which businesses will resurface like phoenixes, perhaps with new business models? If you can force yourself to think, not just about what you're reading today but how it impacts all of us tomorrow, you will be in a stronger position to succeed right now.

The Last Word on Dinner Conversation

When you're at a business dinner, you always want to present the best *you* possible. Table manners exist so that we can eat meals without alarming, disgusting, or amazing the other people at the table. It also really helps to come to dinner with a positive attitude. Avoid cynicism, dark humor, and negativity.

Let's suppose that someone on the team mentions that he practices yoga. Rather than saying something polarizing such as, "Yoga is for people who aren't good at real sports," try to take a more even-keeled approach.

"You're into yoga? That sounds interesting. Tell me more about it. Are those positions easy to master or are they deceptively difficult?"

The quick lowdown on humor: Sarcasm is difficult to pull off without sounding petty. And even gentle humor is often lost on people. The path to a hellish meal is paved with good intentions.

Finally, try to look as if you're having fun, even if you aren't. Take these time-tested words as your mantra and, "Fake it till you make it." The first few formal dinners may intimidate you, but with practice comes perfection.

---

5. *Good Eye Contact Is the Secret of Good You Contact*™

You've always believed that good eye contact is imperative for closing deals, but Joe Client is shifty-eyed and his boss Bentley has a bit of a roving eye. So whenever you eat dinner with them you feel as if neither of them ever glances in your direction. You haven't a clue as to whether or not they're enjoying themselves. Fortunately, as you learned from a sticker affixed to your boss's clipboard, "There's no i in team." You're delighted to let others on your team entertain the clients with fascinating play-by-plays of the most recent football rout over dinner while you pick up your colleagues' slack at the office.

268 When people ask, "How are you?" do they want a real reply?

A. If you can answer the question with enthusiasm, people will be happy for you.

"I'm doing well, thank you, and I'm so happy to be at this conference," is a reply that will stead you well. People enjoy vitality. And optimism is contagious. Feel it and pass it along. "I stayed up really late last night and feel strung out. If I don't get some coffee in my system I'm going to pass out!" is too much information. The former statement is likely to make your listener feel a tiny bit more enthusiastic about whittling away his own day at the conference; the latter may depress him or make him feel anxious. Don't let people in so much if they're likely to find something negative. It could deflate their own moods.

If you don't feel enthusiastic, try faking it until you feel it. Hold yourself upright, look the person in the eye, and just pretend that you're feeling good. It may jolt you into a better frame of mind—if only temporarily.

Are Moods Contagious?

"Emotions are contagious," wrote the Swiss psychoanalyst Carl Jung. New data seems to concur. Moods like cheerfulness, irritability, and melancholy get passed on from person to person within the same social circle, which has major implications for residents of the office beehive.

Evidence shows that watching someone express an emotion can invoke the same mood in you—especially if that person happens to have a particularly expressive face. Good moods can be passed along as well as negative ones, so follow the directive in a popular Broadway musical number and "Put on a happy face."

But take care not to overdo it. A study by the University of Florida found that while charisma can be an effective motivator, overexuberance can sometimes have the opposite effect. Don't talk too loudly or wave your hands too much, or you might inadvertently set off the "fight or flight" syndrome in your employees.[31]

Musical Numbers That Double as Superb Etiquette Advice

Song	Musical
"Put on a Happy Face"	*Bye, Bye Birdie!*
"Let the Sunshine in"	*Hair*
"I've Got Confidence"	*The Sound of Music*

---

269 Your boss fidgets like a child when he's near you and can't look you in the eye. Should you broach the topic—or let it go?

A. What topic?

Courtesy begins when you give people the benefit of the doubt. This maxim doesn't just apply to the courtesy you show others. Sometimes you need to give yourself the benefit of the doubt, too.

There could be numerous reasons why your boss doesn't seem riveted. Your presentation could be too long, or perhaps it's poorly organized. But it's equally likely that your boss may simply feel overcommitted this afternoon for reasons that have nothing to do with you. He doesn't have any time to give you but, for whatever reason, decided not to cancel your meeting.

Your boss could even have ADHD (Attention Deficit Hyperactivity Disorder). Does he tap his foot, chew gum a lot, or constantly check his watch for microscopic movements of the minute hand? New studies show that fidgeting may actually help some ADHD adults concentrate better! So before you blame yourself for making your presentation deadly dull, try to assess why your boss is behaving like a jumping jack-in-the-box.[32]

270 **Whenever you give a presentation to a particular client, he looks as if he's falling asleep! You're not sure whether this is his normal behavior pattern with other people or just with you. What are the rules, if any, about discussing it with him?**

A. Let it go.

You dotted every i on the report and crossed every t, and now your client looks as if he's going to reward all of your hard work with a bunch of zzz's. "Wake up," you feel like shouting in his face. And yet, you resist. What self-control you have!

There are four ingredients that season the stew of a successful presentation: good eye contact, depth of homework, clear and obvious next steps, and your own passion for the project.

How do you know if you've maintained good eye contact? If you can't cite the color of your client's eyes with 100 percent certainty, then it's a sign that you haven't spent enough time peering into them.

When you do your homework, dig deep. But then, topline your findings. Condense your topic so that your listeners can easily take away a few key points—preferably without writing them down.

Plot out the next steps: Your talk should suggest an obvious timeline. The necessary steps should be clearly delineated. Consider delegating different tasks to teammates to help generate interest and build momentum.

Lastly, make sure that you feel deeply moved about the project. Force yourself to fall in love with the assignment so that you'll be able to convey your enthusiasm for it in a sincere way.

That's a Wrap

1. Don't talk about business until dessert.
2. Researching someone else's interest for just sixty seconds a day will give you enough background to be able to raise the topic in a casual conversation, and the effort will be much appreciated.
3. Sex is a total turnoff in business conversation.
4. Don't let a discussion about today's headlines devolve into a screaming match about morality. Know when you are approaching a potentially explosive topic and withdraw quickly.
5. If you don't know the color of someone's eyes after talking to him for over half an hour, then you haven't established enough eye contact.

IV

Etiquette-Challenged Scenarios

Most of us were born with stainless steel spoons in our mouths—not silver. We didn't grow up in manors. We never went to Charm School. Correct manners are alien to us. Unlike the Silver Spoon Set, we need to work. But we often lack the polish we need to "work it" at the office to get ahead. When there are sticky situations at the workplace, or when we find ourselves laboring under a boss with a particularly bad vice, we don't know where to turn for honest advice. We can raise the issue with the HR department but that makes us feel like vicious scandalmongers. Part IV will help us conquer these issues so that we can carry on with poise and elegance.

CHAPTER 19

Sticky Situations

Benjamin Franklin once said, "It takes many good deeds to build a good reputation, and only one bad one to lose it." Echoing the founding father, Warren Buffet cautioned, "It takes twenty years to build a reputation and five minutes to ruin it." Sticky situations at the office challenge our mettle, forcing us to reach deep down inside to maintain our equanimity.

But when we retain our composure, our good reputation stays intact and we find ourselves able to handle rapacious bosses, secretive employees, despondent juniors, underperforming underlings, teammates, and others who may be trying to buy our approval, stab us in the back, or sabotage our efforts in countless nefarious ways.

Staying in control in a chaotic situation is one of the smartest ways to tip off management that you're ready for more responsibility. And flawless manners help you attain control by giving you the tools, language, and cool professional distance required to succeed.

As the former CEO of GE, leadership guru, and *Business Week* columnist Jack Welch once advised, "Control your own destiny or someone else will." This chapter teaches you how to keep your head when all around you are losing theirs and (sometimes) blaming it on you.

1. Is She or Isn't She? (Married/Taking Maternity Leave/Looking for a Job)

"Just find out, okay?" your boss roars at you first thing this morning. "O-okay," you stammer, as always, completely befuddled about what he's asking you to do. "I'd do it myself," he mumbles under his brimstone breath, "but, uh, you're better than me . . ." Seeing your quizzical look, he fills in the blank. "With PEOPLE. You're better than me with people!" he screams before leaving you to your own devices. About three hours later, you inch back to his office to continue the conversation. "What is it you need me to do, Boss?" you ask with cheery bravado. "Find out if your assistant will be leaving us," your boss says in a demure voice, soft as a pussycat. He must have taken his meds in between.

271 **Rumors fly that your assistant's recent trip to Las Vegas turned into a mad dash to the altar. She hasn't breathed a word about it to you. Do you have to hire a personal detective to discover the truth?**

A. When someone's status changes, it behooves you to find out the implications.

When your assistant has been single and carping about it non-stop for months, it's hard to wrap your head around the fact that she might have tied the knot over a weekend. Nevertheless, when an employee's status changes it could have a far-reaching effect on the rest of her life. Where does her new husband live, and will she be joining him? These are reasonable questions to ask as they have an impact on your company. Your assistant may not be a "rock star," but replacing her could still take several months.

When you approach her, try to show some sensitivity to the fact that she hasn't sought you out yet to discuss her plans. Also, show empathy—it's the secret ingredient of all productive conversations. You should feel happy for her even if her spontaneous decision means that she may have to leave.

"I heard through the grapevine that you have some happy news," you can say. "So first off, best wishes. I am so happy for you both." Then, try to draw her out about their future plans.

THE STRAIGHT SCOOP

Sometimes it's easier to extract valuable information when you approach someone as a friend rather than as a superior.

---

272 Your employee looks as if she's six months pregnant and you doubt it's due to the company cafeteria food! You need to know if she will be taking maternity leave. You understand that it's impolite to pry, but can't you just ask her anyway? Business is business!

A. Don't even think about it.

You can't ask, and she'll tell you when she's good and ready.

Tease an employee about being pregnant, and your company could have a big, whopping lawsuit on its hands based on "hostile environment." Women do not take kindly to little jokes about pregnancy or their condition! Charges of discrimination based on pregnancy are also hard to fight in court. And court cases of this kind are on the rise.

Two Acts Designed to Protect the Working Pregnant

Your company doesn't necessarily have to give a pregnant worker paid maternity leave, but it will probably need to comply with the Pregnancy Discrimination Act (PDA) as well as the Family and Medical Leave Act (FMLA).

The PDA protects employees and applicants from discrimination based on "pregnancy, childbirth, and related medical conditions." According to law, you can't fire a pregnant worker because of her condition or force her to take leave—as long as she's physically capable of performing her job. Women who take maternity leave *must* be reinstated under the same conditions as employees returning from disability leave.

Eligible employees can take up to twelve weeks of unpaid, job-protected FMLA leave. And new parents—both men and women—can take FMLA leave any time within the first twelve months after a child's arrival.

273 **Your assistant has traded her gray flannel pants and rumpled jacket for a navy pinstriped suit. For the first time in months, her hair and fingernails actually look kempt. Plus she's carrying an executive leather briefcase as she leaves the office for lunch. Can you ask her if she's looking for a job?**

A. Not on that basis, no.

Don't jump to conclusions based on only partial evidence. It will make you look paranoid, and paranoid people are difficult to work for. Your assistant may be spending the evening with someone whom she cares to impress (like her mother), or she could have made some sort of a resolution six months ago to clean up her act that she's finally following through on.

However, if you hear through a reliable source that your assistant is seeking employment elsewhere, it's smart to discuss the rumor with her if you have any interest in keeping her. In a non-threatening way, you might ask her if she's looking outside the company, what her long-term career goals are, and if she has any frustrations with her current position.

Whatever Happened to the Corporate Ladder?

The corporate ladder used to be an apt metaphor for describing a relatively successful person's projected career path. Someone entering a field straight out of college would essentially start at the bottom rung of the ladder, and with some luck, pluck, and much hard work, continue to climb, rung by rung, until he reached a level near the top. If someone under him on the ladder edged him out of the way, the employee would go find a job at a competitive organization at approximately the same rung, and for probably even more money, and continue the upward ascent.

But much has changed in the last ten years. Numerous companies have shed layers and layers of people, contributing to so-called "flat" organizations without many rungs. Some dot-com bubbles have burst. And some fields have imploded upon themselves, and are now searching for new business models.

Today, most companies don't plot out their employees' career paths. Workers are responsible for figuring out their own paths. Some tools, such as 360-degree evaluations, may help. But a mentor who's interested in someone's personal development can help even more.

Great business etiquette is not just about retaining your composure during the heat of an argument or being able to eloquently persuade someone to your way of thinking. It's also about taking a genuine interest in the lives and careers of those around you.

2. The Catch-22 of Negative Feedback

You were infinitely happier before the consultant swept in and taught you all how to manage each other. Now everyone on the team has taken a confidential personality quiz and you are all expected to productively air your grievances, "map out innovative solutions," and "experiment with wearing each other's hats," whatever that means. Personally, you don't like wearing a hat unless it's navy and you have no desire to wear anyone else's—especially if there is sweat under the hat brim. You believe that you have always been a fair boss; however, under the new "get it all out in the open" rules, three people on your team have already volunteered that they'd respect you far more if you stood up to Satan once in a blue moon. Meanwhile, Satan has expressed that you'd better whip everyone on the team to start working harder, or they will all lose their jobs.

Outlook Determines Outcome

Given a choice, most people prefer to work with sunny, optimistic people. Studies show that optimists are hired more often for a job (even when the people doing the hiring happen to be pessimists). Everyone in business experiences setbacks; but optimists bounce back from adversity faster than pessimists and so they are more likely to be "up at bat" again for the next assignment. There is also compelling medical evidence to suggest that optimism improves overall health. Or as a wise man named *Anonymous* once said, "Attitude determines Altitude."

274 Your corporate culture encourages 360-degree evaluations where everyone critiques everyone else. You feel like you're always inflating everyone else's grades just to stay popular. Is that the only way to receive great evaluations yourself?

A. Give people constructive criticism rather than destructive.

Some people love 360-degree evaluations. These feedback junkies view the evaluations as "honesty mirrors," reflecting insights about themselves that they never saw before. "Mirror, mirror on the wall, who's the fairest manager of all?"

Others despise the evaluations, feeling (sometimes justifiably) that they are a means for some peers and direct reports to "punish them" and hurt their chances for promotion. For while the evaluations are supposedly anonymous, depending on the size of your company and certain people's uncanny ability to "write like they speak," it's often not all that difficult to piece together who said what about you.

One company may use 360-degree evaluations as an adjunct tool only for developmental purposes; another may use the feedback loop to decide important matters, such as raises.

As a general rule, if employees believe that their answers will stay anonymous and that there will be no recriminations for speaking the truth, the evaluations will be less lenient. So if you feel like you need to inflate every-one's grades just to stay in your team's good graces, it may be because you fear retribution. You may want to ask your boss or an HR person about tweaking the evaluation process to make it more puncture-proof.

275 **Your boss rides roughshod on the troops, including your direct reports who seemingly despise him. Is there any way to encourage him to be a bit nicer to people, or is that completely impossible?**

A. If you can make your suggestion sound like it's your boss's idea, you might have a shot.

Dale Carnegie said it best: People hate to be criticized. So take care to frame any criticisms as suggestions or experiments rather than as concrete necessities. When you use the word "we," you also position yourself better as part of the team.

"Danny seems like he's been a bit despondent lately. I already told him what a fantastic job he did on the customer tracking survey and was won-dering what we might do to get him fired up about his next project. I was thinking that maybe we should give him more responsibility and let him try to manage a mini-team."

Why This Technique Works

Your boss has nothing to lose. If, for whatever reason, Danny can't handle the new role, then it was only temporary and your boss looks magnani-mous for having given Danny the chance. If, conversely, Danny turns out to be a genius manager-in-training, your boss will look like a mastermind for having "discovered" him. You will talk to Danny, clearly explaining that the new responsibility is an acknowledgment of his past performance. It's not a promotion; it's simply an experiment. But in the interim, Danny will feel as if his accomplishments are being recognized—by both you and the boss.

276 **Is there a humane way to fire someone?**

A. Yes, and it's not via email.

Issue a warning.

A warning given in time to a receptive employee could help her save her job. While no one likes to hear that she's underperforming, the red flag at least gives the employee a chance to turn things around.

A warning is some advance notice that things aren't working out in the way that you (or the company) had hoped. It's an opportunity to state the problem without ambiguity and generally carries an implied threat. "If things don't change radically within three weeks, then, unfortunately, we will have to let you go."

Do your due diligence on company policy before you sit down with your employee. Gather any paperwork that you may need in advance, fill it out, and begin to establish the paper trail on the employee for your company's in-house lawyers.

Even if you don't particularly like the employee, it sometimes makes sense to negotiate with your boss on her behalf. Try to have your boss agree that if the worker solves the issue in the allotted time frame, then she can stay with no recriminations. Allowing her to stay will save the company money in terms of her severance package, unemployment insurance, training costs for her replacement, plus a mountain of paperwork.

If she works to bring up her performance, it means that she really wants to stay. You can help her and, in the process, gain an ally for life.

For Extra Credit

Try to "be there" for her as much as possible during the probationary period. Set up times with her when she can give you any progress reports. Halfway through the probationary period, you may want to let her know whether or not her efforts seem to be paying off.

3. *Unwanted Gifts and Lavish Attentions*

To you, they are like members of your family even if there are no genetic similarities. There's the smart one (in this case, perhaps more like the "smart-ass one"), the black sheep (your assistant, Ashley), the dumb one (the new intern is no rocket scientist), and you love them all! They may grumble when you implore them to stay late, but they do it out of the goodness of their hearts. And, as a result of their hard labor, sales for the year were only 10 percent down. ("Down," you have it on firm authority, is the new "up.") It only feels right to buy each member of your cracker-jack team a small, personalized memento as a token of your appreciation and hope your company won't take issue with it.

THE STRAIGHT SCOOP

Spend an equal amount of money on each gift, and keep the presents business-oriented and inexpensive. Mugs, mouse pads, and funky (albeit cheap) pens are probably acceptable, but you *must* check your employee handbook for the rules that govern your company! While many self-proclaimed etiquette gurus suggest giving gifts such as homemade cookies, often that's actually *inconsiderate* if you know for a fact that someone on your team is dieting, and just after any major holiday, who isn't?

---

277 Your underling returns from his vacation in Madrid with gifts galore. At first, you're thrilled when you open yours—the watch is stunning and coordinates with everything you own. But later, you overhear one of your employees speculate that your gift must have cost many Euros. Do you assume that she's ill-informed or look the proverbial gift horse in the mouth and tell him that you can't accept his present?

A. Say, "Thanks, but no thanks."
Peek inside your company handbook. The rules differ from company to company. Many companies prohibit their employees from accepting any gift that has more than a token value. But what constitutes a "token"

amount can vary. (Federal employees cannot accept *any* item of monetary value.)

If you can't accept a gift, blaming it on your company's corporate policy should help alleviate any hurt feelings—except for yours, of course. You love that watch! But in all good conscience, you can't accept it.

For Extra Credit

Be sure to report any gifts that you suspect may be too extravagant. Remember always that correct etiquette mandates that you follow the spirit of the law, not just the letter. "Everyone does it" is no justification. You're not "everyone," and, anyway, sometimes "everyone" can be wrong.

Scripting Yourself

When refusing a gift, always thank the person. You're thanking him for thinking of you. If you are returning a present from a client or someone outside of your company, it's sometimes easier to write a handwritten note accompanying it by way of explanation. You can use this script and customize it with your own language:

Dear Paul —

I sincerely appreciated the lovely Waterford pitcher that you sent, but my company expressly forbids me from accepting lavish gifts of this kind. I hope you will understand that I am simply "following orders" and that I sincerely appreciate both the thought and our strong business relationship. Happy holidays to you, Stella, and the kids.

All the best,

The Rules on Gifting Are Tightening

According to the *2008 Plum Book,* which outlines ethical consider-ations for federal workers, "Employees shall not solicit or accept any gift or other item of monetary value from any person or entity seeking official action from, doing business with, or conducting activ-ities regulated by an employee's agency, or whose interests may be substantially affected by the performance or nonperformance of the employee's duties." [33]

278 A vendor always gives you a small present at Christmas— usually a bottle of wine. This year, the vendor sent you a bottle of your favorite cologne instead. Should you accept it or not?

A. Absolutely not.

It may strike you as ironic that a vendor sniffed out your favorite cologne when no one else in your life has ever done so. And when you really love a present, it feels downright wrong to refuse it. Nevertheless, intimate gifts have no place in business, and unfortunately, accepting one sends a mes-sage too.

Just thank the vendor for the thought but explain that you can't keep it. "Thank you, but I really can't accept such an intimate gift," will convey the right message.

Don't send your vendor a message of hope when he doesn't have a prayer.

279 Every time you visited the client at his office, you mentioned how much you admired his black canvas director's chair with the silver company logo emblazoned on it. This year, he sent you one for your birthday. Is it okay to accept it?

A. Double-check your company policy and be sure to report the gift.

The director's chair could have been a premium that was manufactured in bulk several years ago, which will make assessing its true value challenging. *From your standpoint, the key consideration is to report it.* Talk to your boss first and then to someone in the HR department to find out your next step. Your company may have no issue with your accepting the chair, but you *must* alert them about it. If you're going to sit on that director's chair, you'd better make sure that your butt is well covered!

─────────────────── **THE STRAIGHT SCOOP** ───────────────────

As of this writing, there is not one standard gift policy that applies across to the board to all public companies.

Is There a Middle Ground Between Accepting a Gift and Refusing One?

No doubt about it, refusing a gift can be very awkward. It will surprise the giver in an unpleasant way and may have shadow recriminations down the line. If your company's policy is clearly stated, refusing a gift is a bit easier. You're simply upholding what the company dictates. However, if the company policy is fuzzy, then there may be some latitude in how to handle the receipt of a gift. For example, you might be able to say that you appreciate the thought, but your company has some general guidelines about receiving gifts and this one present, as gorgeous as it is, seems to be pushing the limit. Perhaps you can accept it with gratitude this one time with the understanding that you cannot accept any more gifts like this down the road. *Again, the most important thing is to report the gift and follow company directives on how to handle it.*

    While you're brushing up on your company policy about gift giving, also review what it says about Travel and Entertainment expenses.

How to Not Make a Client Feel Mighty Miffed about Your Gift
Always check the policy of your client's company before purchasing a holiday present for him. His company could be even stricter about accepting gifts than yours. Stranger things have happened.

People Who Can't Accept Gifts
1. Government employees
2. Journalists
3. People who influence purchase decisions

---

4. *The Vicious Rumor Mill*

You're convinced that the rumors all start in the little room where the new business supplies are stored. People scurry in and out of that room all day long like squirrels hoarding their winter nuts. And, as the assistants scoot past the associates and the vice presidents fly past the senior vice presidents, little tidbits of information are exchanged. "Big Sister's moving up, Big Brother's moving out." "Layoffs before Christmas." "A strange man wearing a burgundy raincoat was in the boss's office for sixty-five minutes yesterday. What do you think it means?" You do your best to keep your head down and your door open, but you'd have to be deaf, dumb, and blind to ignore the chatter. Hear no evil. See no evil. And what? You don't know what!

280 Rumor has it that your company is merging with another. Your client told you the bad news, and it hasn't been confirmed or denied by anyone inside your own company. How do you arrive at the truth?

A. Approach your boss and let him know what you've heard. Together, design a strategy.

Bad news travels at the speed of a rumor. Many of the details may not be accurate. But often, the core kernel of a rumor is true. That's why it's imperative to find someone in a position of power and ask him what he knows. Conversely, you do not want to prattle about the rumor—and possibly lend it credence—with those who have no idea whether or not it's unfounded.

If the rumor is true, advise your boss that speculation of a buyout will not stay contained for long and offer to work with him on a strategy for letting staffers know. You can call an "all hands" meeting and alert the team that change is in the air. Even if the scuttlebutt turns out to be false, it's a good idea to discuss it openly so that workers won't panic needlessly about their own job security.

281 You've heard that someone on the team is seriously ill. Do you offer your condolences or not?

A. Yes. Don't treat her like she has cooties.

It's safe to assume that if you know about a colleague's illness, the news is "out there." Don't spread the gossip, but feel free to act on the information by reaching out to her. Express your sympathy. "I just heard the news and I'm sorry," or words to that effect will show her you care. "Let me know if there's anything I can do" tells her that you're accessible if she needs a buddy during these distressing times.

Don't be shocked if some of your colleagues make no effort to reach out to her. On some primal level, they may fear becoming contaminated themselves, even if she isn't the slightest bit contagious in the medical sense. As Robert Greene asserts in his book, *The 48 Laws of Power*, "Infection: Avoid the unhappy and unlucky."

Whether or not others extend their best wishes for a speedy recovery, you should. It's the right thing to do. And if you're truly concerned that her bad luck will rub off on you, just take an extra-long shower tonight.

You're gonna wash her rotten luck right out of your hair.

282 Someone informed you that your best buddy at the office is going to get the ax. What should you do?

A. Nothing. Your responsibility to the company trumps loyalty to your friend.

Companies can be heartless places, well reflected in the popular literature about them. We would never need to read books such as *How to Work for an Idiot*, *The No-Asshole Rule*, and *Bad Bosses, Crazy Coworkers & Other Office Idiots*, if in fact all those for whom we ever labored were charming and considerate creatures! Nevertheless, you must resist the temptation to give your friend advance notice of his firing.

You may not wear fatigues to work every day, but you are still a soldier for the organization. You must remain loyal to its directives even when you heartily disagree with them. Giving your friend the inside scoop is highly unprofessional. It will also disrupt whatever timing reasons upper management has for withholding the information from him. They may need a particular person to come back from vacation before they can convey the sorry news.

Finally, once you give your buddy the heads up, he'll tell everyone else on the team, which will certainly kill morale. The scuttlebutt squad will squander valuable company time gossiping behind closed doors before the news is even official. Workers will frantically speculate over whether his firing was an isolated incident, and no one will know.

Empathy and Sympathy

"It's a blessing in disguise," "look for the silver lining," and "years from now, you'll look back and realize this is the best thing that ever happened to you" are patronizing statements, spoken by the well-intentioned but ill-informed.

Not every firing is a blessing—not when the person is out of work for months and has to downgrade his living arrangements as a result. The silver lining, *if* it exists, often takes years to discover. For example, if someone uses a firing to find a new career for himself, that might be an example of improving his lot. But switches like that often take a long time to manifest. In the interim, he needs to pay his rent. At least, "years from now you'll look back" takes into account that the healing process doesn't happen overnight!

Instead of dismissing someone's pain with a cliché, try expressing your empathy with a statement that mirrors how your friend feels. "I'm so sorry that you have to experience this," is always appreciated. "Let me know if there's anything I can do," is ideal—if, in fact, there are ways you can help. If you're willing to critique your friend's resumé or provide him with some contacts, that statement is appropriate. Depending on your friend's emotional state, you might also offer to treat him to a drink or dinner if he wants to talk to you further.

5. When Your Reputation Is on the Line

You remember reading in some management manifesto that the "ability to adapt to change" is a predictor of one's success. But secretly, you wish that things would go back to the way they were. With all of the consultants running around your office and the stench of layoffs in the air, your teammates are always holed up somewhere gossiping instead of being down in the Cube Farm working. You can't find them when you need them, and it's interfering with your ability to get your own work done. Lately, there have been so many pesky management issues to resolve that you no longer feel like a player who makes rain fall. (You're just trying to keep your head above water.) With the top brass hunkered down behind closed doors and your own people missing in action, you wonder if your own reputation is beginning to tarnish and if there's anything you can do to quickly buff it.

283 **Your boss wants you to play "bad cop" and fire six people. If he tells you to jump off a cliff, do you have to?**

A. Yes, that's in your job description.

Call it "Kill the messenger" syndrome. You may have given your employee the best reviews that she ever received. You may have even tried to save her job. It matters not. She still wants to kill you.

Ironically, if you can maintain some emotional distance by keeping the firing somewhat impersonal, it will be better for both you and the unfortunate victim. (Rent the movie *Up in the Air* for inspiration.)

Find out beforehand what the official story is about the person's termination. Is it performance-related? A simple, "I've been asked to let you know that the company will have to let you go" will communicate more than enough information. Is it a downsizing? "Due to the recent restructuring, the company has been forced to lay off some people. I'm sorry to tell you, that, effective immediately, your services will no longer be needed."

Be sure to have an HR person in the room with you, and if you're given a script, stick to it. Don't make any promises you can't keep, such as saying that you'll help the employee find another job.

284 The Watercooler Wag wants to apply to graduate school and incorrectly assumes that you'll be delighted to write a recommendation for her. How do you dissuade her from this notion?

A. Be honest, but vague about your reasons.

If you can't, in all sincerity, craft the type of reference that will help someone at your office advance to the next stage of her career, it's far kinder to admit it.

"I'm not sure that I know you well enough to write the outstanding recommendation you deserve. You're probably better off asking someone who knows you a little better than I do," is the white fib that salvages the situation and spares feelings.

Any reference that you write needs to be the equivalent of an "A." Otherwise the person in question probably *won't* get into the grad school or the co-op or the training program of her dreams.

Today, things are brutally competitive and everyone needs the most glowing recommendations they can get.

It's a jungle out there.

$\mathcal{285}$ You are finally promoted. Yeah! However, once the congratulatory email is dispatched, someone on your team gripes that she was overlooked. And she's expressing her feelings to anyone who'll listen to her, which is everyone. What should you do?

A. Sit tight, and hold onto your hat.

Never fear, your company won't rescind its offer. Her complaints, if bolstered with sage arguments, may make your boss and others in top management consider her for some future promotion down the line. But if she seethes and acts resentful, her remonstrations may actually hurt any chances she has for advancement.

In any case, don't fret about her grumbling. Your job is to step into an exciting new management role and prove to your boss that he was right to pluck you for this job. Keep your chin up, but your head down. It's time for you to get back to work!

That's a Wrap

1. Just because your boss asks you to find out something personal about one of your employees doesn't necessarily mean that you should.

2. Everyone hates to be criticized. So try framing any criticisms as constructive suggestions instead.

3. Check the company handbook on policy before accepting or giving any gifts.

4. Don't spread rumors, but if there's one floating around that impacts the fate of every person in your company, try to find out whether it's true and devise a strategy for open discussion.

5. If someone challenges your promotion, keep your manners well buffed. You need to prove that management made the right decision by promoting you.

CHAPTER 20

Advice for Handling Vices, Yours and Other People's

The biggest problem with vices is how quickly they can degrade one's reputation and lead a career into a downward spiral—sometimes, all the way to ruin.

This chapter tackles the biggest reputation saboteurs and teaches methods for coping with them. Does someone in a position of authority have a predilection for generous alcohol consumption? And if so, should you ignore the problem or take some responsibility for it?

Is an assistant who smokes too much a liability only to herself? Or is her habit sucking up so much company time that, in effect, it's unfair to the non-smokers?

Pick up pointers for dialing down drama-queenism (both yours and other people's), and learn why stiff upper lipism is one trait that higher-ups seek. Humorlessness and blowhardism may not be the marquee vices on the "Seven Deadly Sins" list, but perhaps they should be.

If you're guilty of any of these vices, this chapter will help you recognize it.

And self-knowledge is the first step to changing the course you're on.

Do you know others who indulge? Here, find skillful ways to coax them to more productive behavior.

1. A Predilection for Generous Alcohol Consumption

Your recent promotion completely changed your relationship with Satan. Suddenly, you find him to be the world's greatest boss! He has no problem delegating work to you. He trusts you to run huge portions of the business unsupervised. He's even the life of the party, that is, if he ever gets to the party. Lately, his absences have become more noticeable. You take no issue with his two-hour lunches, except when he forgets what he said beforehand. You just wish that he wouldn't skip out on so many meetings with clients and important prospects. Should you continue to keep your boss's secret bottled up? Or, by keeping his secret, are you behaving almost as irresponsibly as he is? When your boss is pursuing a crash course to his own destruction, what, if anything, should you do about it?

286 **Your boss drinks like a fish. You've had to pour him into a car service home on more than one occasion. Do you tattle, try to scare some sobriety into him, or put on your handy pair of blinders?**

A. Wear blinders.

You are not your boss's keeper. Unless the words *Chaperone* or *Nursemaid* are part of your job description, you should avoid these roles like Swine Flu. Did your boss don a lampshade at the last office Christmas party? Close down a few restaurants after dancing on the tables? Does he keep a bottle of moonshine stashed in his desk to cure his mysterious morning malaise? Never add to his troubles by giving him the disapproving eye or squealing to the higher-ups. Your job is to write research reports, remember?

287 **The president of the office corners you in the hallway one morning and asks if your boss has been drinking on company time. Do you tell the truth or feign a coughing attack and hightail it to the watercooler?**

A. Tell the truth—but sidestep the question.

No doubt the company president heard a rumor about your boss's nefarious tippling habit and seeks verification from a reliable source. You should feel honored that *you* are the source; it's a sign that he trusts your judgment.

However, his question is also a test of your character and one you can't afford to fail. Remember Benjamin Franklin's cautionary note about the one bad deed that can harm a good reputation. Squealing is that one bad deed. Frame your boss's drinking as a "problem" and you show yourself to be disloyal. This black mark on your character will linger *long* after your boss is put on probation.

As you mentally weigh the cons of full disclosure, the company president taps his foot impatiently while your boss's career hangs in the balance.

The correct response: "I think we *all* had a little too much eggnog at the office Christmas party. Boy, even the Accountant was swing dancing with our receptionist. What a great party!"

Why This Technique Works

You've told the truth but adroitly sidestepped the real question, which is about your boss's propensity to drink during the daytime. Congratulations. Your tap dancing skills are to be commended. Discretion is often the better part of showing yourself worthy of a promotion.

288 Woops! Your boss never showed up at the new business pitch this morning. Do you cover for him or blow the whistle?

A. Cover for him—unless it's a recurring pattern.

Give your boss the benefit of the doubt. He could have: overslept, missed the train, realized he didn't have enough money for a cab to the meeting, stood in an interminable line at the ATM machine, only to get stuck in the elevator en route to the wrong floor, and then slipped on a banana peel! Some or all of this could have happened. People are only human.

On the flip side, alcoholics can be absolute geniuses when it comes to inventing all sorts of rationales to explain their curious absences. Remember that "half of life is showing up"; and when it comes to new business pitches, the percentage is considerably higher!

If your boss's self-destructive pattern continues, eventually it will jeopardize the business and cause clients to pull out. At that point, you will have no choice but to speak up. The trick is to do it with sensitivity. Don't be the proverbial messenger that everyone wants to shoot.

Find an HR person; tell her that what you are about to reveal is confidential; and ask her to discreetly check the facts without mentioning your name. She and others in her department may be able to recommend a rehabilitation program for your boss.

2. *Cigarette Smoking*

She's a rebel with a cause: smoking. Your assistant is part of the posse that lurks outside of the office building with the other freezing outcasts. They shiver around the lone iron standing ashtray. As you pass the scraggly crew this morning, your assistant Ashley flashes an impish, yellow-toothed grin. Dashing outside at 3 PM for a quick coffee run, you can't help but observe that she's still planted to the spot, a fresh box of Marlboro Lights peeking out of the top of her pants' pocket like a smoking gun. When you leave at night, Ashley is still glued to that iron lung—er, ashtray. With hundreds of intelligent people kicking the habit every week, why does your assistant have to be the last smokeaholic in America?

 Your assistant reeks like an ashtray. Do you leave a box of breath mints for her as a subtle hint or go all out and spring for a bottle of mouthwash?

A. Neither. Use the power of numbers to help her smell as fresh as a daisy.

Where there's smoke, there's ire—yours, mainly.

You can ban smoking from your home; you can vow to hang around only non-smokers; but in business, it helps to appear non-judgmental. You will have to figure out how to frame and air the issue with the moxie of a Machiavelli.

Fortunately, there is power in numbers. If you are the only one who is bothered by her smoking, consider approaching a third party: the HR manager. You might explain that you're seeking her counsel in confidence because the *last thing* you want to do is offend your employee but the scent of tobacco clings to her breath and clothing and you're concerned that potential customers may be turned off. Then ask if the HR person might step in and leave your name out of it. (HR managers take scores of seminars on how to tackle issues far more sensitive than this one.)

When the HR manager raises the smoking issue with your assistant, the manager will also use the power of numbers to bolster her case. She'll no doubt tell your employee that someone stepped forward to complain and that she's not allowed to share who it was, but the problem can be easily remedied with the help of a great drycleaner, a secret stash of breath mints, and a quick swab with a toothbrush after lunch.

If others on your team are also carping about your assistants pungent aroma, then you'll have even more leeway with your approach. The power of numbers is on your side. You can either talk to the HR manager and explain that several people have noticed the problem or take out your problem employee for a "sandwich."

In this case, a sandwich is not a slice of Havarti cheese nestled in between two pieces of sourdough but an approach to solving numerous types of office frictions. (See "The Sandwich Approach to Offering Criticism.")

290 **Your assistant's smoking breaks add up to a lunch break. And that's before lunch. Any ideas on snuffing out her errant behavior?**

A. Start altering her work assignments.
Start piling on the work projects. If she fusses that she has too much work on her plate, gently advise her that if she would take fewer breaks it would free up her time for real work.

Why This Technique Works

You've avoided treating your assistant like an imbecile by lecturing her on the dangers of smoking. She's well aware of the hazards and has chosen to ignore them. Instead, you have given her a cogent business reason to curb the habit: It's interfering with her ability to get her work done. Finally, you've accomplished all of this without adopting the stern tone of a disciplinarian, or her mother, or any of the people that probably made her pick up the filthy habit in the first place.

291 Your assistant's smoking hack is disturbing the peace on the floor. The non-smoking natives are growing restless. "Why does she always cough?" they ask. "We can't concentrate." How do you handle this second-hand smoking dilemma gracefully?

A. Bring your assistant cough drops and a box of Kleenex.
Play it straight. Tell your assistant that you're worried that she may be coming down with a terrible cold. Several of the people at the office have heard her coughing and are concerned about her health.

The "Sandwich" Approach to Offering Criticism

It smells bad. Yes, your assistant's smoky odor is annoying, but your teammates reaction to it is even more so. It's time to try the "Sandwich approach." Take your assistant out for a cup of coffee. A real sandwich isn't mandatory.

Tell her how much you enjoy working with her (if true). Then gently switch the topic. "I have received a tiny bit of negative feedback about you," you might offer, "but I think there's a fairly easy solution. Some of the team members have noticed that you have a strong tobacco scent. I appreciate that you probably don't want to quit, and I'm not going to pretend I'm the surgeon general, but you may want to bring some toothpaste to the office and brush after you smoke or pop a Breathsaver after every butt or both."

Then close your conversation with something glowingly positive. "Again, in general, I'm delighted with your performance and know that you'll work hard to correct this."

The Zero Tolerance Policy
Some companies have no tolerance for smokers and won't even hire them. Drug testing is on the rise as a way of weeding out smokers who are job applicants. While some may call this "discrimination," smokers should be aware that, in general, there's much less tolerance for the tobacco habit these days than in years past.

---

3. Drama Queen-ism to an Excruciating Degree

Clearly, his talents are going to waste. With this kind of acting talent, he should be in a stage production of *King Lear*, instead of staging filibusters in the office hallways about every little thing that goes awry. His histrionics are legendary and you have no idea what value he contributes to the company. But for the moment, your charge is to tolerate him. Or is it? When your direct report is holding you hostage at a play that you don't want to attend, is it possible to sneak out of the performance before the final curtain call? Can you demote him to more of a backstage role? Or can you offer him a starring role—but in a different department?

Who Knew?

The American Psychiatric Association defines Histrionic Personality Disorder (HPD) as a "disorder characterized by a pattern of excessive emotionality and attention-seeking, including an excessive need for approval and inappropriate seductiveness, usually beginning in early adulthood." These individuals are lively, dramatic, enthusiastic, and flirtatious.[34]

292 Your local Drama Queen spins tall tales for maximum effect. How do you tell him to zip it?

A. Every Drama Queen needs an audience. Pawn yours off on someone else.

Your Drama Queen was on a roll last week. "OMG!" he said, running up to you breathlessly, "the client was so distraught that she practically jumped out of a window. But the window wouldn't open, and so she just fumed until her face turned purple." You want to believe him, but it's hard for you to imagine any client going ballistic over the field report that you read. It's pretty tame stuff and contains nothing that the client hasn't heard a thousand times before.

First, confirm with your client that your interpretation is accurate and that there's nothing new you need to know. Then, if you must keep the Drama Queen on staff, find someone to act as a buffer. There may be some hard-working, deserving soul who would really appreciate the supervisory opportunity while you definitely don't need the aggravation.

Why Drama Queens Should Temper Their Flair for the Dramatic

Being a Drama Queen flies in the face of professionalism. Why? Isn't the Drama Queen just adding some excitement to all of our humdrum lives?

No, he isn't. Professionals are paid to solve problems. But Drama Queens get a special joy out of heightening problems. Every molehill turns into an abnormal mole, which needs a surgeon's scalpel. And unfortunately, *you* are that surgeon. You're being called upon to investigate issues and per-ceived disputes that don't really exist when you need to devote your efforts to scourging the problems that do.

Even in the face of big troubles, a measure of stiff upper lipism is gener-ally a quality that most managers appreciate. Always try to think of potential solutions to a problem before screaming about it from the rooftops.

293 When you offered constructive criticism to an underling, she burst into tears. Is she just acting melodramatic, or are you a dastardly villain?

A. Get a second opinion.

It's true that everyone hates to be criticized. But it's also true that, left to her own devices, everyone would give herself an "A+" for her on-the-job performance and expect a massive raise as a reward. As a manager, part of your challenge is to not only be considerate and courteous but also to manage your employees' expectations.

Write up a report of the incident. Include as many pertinent details as possible. What were the exact words that you used? How did your underling respond? Imagine that you're a screenwriter and work to capture snippets of dialogue. Draw a picture with your words about your employee's mood. Was she as carefree as a songbird when she first flitted into your office, or could you tell immediately that something was wrong? (Your negative criticism could have inadvertently pushed her over the edge.) Did your remarks truly surprise her, or do you suspect that she's heard the identical feedback from others? If possible, construct this report within two hours of the incident while the memory is still oven-fresh in your mind.

Then solicit some feedback of your own. Ask a trusted mentor at the company if she feels that you handled this confrontation properly. Discuss the conversation with your direct supervisor as well. You wish to do two things: 1) make certain that he'll support you in the event that your underling makes a formal complaint to HR, and 2) find out if there was kinder way to handle your employee while still delivering the bitter pill of criticism.

294 The new intern speaks through his nose instead of his mouth. Every time he poses a question, you just want to put on your earphones and hide. Just hearing him speak sets your fragile teeth on edge. Can you offer to buy him voice lessons?

A. Stop acting like a Drama Queen yourself, and deal with it.

Be grateful that you work at a company where not everyone grew up in the same town and different points of view are tolerated. If you have difficulty understanding him, feel free to say so and ask him nicely to repeat the question. But don't dismiss him out of hand just because he's not a Stepford employee.

4. Blowhardism

In your opinion, windbags are aptly named. Cut one off mid-sentence and it seems to take the wind right out of his bags. Avoidance doesn't work either. It's almost as if the windbag gets wind of it and makes a special point of sailing by your office to torment you. Your boss's boss is a windbag of the thirty-knot variety. No conversation with him ever transpires in under fifty minutes. As you are sipping your 3 PM latte in silence, you feel a draft coming on. It's the windbag rounding the corner blowing on everybody he sees. Should you close your door? Feign that you're on an important call? Duck into the rest room? When you have a windbag in your office, is there anything that you can do to avoid the full gale of his personality without bringing on the dreaded wind chill factor?

295 **Your boss's boss blathers like it's going out of style (which, in your opinion, it already has). When the man on top is a chatterbox, is there any way to politely screen him out?**

A. You can't totally block him, but you can commit more items to paper.

Chatty Cathys and Charlies crave attention. Maybe they felt abandoned as children and never recuperated. To make certain that they'll never feel as pained again, they have no hesitation about trapping you in a corner until they're talked out. You try to edge away, but they won't let you.

Similarly, you can't just plug them out with earphones. Chatterers have no problem turning the music down when it's their turn to speak.

A cleverer method is to devise a communication strategy where important facts are set down on paper so that the blabbermouth has some real items he can react to and discuss. Did the client meeting go smashingly well? Did you secure a new piece of business? Do you have to retool some of the thinking that went into the pitch letter?

Commit everything to a conference report and email it to your boss's boss. By making your reports to him one of your top priorities, you will help fulfill his chronic need for attention. And when he circles around to you, at least he'll have something important to say.

Six Ways to Bid So Long, Farewell to a Magpie
1. "I know you're busy."
2. "I'll let you go."
3. "I know your time is valuable, and so I'll let you get back to work."
4. "Let me circle back to you later, once this deadline passes."
5. "I can't wait to hear more about it. But unfortunately, I'm late for a meeting."

296 **The Chairman Emeritus rambles on about events that happened all the way back in the pre-Twitter Age. He remembers the way the company operated before the merger, before the move, and before any of the other top managers arrived. He talks about the "glory days" of yesteryear non-stop. Is there any way to stop him?**

A. No. Hear him out, and you may learn something.

Old-timers can be very instructive on matters of corporate culture, so show some deference. Listen attentively to these "tribal elders" and you could amass a thesaurus's worth of knowledge on corporate values, strategies for success that worked in years past, and initiatives that flopped that should never be repeated. View your elder as one of the rare keepers of institutional knowledge and vow not to be one of the swine before which he drops his pearls.

297 **Now that you're in management, you would like to officially kill the status meeting. Good idea or bad?**

A. Terrible.

For better or worse, meetings are part of your corporate culture. You weren't promoted to change the culture but to carry it forward. Think in terms of evolution, not revolution. Small tweaks are probably acceptable; dramatic overhauls are not.

Do meetings now run for thirty-five minutes? You can snip a throat-clearing introduction here or an unnecessary agenda item there to bring down the time to thirty minutes. You can also modify the culture, bit by bit, by making small refinements and then testing them to see if they work.

If your company has a sales force, perhaps you can suggest teaming up your best salespeople for a major drive. If your company is divided into large teams to service clients, maybe you can experiment with a new rotational structure for a brand new client. But take care to take only mini steps.

You never want to frighten anyone in top management or make your boss question his decision to promote you. You also don't want to confuse the people on your team. There will be some who, resentful of your advancement, will resist it with every fiber of their beings. Don't give them the ammunition.

You may want to tighten your political hold before making any substantive changes.

───────────────── THE STRAIGHT SCOOP ─────────────────

Once you've been promoted, it's even more important to continue to do the same great job that you have been. Don't worry so much about improving *the process*. Concentrate on actions that will lead to *tangible results*. Can you add a brilliant angle to a project? Can you write a stunning numerical analysis? Can you conduct some consumer research that will unmask the competition? You can, and you should.

5. *Humorlessness, Except When in Germany*

Ever since your company merged with the boutique in Bethesda, life has been grim. No one even cracks a hale "Hey there," much less a joke. Clustered behind closed doors, there are two cliques developing—the Us-es versus the Thems. But even among the formerly chipper Us-es, hilarity is as constrained as a girdle. The Thems march to their assigned bunkers each morning, serious, saturnine, and sedate, and barely speaking to each other. Oh, what you wouldn't do for the old light-hearted banter of yesteryear. It may sound like the lyrics from a certain Joni Mitchell song, but you really didn't know what you had till it was gone!

───────────────── THE STRAIGHT SCOOP ─────────────────

A sense of humor is a serious asset. It lends you a fresh perspective and allows you to observe the irony even in adverse situations. Having a sense of humor about yourself lets you control situations. Things may not always go your way, but if you can laugh them off, they also won't impact you as much. Dwight Eisenhower said it best: "A sense of humor is part of the art of leadership, of getting along with people, of getting things done."

298 You told a joke in the meeting. SPLAT! That was the sound of the joke falling flat on its face. No one laughed. They didn't even crack a smile! Should you stop trying?

A. Practice your sense of comedic timing.

Billy Crystal wasn't born in a day. Well, maybe he was, but his fabulous comedic timing took years to develop. Watch funny people say and do funny things, and your sense of humor will become sharper and more refined. Ellen DeGeneres is funny. Alec Baldwin can be very funny. Whoopi Goldberg is funny. Pick a comedic mentor. Mimic what he or she does. And then start practicing it in front of an audience.

Read something humorous, such as a comic strip, before you arrive at the office. Ask friends to send you Internet jokes. (Granted, they're not a laugh riot, but they can still get your comedic juices flowing.) Keep a humor diary of the most hilarious lines that you hear all week and simply recycle one or two of them to bring some joy to a meeting.

You don't want to be a professional comedian. (If you do, you're in the wrong field.) But infusing your office with some occasional lighthearted banter is a noble endeavor.

299 You're plumb in the middle of a shaggy dog story when suddenly you have the urge to bow out. You can't remember the punch line. How do you save face?

A. Make something up—fast.

It's the joke equivalent of giving a presentation to your entire sales team— naked. Except that this isn't some dream. And you *can* control the outcome. Just say anything that continues the story with the same characters that you've already introduced: "And so the chiropractor said to the nurse, Honey, you're breaking my back!" Then ask the folks at your office, "Do you get it?"

When they stare at you as if you're an alien from another galaxy just here on borrowed time, simply say: "Oh, what a relief! I didn't think it was funny either. Thanks for proving it to me. I really depend on you guys."

They will probably think you're zany, but tolerable, in the same way that a Gracie Allen routine is, or the cast is from the hit TV show, *The Office*.

People don't always have to laugh with you. Sometimes, they can laugh at you. As long as they like you, who cares?

How to Get a Sense of Humor—Pronto

1. **Hang out with funnier people.** Laughter is contagious, so even if you're not the one who's cracking the jokes, other people's humor will rub off on you.

2. **Collect jokes and start a joke scrapbook.** Did you receive a funny Chinese fortune in a cookie or stumble on a cartoon that made you smile? Paste them into your scrapbook. Jay Leno got a kick out of ads with typos in them. It's your scrapbook, so you can put anything you want inside. Just don't leave the scrapbook at the office. You wouldn't want your personal scrapbook of hilarity accidentally falling into the hands of someone who may not get the joke.

3. **Read funny books.** Start with Jonathan Swift, P.G. Wodehouse, and Ogden Nash. Then graduate to Woody Allen, Douglas Adams, and Jeff Foxworthy.

4. **Analyze this.** Figure out what makes something funny. Then weave the same technique into your conversations. Here's a conversation between Chandler and Joey on the old *Friends* TV sitcom. It's funny because Ross seems to be answering a completely different question than the one Chandler asks.

    Ross: What are you doing?
    Chandler: Making chocolate milk. You want some?
    Ross: No thanks, I'm 29.[35]

    Often there's a kind of truth in a joke that runs counter to the logic that the joke has already set up. The distance between the two "truths"—both equally valid—is what makes us laugh. Here's a good example from Douglas Adams: "Anyone who is capable of getting themselves into a position of power should on no account be allowed to do the job." [36]

5. **Watch sitcoms.** *The Big Bang Theory* and *Two and a Half Men* are both hysterically funny in different ways.

300 You have been perfecting your sense of humor for months and have a great impersonation of the boss. Lowering your voice and letting your eyelids burn just the way he does when he's on a tear, you are giving the performance of your life. Everyone on the team is rolling in the aisles laughing when suddenly he emerges from behind that giant square industrial pillar. "In my office . . . now!" he belts, fire flaying from his dragon-like nostrils. What do you say?

A. "I'm sorry."

Do not delay. Follow your boss into his office, quietly close the door, and deliver a swift, heartfelt apology. You will need to reach down deep inside yourself to feel your humility.

"I'm sorry if that came off as insensitive," you can tell him, "and if it hurt your feelings. I feel really badly about making a joke at your expense. I am going to ask your forgiveness and promise I will never do it again. Is there any way that I can make it up to you?"

When he keeps you in the office toiling away until midnight on a clerical task that your assistant Ashley could probably perform with her eyes closed, remind yourself to never do impersonations of anyone at the office while inside the building!

Walls have ears, you know.

For Extra Credit

If you can pepper your apology with some flattery, all the better. Here's another script that you can try: "I'm a great admirer of yours and probably just imitate you because I really enjoy working for you. That said, please accept my sincere apology. I shouldn't have been having fun at your expense and promise I won't anymore." Take these words, amend them, and make them your own. And stop squandering your talents on imitating your boss! Go sign up for amateur hour at a comedy club instead.

It's No Laughing Matter

When you're at the workplace, you need to be a bit cautious. Try to screen jokes in advance to make sure that no one will be offended. Think of all of the jokes floating through cyberspace about the various differences between men and women. Someone without a sense of humor could easily read one of those jokes and feel like half of the population was being insulted!

Stay away from all ethnic, racial, religious, or gender-based jokes. You may well wonder what sort of joke that leaves. It leaves the well-told anecdote. When you observe something about human nature that's offbeat but indelibly true, the result can be fairly whimsical and no one will feel hurt or demeaned.

301   It's a cruel joke. You have all of the trappings of a top manager except for the paycheck. You have a window office, bottom line responsibility, and authority over others, but your salary is still middle-of-the-road. What can you do to persuade your boss to reward you in the manner that you deserve?

A. Make the case.

If you've been working at the company for a while, your boss and others may still see you as a "child." But you're a grown-up who has taken on scores of new responsibilities and used your command of etiquette to pitch and win new business, placate annoyed clients, douse email flames, and manage staff. At every turn, you've demonstrated skill with the way you handle clients as well as internal politics. When your boss asked you to embrace the social media drive in addition to all of your other responsibilities, you nobly rose to the occasion.

Now it's time for you to be brave and ask for the remuneration that you so richly deserve.

"Hi, Boss. I was wondering if you might give me that raise you promised me eight months ago. There's been a tremendous amount of staff turnover, but as you can see, I'm loyal to you."

Bring in your glowing emails, your sales projections, and your phenomenal reports. Discuss the growth plan that he helped you craft at your insistence. Talk about how you want to stay at the company.

Today, finally, you will prevail.

Put Your Manners to This Test

Manners defer to the common good over individual gain. Every time you ask, "What would the world be like if *everyone* did this?" the world becomes ennobled and a slightly better place. Use this as a litmus test for whenever you face a manners conundrum at the workplace.

Let's review the boss with the drinking problem again, with this litmus test in mind.

If everyone at your office pointed fingers every time anyone had any sort of a problem, the office would become an intolerable place to work. That's an excellent reason to *never* tattle on your boss—as long as his self-destructive behavior isn't hurting anyone besides himself. Even if his drinking problem spirals to the point where it gets on his boss's radar, it's *still not your job* to out him—as doing so will likely get him in a heap of trouble and harm your own career prospects.

However, if your direct supervisor's addiction mushrooms and he continues to miss important meetings, then, ask yourself again: "What would this office be like if *everyone* did this?"

All of your clients would leave and there wouldn't be any meetings to attend!

At that juncture, your moral compass will point you in the right direction, which, by necessity, will entail speaking up. When you do, be tactful and raise the issue in a way that leads to solving the problem—without causing your boss needless embarrassment.

That's a Wrap

1. Don't tattle on your boss unless his antics start to jeopardize the business.
2. Find creative ways to enforce productive change that don't involve heavy lectures.
3. Your best defense against a Drama Queen is to put someone else in charge of him.
4. Before you dismiss a blowhard as not worthy of your time, assess if there is something that he can teach you about the business.
5. A sense of humor should be nurtured because it's a handy business tool to have at your disposal.

The 4 C's of Etiquette—Courtesy, Consideration, Camaraderie, and Class

Emily Post once said, "Manners are a sensitive awareness of the feelings of others. If you have that awareness, you have good manners, no matter what fork you use." [37]

One way to retain that sensitivity is to consider etiquette as a system based on four key facets. The facets are easy to remember because each starts with the letter "C," just like the 4 C's of buying a diamond. The 4 C's of proper etiquette are: courtesy, consideration, camaraderie, and class.

Courtesy involves listening over talking, not interrupting someone, not "trumping" someone's story or stepping on his lines, being especially sensitive to the needs of the elderly, standing when someone enters a room or your workspace if possible, and using phrases such as "Please," "Thank you," and "Pardon me."

Consideration acknowledges that there are many other people sharing a limited amount of space on planet. Whenever possible, you don't want to grate on their nerves. Consideration covers keeping your voice down, not cutting people off in lines or on highways, not making one's space untenable either by allowing loud noises into it or by keeping it so messy that it's unbearable to work in.

Camaraderie means thinking of yourself as a team player and not always trying to angle to get ahead or promote your own achievements. Do your best not to keep a meticulous accounting of every favor you are ever owed, or you will feel miserable. Know that when you feel like you are part of a team, everyone will enjoy working with you, and that this benefit far outweighs the benefits of constant self-promotion and horn-tooting.

Class concerns your demeanor, which should aim for cordial rather than dour. It also involves tempering your sarcasm, especially if the humor is at someone else's expense. Be pleasant and do your best to please, even when others are unpleasant or direct their foul moods at you.

Etiquette is based on a system. Over time, the system will work for you—if you can only get out of your own way long enough to allow it to.

Why Manners Still Matter
in the 21st Century

In 1624, John Donne wrote, "No man is an island."

These words are as true today as they were almost four centuries ago. We depend on each other for survival. And nowhere is that more expressed than through our technology.

We can hide behind our computers, and then Facebook comes along and figures out a way to move the watercooler online. Suddenly we are all importing our contacts that we've known since childhood—and sharing them with passing acquaintances-of-acquaintances—until our networks mushroom exponentially into hundreds of people. We can resolve to never leave our cocoons and pods, and then foursquare invents a geolocator that rewards us for venturing out to different venues and sharing our own experiences with thousands of friends in our various networks.

We can determine that our real life is so challenging that we'd prefer to live out our fantasies in the virtual world known as Second Life. But we create avatars in our own images that look exactly like ourselves. And then we import our businesses into Second Life and conduct meetings from our first life in Second Life!

There is no escape from other people!

In the United States we are a nation of three hundred million people, all of us colliding into each other in both our real and virtual lives at the speed of thought multiple times a day. Manners—from the most trivial, "Excuse me," to the courtesy extended when you rise to give someone elderly your seat on the bus, to tamping down an email flame, to keeping your voice low and pleasant when you are in public—are simply a means for us to negotiate our way through the crowds that inhabit all of our worlds.

In meetings, we want to engage and persuade other people. Online, we want to connect with them. And over meals, mainly, we may want to engage, persuade, connect and entertain them. Above all, we don't want to offend them!

In her watershed book, Emily Post agreed with John Donne when she wrote, "Every human being—unless dwelling alone in a cave—is a member of society of one sort or another."[38]

Modern etiquette simply spells out today's rules for negotiating these new, ever-expanding, ever-changing, and thoroughly intertwined societies.

Quiz Answers

1. B (See Chapter 1.)

2. D (See Chapter 3.)

3. B (See Chapter 1.)

4. A (See Chapter 2.)

5. D (See Chapter 5.)

6. A   While answer 6D seems like the more considerate policy, it alerts your interviewer even earlier to the fact that you're running late. If she's the type to stew about small breaches, it gives her five more minutes to conclude that you're not the right person for the job. It's savvier to call the moment you were supposed to arrive, profusely apologize for your lateness, and tell her when she can expect you.

7. B (See Chapter 14.)

8. B (See Chapter 14.)

9. C (See Chapter 1.)

10. D (See Chapter 5.)

End Notes

1. For further reading, see Keith Ferrazzi with Tahl Raz, *Never Eat Alone* (New York, Random House, 2005), p.152-154.

2. USDOT Public Affairs press release, "U.S. Transportation Secretary Ray LaHood Announces Federal Ban on Texting for Commercial Truck Drivers," February 26, 2010, http://www.dot.gov/affairs/2010/dot1410.htm (accessed March 14, 2010) and reprinted with permission from Justin Nisly at Justin.Nisly.ptt@dot.gov.

3. Susan Dunn, M.A., "Two Good Reasons Not to Use Your Cell Phone in the Car," 2004, http://www.talewins.com/protectyourself/cellphones.htm (accessed March 14, 2010).
    The University of Toronto study was also referenced in: http://www.dartmouth.edu/~chance/course/Syllabi/97Dartmouth/day-1/phone-2.pdf which is a pdf of the following article from *The New York Times*: Gina Kolata, "First Proof, Driving While Talking on Phone is a Hazard," *The New York Times, A-30, February 13 1997*.

4. Kenneth H. Beck, Fang Yan, and Min Qui Wang, "Cell Phone Users, Reported Crash Risk, Unsafe Driving Behaviors and Dispositions: A Survey Of Motorists In Maryland," *Science Direct*, 2007, http://www.sciencedirect.com/science?_ob=ArticleURL&_udi=B6V6F-4R4692G-2&_user=10&_coverDate=12%2F31%2F2007&_rdoc=1&_fmt=high&_orig=search&_sort=d&_docanchor=&view=c&_searchStrId=1209192410&_rerunOrigin=google&_acct=C000050221&_version=1&_urlVersion=0&_userid=10&md5=9511ca2f434b228e7a2162068c0c7a25 (accessed March 14, 2010).

5. Cado Parish Press Release, "Sheriff Hathaway Offers ATM Security Measures," March 9, 1998, http://www.caddosheriff.org/pr/releases/backgrnd/atm.htm (accessed March 14, 2010).

6. For further reading, check out "Obama's Bow in Japan Sparks Some Criticism," Associated Press, November 16, 2009, http://www.msnbc.msn.com/id/33978533/ns/politics-white_house/ (accessed March 14, 2010).

7. For further reading, see: Chris Casacchia, "Sound Off: Cultural Differences," *Phoenix Business Journal*, December 25, 2009, http://phoenix.bizjournals.com/phoenix/stories/2009/12/28/focus2.html (accessed March 14, 2010).

8. "Type A and Type B Personality Theory," Wikipedia, http://en.wikipedia.org/wiki/Type_A_and_Type_B_personality_theory (accessed March 14, 2010).

9. For further reading, see "The Halo Effect: When Your Own Mind Is a Mystery," PsyBlog, which references Nisbett, R. E., & Wilson, T. D., "The halo effect: Evidence for unconscious alteration of judgments." *Journal of Personality and Social Psychology*, 1977, 35(4), 250-6, http://www.spring.org.uk/2007/10/halo-effect-when-your-own-mind-is.php (accessed March 14, 2010). See also: "Halo Effect," Wikipedia, http://en.wikipedia.org/wiki/Halo_effect (accessed March 14, 2010).

10. *Wall Street Words*, Houghton Mifflin Company, 2010 (online version); see entry under Financial Dictionary for "transparency" (accessed March 14, 2010).

11. "Tribute to Sergeant Schultz," *Hogan's Heroes* (TV show), http://www.youtube.com/watch?v=34ag4nkSh7Q (accessed March 14, 2010).

12. For further reading, check out: whyiscolor.org at http://www.cis.rit.edu/fairchild/WhyIsColor/files/ExamplePage.pdf (accessed March 14, 2010).

13. Emily Post, *Etiquette in Society, in Business, in Politics, and at Home* (New York, Funk & Wagnalls, 1922) quoted in *Emily Post's Etiquette: A Guide to Modern Manners* by Elizabeth Post 14th Edition, (New York: Harper & Row, 1984), page 469.

14. http://wordnetweb.princeton.edu/perl/webwn?s=monologist; see entry under "monologist."

15. "House Rules and Club Policies," Columbia University Club of New York website, http://www.columbiaclub.org/house_rules_club_policies.html#cellularPhone (accessed April 1, 2010).

16. As quoted in: Jim Brossman (editor), *Town & Country Social Graces* (New York, Hearst, 2002).

17. Malcolm Gladwell, *The Tipping Point* (New York, Little, Brown and Company, 2000) as quoted in Keith Ferrazzi with Tahl Raz, *Never Eat Alone* (New York, Random House, 2005).

18. For more reading, see: "Net Lingo List of Internet Acronyms & Text Message Jargon," http://www.netlingo.com/acronyms.php (accessed April 1, 2010).

19. For more information on TigerText, see iTunes Preview at: http://itunes.apple.com/us/app/tiger-text/id355832697?mt=8 (accessed March 14, 2010).

20. For more reading about foursquare, check out the foursquare website at: http://foursquare.com/help/ (accessed March 14, 2010).

21. Jacqui Cheng, "Does This TV Make Me Look Fat: The Extra 10 Pounds Myth," ars technica, http://arstechnica.com/gadgets/news/2009/08/does-this-camera-make-me-look-fat-the-extra-10-pounds-myth.ars (accessed March 14, 2010).

22. For more reading, see the Yale University website at http://www.library.yale.edu/training/netiquette/flames.html (accessed March 17, 2010).

23. For further reading, see Privacy Rights Clearinghouse website at http://www.priva-cyrights.org/fs/fs7-work.htm#3b (accessed March 15, 2010).

24. Urban Dictionary, see entry under Esex at: http://www.urbandictionary.com/define.php?term=Esex.

For further reading on avatars, check out:

25. Byron Reeves and Leighton Read, "Avatars in the Workplace," *The Harvard Business Review* blog (January 21, 2010) at: http://blogs.hbr.org/cs/2010/01/avatars_at_work.html (accessed March 15, 2010).

26. Sean Silverthorne, "Use Avatars to Improve Virtual Meetings," The View From *Harvard Business* blog, (January 22, 2010) at: http://blogs.bnet.com/harvard/?p=5316 (accessed April 1, 2010).

27. Emily Post, *Etiquette in Society, in Business, in Politics, and at Home* (New York, Funk & Wagnalls, 1922). Introduction by Richard Duffy (accessed online). http://www.bartleby.com/95/101.html (accessed March 15, 2010).

28. "Bread and circuses," Wikipedia, http://en.wikipedia.org/wiki/Bread_and_circuses (accessed March 15, 2010).

29. For more reading about how alcohol affects men and women differently, see: The University of Lethbridge Alcohol Awareness website at: http://people.uleth.ca/~c.wheeler/AlcoholWebSite/pages/for_girls.htm (accessed March 15, 2010). Dietary Guidelines for Americans USDA website at: http://www.health.gov/DIETARYGUIDELINES/dga2005/document/html/chapter9.htm (accessed March 15, 2010).

30. "Sprezzatura," Wikipedia, http://en.wikipedia.org/wiki/Sprezzatura (accessed March 15, 2010).

31. For further reading on the affect of one's mood on others, see: Daniel Goleman, "Happy or Sad, a Mood Can Prove Contagious," *The New York Times*, Science Section, October 15, 1991 (accessed online). http://www.nytimes.com/1991/10/15/science/happy-or-sad-a-mood-can-prove-contagious.html?pagewanted=1 (accessed March 15, 2010).

    Kathryn Matthews, "Marital Mood Leak: Feelings May Be Contagious," Oprah.com, September 19, 2008 (accessed online). http://www.oprah.com/relationships/Your-Spouses-Mood-May-Be-Contagious (accessed March 15, 2010).

32. Roland Rotz, PhD, and Sarah D. Wright, "When ADHD Kids Fidget: Better Focus Through Multitasking," *Additude* magazine (accessed online). http://www.additudemag.com/adhd/article/3967.html (accessed April 1, 2010).

33. "Ethical Considerations for Federal Employees," *2008 Plum Book* (accessed online). http://www.transitionjobs.us/ethical-considerations-federal-employees (accessed March 15, 2010).

34. "Histrionic Personality Disorder," a Wikipedia, http://en.wikipedia.org/wiki/Histrionic_personality_disorder (accessed March 15, 2010).

35. Memorable Quotes from "Friends," The Internet Movie Database, http://www.imdb.com/title/tt0108778/quotes (accessed March 15, 2010).

36. Funny Douglas Adams Quotes—Funny Quotes by Douglas Adams, http://www.basicjokes.com/dquotes.php?aid=140 (accessed March 17, 2010).

37. Emily Post quote: http://thinkexist.com/quotation/manners_are_a_sensitive_awareness_of_the_feelings/205405.html (accessed March 31, 2010).

38. Emily Post, *Etiquette in Society, in Business, in Politics, and at Home* (New York, Funk & Wagnalls, 1922) (accessed online). http://www.bartleby.com/95/1.html (accessed March 18, 2010).

Recommended Reading & Other Resources

Books

1. Awl, Dave. *Facebook Me! A Guide to Having Fun with Your Friends and Promoting Your Projects on Facebook.* Berkeley: Peachpit Press, 2009.

2. Carlson, Richard. *Don't Sweat the Small Stuff...and It's All Small Stuff.* New York: Hyperion, 1997.

3. Carnegie, Dale. *How to Win Friends & Influence People.* New York: Pocket Books, 1936.

4. Claxton, Lena, and Alison Woo. *How to Say It: Marketing with New Media: A Guide to Promoting Your Small Business Using Websites, E-zines, Blogs, and Podcasts.* New York: Prentice Hall Press, 2008.

5. Comm, Joel. *Twitter Power: How to Dominate Your Market One Tweet at a Time.* Hoboken: John Wiley & Sons, 2009.

6. Diran, Kevin Michael, EdD. *How to Say It: Doing Business in Latin America. A Pocket Guide to the Culture, Customs and Etiquette.* New York: Prentice Hall Press, 2009.

7. Frankel, Lois P., PhD. *Nice Girls Don't Get The Corner Office 101: Unconscious Mistakes Women Make That Sabotage Their Careers.* New York: Warner Business Books, 2004.

8. Gillin, Paul. *Secrets of Social Media Marketing: How to Use Online Conversations and Customer Communities to Turbo-Charge Your Business!* Fresno: Quill Driver, 2009.

9. Goldsmith, Marshall. *What Got You Here Won't Get You There.* New York: Hyperion, 2007.

10. Greene, Robert. *The 48 Laws of Power.* New York: Penguin, 2000.

11. Martin, Judith. *Miss Manners' Guide to Excruciatingly Correct Behavior.* New York: W.W. Norton & Company, 2005.

12. Morrison, Terri, and Wayne A. Conway. *Kiss, Bow, or Shake Hands.* Avon: Adams Media, 2006.

13. Oliver, Vicky. *301 Smart Answers to Tough Interview Questions.* Naperville: Sourcebooks, 2005.

14. Oliver, Vicky. *Bad Bosses, Crazy Coworkers & Other Office Idiots.* Naperville: Sourcebooks, 2008.

15. Post, Elizabeth L. *Emily Post's Etiquette: A Guide to Modern Manners 14th Edition.* New York: Harper & Row, 1984.

16. Post, Elizabeth L. *Emily Post's Etiquette: The Definitive Guide to Manners 17th Edition.* New York: HarperResource, 2004.
17. Post, Emily L. *Etiquette in Society, in Business, in Politics, and at Home.* New York: Funk & Wagnalls, 1922.
18. Sutton, Robert I. *The No-Asshole Rule: Building A Civilized Workplace and Surviving One That Isn't.* New York: Warner Business Books, 2007.

Great Organizations

Dale Carnegie® Training http://www.dalecarnegie.com/about_us/about_us.jsp

Toastmasters International http://www.toastmasters.org/

Websites for the Business Traveler

1. www.cyborlink.com
2. http://ediplomat.com/, see "Cultural Etiquette"
3. www.ExecutivePlanet.com
4. www.kwintessential.co.uk/resources/country-profiles.html
5. www.petergreenberg.com, see "Business Travel"

The Straight Scoop

If you have a question about business etiquette or just need some friendly advice, you can email me once. And I do promise to return your first email. So save it for a time when you could really use the help! Good luck with all of your business pursuits. vicky@vickyoliver.com

About the Author

Vicky Oliver's savvy career advice has been featured in over 300 media outlets, including *The New York Times, The Wall Street Journal,* the *New York Post, LA Times, Chicago Tribune, Esquire* magazine, *Essence* magazine, and Bloomberg TV.

Her first book, *301 Smart Answers to Tough Interview Questions,* a national bestseller now in its third U.S. printing, won the 2010 Eric Hoffer award in the Business category. The book has been translated four times and is sold in twelve countries.

Her second book is called *Power Sales Words: How to Write It, Say It, and Sell It with Sizzle.* Her third book, titled *Bad Bosses, Crazy Coworkers & Other Office Idiots,* won the National Best Books 2009 Award for Best Business Careers Book and was a 2010 International Book Award finalist in the Business Careers category, a 2010 International Book Award winner in the Business Reference category, and won an Honorable Mention in the 2010 San Francisco Book Festival. It's now in its second printing.

She also gives seminars on job-hunting, networking, and business etiquette for groups of 50–200.

Vicky Oliver is ever true to her schools. She is currently Chair of the Communications & Marketing Committee of the Brown University Alumni Association (BAA) Board of Governors, President Emeritus and an executive board member of the Brown University Club in New York, co-chair of the Career & Networking Committee of the Brown University Club in New York and its past Secretary, and Vice President of her class at Brown.

Vicky Oliver lives in Manhattan, where she helps people turn around their careers and their lives.